I0796146

THE ILLUSTRATED HISTORY OF THE

HARLEY-DAVIDSON

NITE OWL
DRIVE IN

THE ILLUSTRATED HISTORY OF THE

HARLEY-DAVIDSON

An encyclopedia of the definitive motorbike from classic to custom, with 750 photographs

ROLAND BROWN AND MAC McDIARMID

LORENZ BOOKS

CONTENTS

MOTOR
HARLEY-DAVIDSON
CYCLES

THE WORLD OF HARLEY-DAVIDSON

"If you have to ask..." said the Harley-Davidson slogan, "...you wouldn't understand." Just what is it that makes Harley-Davidson so special? The company makes motorcycles, true, but it is much more than a mere motorcycle manufacturer – Milwaukee makes legends. The company that has become an American icon crafts heavy metal into love affairs, forges lifestyles and fulfils dreams. As much myth as motorcycle – often imitated, never copied – there is simply nothing quite like a Harley-Davidson.

Today, Harleys are as recognizable around the world as the Stars and Stripes, as ubiquitous as McDonald's and as prized for their rugged honesty as Zippo lighters and Levi's. They appear in movies and advertising; they're the wheels of choice for celebrities and stars. Elvis owned one and, according to the T-shirt at least, God rides one too. Harleys have been raced almost since the first one was built. They have been a vivid facet of American life through two world wars, a crippling Depression and the fluctuating fortunes of the current Millennium. Harley-Davidson's is the longest history in motorcycling, almost the story of motorcycling itself, and *The World of Harley-Davidson* is the epic tale of the making of an American legend.

LEFT This Harley advertising from 1920 confirms that the fast-growing Milwaukee firm had a substantial factory and globe-conquering ambition more than a century ago.

THE EVOLUTION OF HARLEY-DAVIDSON

From uncertain beginnings in a Milwaukee basement in 1903, Harley-Davidson has survived and ultimately thrived for more than 120 years. Once the world's largest producer of motorcycles, Harley's sales shrank to a mere 10,000 per year during the 1950s. Increasing competition – first from Europe, then from Japan – brought the once-proud giant to the brink of ruin. Harley limped through the 1970s amid changes of ownership and a moribund model range. By the mid-1980s this vibrant dream factory was effectively broke.

Then came two decades of spectacular growth, as Harley combined inspired styling and marketing with modern manufacturing techniques, before the firm was rocked by problems including the global financial crisis. Recent years have seen an impressive rebirth that has sent Milwaukee's finest charging confidently into the future.

LEFT One of Harley's strengths over the years has been an ability to combine updated engineering with timeless style in models such as the Ultra Classic Electra Glide.

EARLY YEARS

In the early days of the 20th century, young men in dingy workshops across the industrialized world tinkered with an endless array of new-fangled mechanical contraptions. Among them were one Harley and three Davidson brothers whose partnership would lead to spectacular success.

There may have been hundreds of such enthusiastic amateurs in Wisconsin alone, but it was the relatively untutored tinkering of two young Milwaukee men in particular that would give rise to an American legend.

The story begins in 1900 – 15 years after Gottlieb Daimler created the world's first powered two-wheeler and only six years after the first production machine – when William Sylvester Harley and Arthur Davidson got together in a Milwaukee basement with motorcycling in mind.

Information from these early years is sketchy, so the inspiration for their enthusiasm is unclear. A primitive motorcycle was demonstrated by its creator, Edward Joel Pennington, on nearby Wisconsin Avenue as early as 1895, though it's not clear whether the duo actually witnessed the event. They are known to have been impressed by a variety act five years later, however, in which comedienne Anna Held rode a French-built motorcycle across the stage of Milwaukee's Bijou theatre.

William Sylvester Harley was just 20 at the time, Arthur Davidson a year younger. The pair had been friends since their school days and, by accident or fate, had already accumulated some of the skills their dreams required by the time they began working together in that Milwaukee basement. Harley

ABOVE The founders, from left: Arthur Davidson, Walter Davidson, William Harley and William Davidson.

BELOW What is believed to be the very first production Harley-Davidson, now fully restored, has been on display in Milwaukee in recent years.

RIGHT The Model 5D twin from 1909 was essentially two singles on a common crankcase. Valve gear problems meant that only 27 were built. Production of an improved version began for 1911 with the Model 7D.

worked as a draughtsman and had six years of experience in bicycle manufacturing; Davidson was a pattern maker with the same company as Harley, working on small petrol (gas) engines. They were also fortunate enough to have working alongside them a German colleague familiar with pioneering European motorcycles. Work on the first Harley-Davidson engine began in 1900 or 1901 and was probably based on one of the do-it-yourself kits then available, itself roughly based on the French De Dion-Bouton design. A drawing dated 20 July 1901 shows a 7.07cu in (115.8cc) engine with a bore and stroke of 2 x 2.25in (50 x 55mm). When installed in a bicycle, power proved deeply disappointing.

At least one more prototype followed, including a machine capable of "thrilling speeds up to 25mph" and measuring 10.2cu in (167cc). It soon became clear that their venture required more expertise if it was ever going to get up to speed – beginning with the need for a skilled mechanic. Fortunately, Arthur's brother, Walter Davidson, was just such a man.

ABOVE America's early road network was primitive, but motorcycles proved easier to manhandle than cars.

RIGHT Harley production began in 1903 in this small shed in the Davidson family's back yard at 37th Street in Milwaukee, here pictured years later in the shadow of the factory.

LEFT By 1913 all Harley twins enjoyed all-chain drive, although the basic Model 9A single (below) continued with leather belt drive.

LEFT As early as 1912, Harley-Davidson was focusing on its "new type" motorcycles' attributes of safety, comfort and fuel economy in its advertising material.

BELOW A well-to-do couple with a Model 9A, pictured in 1913.

Walter was working as a railroad machinist in Parsons, Kansas, at the time, but was due in Milwaukee for the wedding of a third Davidson brother, William A. (Bill). Arthur wrote to Walter, offering him a ride on their new motorcycle. It was only later that he discovered ("imagine my chagrin") that he would have to help build it first. He must have liked the idea though – enough to find work in Milwaukee and join the team. The founders became four when William, the eldest Davidson brother and a foreman railway toolmaker, jumped on board – and the four began the ride of their lives.

The machine recognized as the first true Harley-Davidson engine was built during 1902–3, by which time locally built Merkel and Mitchell motorcycles were already a familiar feature of Milwaukee life. Bore and stroke were 3 x 3.5in (76.2 x 88.9mm) for a displacement of 24.74cu in (405cc) but the Harley-Davidson engine incorporated many technical refinements. The new engine was of F-head layout, with much larger cooling fins than before, as well as much larger flywheels – almost 10in (250mm) across. Some of the machining was done on a lathe belonging to a friend, Henry Melk, while other parts were crafted illicitly as parts for foreign sales in the tool rooms of William A. Davidson's employers, the Chicago, Milwaukee and St Paul Railroad. Legend has it that the first carburettor was made from a discarded tomato can (although this could as easily refer to the 1901 engine), and Bill Harley later described its spark plug, which had cost the princely sum of $3.00, as being "as big as a doorknob".

Assistance with the design came from Arthur's childhood friend, Ole Evinrude, who was already making liquid-cooled engines of his own and would later find fame with his outboard motors. Evinrude is credited with setting up the carburettor, but other components – notably the roller tappets still used on Harleys today – may have been his idea as well. Scaling 49lbs (22kg), this engine was installed in a loop frame similar to the existing Merkel design, in the Davidson family's back yard at 315 37th Street. The site, known as 38th Street today, is now owned by the giant Molson Coors Brewery and is little more than a stone's throw from Juneau Avenue.

BELOW The inlet-over-exhaust valve layout is clearly seen on this early "Renault Gray" single.

ABOVE Team Harley in 1915, from left: Otto Walker, Harry Crandall, Joe Walter, Red Parkhurst, Alva Stratton and Ralph Cooper.

BELOW This celebratory restoration of a 1913 single shows an image of the first factory (which was located on Juneau Avenue, Milwaukee) on the tank.

ABOVE William S. Harley on the left and Walter Davidson on the right getting a motorcycle over the rocks of a creek, 1912.

THE HARLEY-DAVIDSON MOTOR CO.

So it was that in 1903 – the same year the Wright brothers took to the air – the Harley-Davidson team created its first motorcycle and readied itself to produce similar machines for public consumption. This handsome machine was gloss black with gold pinstriping, a single-loop tubular steel frame, unsprung forks and leather belt final drive directly from the crankshaft. Additional power was offered by pedals, which also provided the only braking force. It is unclear how many machines were built during 1904 – sources suggest figures anywhere from one to eight, although anything over three seems unlikely. However many there were, each was assembled in a 15 x 10ft shed erected in the Davidson back yard by the boys' father, a cabinet-maker. Modest though it was, the shed bore the legend "Harley-Davidson Motor Co." on its front (and only) door with typical understated pride.

The first production Harley has a tale to tell all of its own. It carried its first owner, a Mr Mayer, for almost 6,000 miles before passing to George Lyon, who covered another 15,000 miles. It was sold in turn to a Dr Webster, followed by Louis Fluke and Stephen Sparrow, who between them clocked up almost another 62,000 relatively untroubled miles (a total of 134,000 km). By 1913, the company decided to advertise the bike's exploits, promoting an image of dependable travel: "100,000 miles on its original bearings and no major components replaced". Harley-Davidson engines were also produced for use in "buckboards" (four-wheel wagons) and the company's earliest advertisements also proposed their use in boats.

Motorcycle production increased to seven in 1905 as the company took on an outside employee and attracted its first dealer, C.H. Lang of Chicago, who would become the largest motorcycle dealer in the country within a dozen years. A year later, in 1906, "Renault gray with red pinstriping" joined black as a colour option, and the model became known as "the Silent Gray Fellow", a name that reflected its quietness and dependability.

Engine capacity had by now increased to 26.84cu in (440cc) and the list price for the latest models was $200.

Production had soared to 50 units by 1906, prompting a move from the company's original hut on 37th Street and Highway Boulevard into its first proper building on the present Juneau Avenue site. The new factory turned out to be sitting partially on land belonging to the railroad. Fortunately, the "factory" was a wooden structure, and at 28 x 80ft (9 x 25 metres) eight or ten people were able to carry it the few feet to its proper location.

Finance for expansion came from a relative, James McLay, known as "the honey uncle" due to his generosity and

BELOW LEFT AND RIGHT An unrestored and original 1915 61-inch F-head twin. Note that pedal assistance is still retained.

ABOVE A rare 1914 Model 10C single with hugely complex two-speed rear hub.

hobby of beekeeping. This affectionate tribute was more appropriate than anyone could imagine, for Juneau Avenue was to become a veritable hive of activity, seven days a week, 365 days a year.

FORGING AHEAD

By 1907, the company was getting serious: it became Harley-Davidson Inc. Walter was the largest stockholder, followed by Arthur, with the two Williams a joint third. A Davidson sister, Elizabeth, also had the good sense to buy Harley-Davidson shares early in the firm's life. (By 1916, Davidson family stockholders would outnumber Harleys seventeen to three.) It was a heady time. The company had already taken on extra staff; William Harley had begun an engineering degree at the University of Wisconsin in Madison; Walter was exploring the mysteries of heat treatment on metals; and Arthur, as company secretary and sales manager, was taking a more professional approach to production and training. The company may have begun as four young men with more enthusiasm than talent, but they had ambitions for the company they had created. That year, they produced no fewer than 150 machines and within 12 months had sold the first of many thousands for police duty.

Even so, it was clear that further progress demanded a more ambitious new motorcycle than the existing single, which in 1909 expanded to 30.17cu in (495cc). By 1908, William Harley had graduated and continued work on a more potent engine. This

BELOW Harley-Davidson motorcycles and sidecars were used by the rural postal service.

BELOW Harley's rapid increase in production necessitated frequent enlargement of the Milwaukee factory.

LEFT By 1917 Olive Green had replaced Renault Gray as the factory colour, here on a Model J twin three-speed.

bore fruit a year later with the launch of the company's first production V-twin, the Model D, essentially a doubled-up single with strengthened bottom-end.

The first such model became officially available on 15 February 1909, although the first working prototype appears to have been built as early as 1906. A press report from the time clearly mentions a 53in (869cc) Harley twin in April 1908, while a privately-owned Harley-Davidson twin won a hill climb event at Algonquin, Illinois, in July that same year.

Whatever its exact development history, the Model D twin was an inlet-over-exhaust valve design with a capacity of 53.7cu in (880cc), developing around six horsepower and capable of a top speed close to 62mph (100kph). The cylinders were splayed apart at the trademark 45-degree angle.

The strength of the Model D twin was amply proven in June 1908 when Walter drove one of his bikes to its first "official" competition success, a two-day endurance run in New York's Catskill Mountains. The sole Harley scored a "perfect" 1,000 points, outstripping all the more fancied runners in a field of 61 machines. Surprisingly – and embarrassingly – the first production twins were beset by valve-gear problems, with production being suspended during 1910.

The factory resisted official racing for several years despite widespread success in competitions. The factory's reluctance continued even when a private owner took the new 61in (989cc) X8E twin (the first Harley with a clutch) to victory in the 1912 San José road race by no less than 17 miles (27km): Bill Harley established a works race department two years later.

A DEPENDABLE TWIN

When the V-engine reappeared as the "50-inch" (810cc) Model 7D of 1911, no expense had been spared and every

BELOW Since opening in 1919, this Juneau Avenue factory has been the home of Harley-Davidson.

BELOW William Ottaway, who was Harley's first race boss, sits astride a 1924 Model JDCA.

ABOVE Gordon, Walter Jnr. and Allan Davidson (sitting on bikes) in San Francisco after a cross-country ride in 1929.

effort made to produce a machine worthy of Harley-Davidson's reputation. Not only had proper mechanical valves replaced the hit-and-miss automatic inlets, an adjustable tensioner had been added to the slippage-prone belt final drive.

Another notable improvement to this model saw the revised powerplant housed in a new, much sturdier frame.

A year later, a 61cu in (989cc) version, the chain-drive Model X8E, reinforced these developments. With its second attempt, Harley hit the nail on the head, and the V-twin took its rightful place in Milwaukee history.

Production in the rapidly expanding company soared to 450 machines in 1908, housed in a new, brick-built factory of 2,380sq ft (221sq metres) and employing 18 people. New machinery arrived almost weekly and was set to work, according to legend, "as soon as the cement was dry", and in what must have seemed like an instant, became obsolete. Two years later, 149 staff were engaged in another new factory – a reinforced concrete structure of 9,520sq ft (885sq metres).

By the time the new 5hp, 35cu in single model (565cc 5-35) appeared in 1913, the company had established a reputation for producing machines that were dependable in both domestic and competitive use. The factory was hurtling ahead as well in this changing age and included a separate Parts and Accessories Department. More than 1,500 employees worked for a company whose manufacturing floor area had grown from nothing to almost 300,000sq ft (28,000sq metres) within a decade. Production rocketed from eight machines in 1905 to 1,149 in 1911 and 17,439 in 1916, the year prior to the United States' entry into the First World War.

Though not yet dominant in the industry, in 1913 Harley produced around 18 per cent of the 70,000 American-built motorcycles.

Very soon, however, all this would change, and much of this energy would be called to the service of Uncle Sam.

BELOW Harley-Davidson's first V-twin engine, introduced in 1909. It displaced 49.5cu in (811cc).

WAR AND PEACE

On 6 April 1917, the United States declared war on Germany. Harley's successful peacetime formula suddenly faced an entirely new set of demands for which, five years earlier, the company may have been ill-prepared. By 1917, however, this bullish, expanding company was ready to go to war for real.

Harley-Davidson supplied the best part of 20,000 motorcycles to the American military in total, the majority being 61-inch twins. Indeed, the war did little but good for the company's prospects. Rival European motorcycle manufacturers were preoccupied by hostilities for a much longer period (1914–18) than those in the United States. Consequently, Milwaukee was able to extend its markets and reputation overseas. By 1918, aided by a $3 million loan from the M&I bank, Harley-Davidson had become the world's largest manufacturer of motorcycles. Within a year, "Hap" Scherer had been appointed Harley-Davidson's first publicity manager. By 1921, machines were being sold through 2,000 dealers in 67 countries, with product catalogues printed in seven languages. As the dust settled on

ABOVE Harley was quick to develop its bikes for war, including mounting them with machine guns.

BELOW Milwaukee-built sidecars proved to be extremely popular for both military and civilian use.

LEFT Board racers were Harleys in their leanest form, stripped of even any semblance of brakes...

BELOW Front brakes finally arrived in the late 1920s, as on this Model J Big Twin.

the carnage of the war, one-sixth of Milwaukee's production was destined for export.

The aftermath of war had other, less predictable side-effects. One of these was the retention of army green as the company colour in place of the pre-war pale grey. Another more enduring effect concerned training. To help military personnel keep Milwaukee's wares reliable, the Harley-Davidson Service School was established in 1917. Initially intended as a military measure and as concerned with riding instruction as mechanics, the Service School soon developed into a crucial arm of the factory's civilian service.

By the eve of the "Roaring Twenties" the Juneau Avenue factory had become a colossus. In 1919, close to 1,800 employees toiled on a floor area exceeding 400,000sq ft (37,000sq metres) to produce 22,685 motorcycles and over 16,000 sidecars. The Model J Sport Twin, unveiled that same year, was unique among Harleys, if not American motorcycles in general. Instead of the "V" layout, the 35.6cu in (584cc) twin adopted a horizontally opposed design, with cylinders that were orientated fore-and-aft. Although

RIGHT Harley's Service School was established in 1917 to train military personnel, and continued to hold an important role in peacetime.

long and unwieldy, the layout offered a very low centre of gravity and a compact width, ideally suited to America's then-primitive road network.

There were other innovations, most of which would stand the test of time better than the model itself. The final drive was sensibly protected from dust in a metal enclosure, lubricated by oil mist from the engine breather. It was also the first model to feature a full electrical system produced by the Harley factory. Although the Sport set many records – Canada to Mexico in less than 75 hours, no easy task even today – its six horsepower engine lacked the bottomless big-inch power America demanded, and was discontinued after 1922.

The 1920s didn't so much roar as whimper where motorcycles were concerned. Much of the blame for the Sport Twin's relative failure lay far beyond Milwaukee's control – 1920 witnessed a major trade recession with a massive over-supply of manufactured goods as global economies struggled to adjust to peacetime trade. One of the consequences was Henry Ford's slashing the price of his Model T car to $395, the same as the biggest Harley twin. The effects on motorcycle sales were inevitable. The trade slump was brief, but America's love affair with the car was not, and neither Harley nor any other bike manufacturer fully recovered their previous momentum.

ABOVE Inventiveness is apparent in this 1919 twin, fitted with stabilizing skis for use in icy conditions.

Milwaukee's sales collapsed from over 28,000 in 1920 to 10,202 in 1921, with sales so poor during that spring that the factory, which had expanded 12 months before, shut down for a month. Sales would not return to 1920s levels for a further 21 years. Most of the machines that were sold during that time were 61-inch V-twins.

Although the Sport failed to make the impact Harley hoped, one of the next models quickly became a Milwaukee legend. In 1921, the V-twin was replaced by the JD and FD, the first 74-inch (actually 74.2cu in/1,216cc) models, with F-head, inlet-over-exhaust (ioe) valve layout. Each example was dubbed a

LEFT Harley produced more than 16,000 sidecars in 1919, but the three-wheeler's popularity was hit shortly afterwards by Ford's keenly priced Model T car.

"Superpowered Twin" in tribute to its 18hp engine and both underwent rigorous pre-delivery testing: yet another Harley innovation.

As for the rest of the range, the 30-inch single had been dropped after 1918. In 1926, a new single – the 21in (344cc) Model A – was introduced, joined four years later by a 30.5in (492cc) sister. In a radical move, Harley-Davidson pioneered the front brake in 1928, just as the company had pioneered kick-starts and three-speed transmissions more than a decade earlier. All models were sold in varied specifications of transmission, valve-gear and power, so that in 1928, for instance, three basic engine types accounted for no fewer than a dozen models. By this time, Harley's only surviving domestic competitors were Indian, Henderson, Cleveland and Super-X.

The last year of the decade introduced the machine that would become Milwaukee's bread and butter. The new WL was a 45in (742cc) side-valve V-twin which supposedly combined the single's agility with the power of the bigger twins. Capped by rakish twin "bullet" headlights, the new model was an instant success and constituted the lowest rung on a V-twin ladder made up of 45-, 61- and 74-inchers. Star billing in the 1929 Harley-Davidson catalogue went to the JDH Two-Cam, which housed a specially-prepared variant of the 74-inch engine that had been developed for the factory's all-conquering board racers.

Billed as "the fastest road model that Harley-Davidson has ever offered to the public", it could probably out-run any other two-wheeler on the American highway. The WL may have been humbler but it proved its worth by keeping Milwaukee's head above water in the years ahead.

The Harley-Davidson Enthusiast

November, 1929

ABOVE *The Enthusiast* magazine, first published in 1916, contained touring stories, race reports and information about clothing and accessories.

ABOVE The 1920s was marked by F-head machines like this 1922 61-inch twin. Flatheads appeared in 1926, the same year as the first overhead valve engines.

RIGHT Before 1927, only a rear brake was fitted onto bikes.

THE 1930s

The 1930s began in high spirits with arguably the most mouth-watering range to come out of Milwaukee for years. All models now had bigger brakes and tyres, improved ground clearance, lower saddles and – best of all – removable cylinder heads.

Dubbed "Ricardo" heads, they were far more practical and efficient than the one-piece iron cylinders previously employed. Although plagued by early problems, the new high-compression 74.2cu in (1,216cc) VL offered fully 15 per cent more power than any previous Harley roadster. A nationwide "open house" attracted customers by the thousands and, with sales quickly up 30 per cent on the previous year, the new decade appeared rich in promise.

There was one cloud on the horizon, however. In October 1929, a few weeks after the 1930 range was unveiled, the Wall Street stock market crashed, sending tremors throughout the American economy and the rest of the world. President Herbert Hoover's initial rapid intervention seemed to stem the tide but economic confidence continued to wilt. In 1930, 1,300 banks went to the wall. Manufacturers in every industry offered incentives to stimulate business, but to no avail. Within 12 months, the mighty Juneau Avenue factory was running at a mere 10 per cent of production capacity and would report a loss of more than $320,000 the following year.

ABOVE By the 1930s all Harleys were flatheads, such as this imposing 74-inch VL from 1933.

By 1933, one quarter of the United States workforce was unemployed. Few people had money to spend on motorcycles. Of hundreds of American bike manufacturers, only Harley and Indian had the financial strength and acumen to survive. Industry-wide production fell from 32,000 to 6,000 units per year by 1933, by which time fewer than 100,000 motorcycles were registered in the whole of the United States. Of these new sales, Milwaukee's share was just 3,703 – its lowest in 23 years.

LEFT 1932 saw the introduction of the enduring Servi-Car, which would continue in production for 40 years.

ABOVE The depressed scene of the 1930s did not deter the enthusiasts from the Blue Comet motorcycle club from Lansdale in Pennsylvania.

Desperately, Juneau Avenue wracked its brains for innovative sales ideas, ranging from savings plans to a medal scheme intended to turn every Harley owner into a salesman. One enduring response was the sale of branded clothing and accessories – a sideline now worth millions of dollars per year. A superficial but significant measure was the abandonment of dull green paint in 1933, in favour of more vivid colours and art-deco graphics which continue to brighten Harley-Davidsons today.

An altogether grittier response was the three-wheeled Servi-Car, a cheap delivery and police vehicle powered by the 45-inch (742cc) Model D engine. Surprisingly, given the fraught circumstances of the time, this three-wheeler was both a sound design and a solid piece of engineering – so tough and enduring, indeed, that it survived

LEFT Harley's 1930s advertising remained bold and optimistic, with bright colours and art deco inspiration.

RIGHT The Knucklehead would prove an ideal bike for stylish touring, as highlighted by this factory publicity shot.

ABOVE The troubles of the Depression encouraged novel art-deco styling, such as the tank badge on this mammoth 80-inch VLH from 1936. The same motifs can be seen even on modern Harleys.

in production from late 1931 until 1974. The true hero of the Depression years was the side-valve twin: cheap to produce, economic to run and maintain, and easily repairable.

Almost on their own, the D and V models saw Harley through the Depression, along with the 30.5in (492cc) single-cylinder machine of 1929. As the financial vice tightened, no other significant new models were developed during those six years.

In many ways, the worst of the Depression also brought out the best in the company. By reducing the length of the working week, as many staff were kept on as possible, although this was less generous than it might appear,

BELOW Drab green was more common. Almost 90,000 of these 45-inch (742cc) flathead twins were built for the military during the Second World War, and thousands served with the Soviet forces.

ABOVE A WLA in desert camouflage stands out against civilian chrome.

since it was partially mandated by the government's National Recovery Administration, and every skilled hand would be needed when the slump finally abated. Prudent financial controls, police and military contracts, novel sales strategies and energetic pursuit of exports kept the company afloat, and by 1934, the books were back in the black.

KNUCKLING DOWN

Painfully slowly, President Roosevelt's "New Deal" began to take effect and, by 1936, the crippling Depression came to a close. New machines began to emerge from Milwaukee, whose 1935 model range had comprised a mere two basic models. These were the 45-inch (742cc) Model R (essentially the D model with light alloy pistons, soon to become the heroic W) and the 74-inch (1,216cc) Model V and its derivatives, now cured of its original and varied ills. Both were side-valve designs, slow and steady, whereas the American public increasingly craved more advanced machines.

The biggest newcomer was the V-twin Model UL. Although still side-valve and visually similar to the proven DL45, it displaced a stupendous 78.9cu in (1,293cc), making it ideal for heavy sidecar use. It was to continue in production until 1945. Most important of all was a new generation of 61-inch (898cc) twin with overhead valves and twice the power of its predecessor. The legendary Model E – the Knucklehead – had arrived.

The 1936 Knuckle could have appeared in 1934 but for government restrictions aimed at reducing employment. For company and public alike, this was frustrating but certainly worth the wait. The Knuckle was a Juneau Avenue first in many respects – the first four (forward) speeder; the first overhead valve roadster twin; the first hemispherical heads. The engine was heavily influenced by the competition experience of the legendary Joe Petrali, Harley development rider and near-unbeatable racer. It announced its arrival by recording a speed of 136.183mph (219.16kph) on the sands of Daytona Beach, Florida. The rider, naturally, was Joe.

With the new model as its flagship, Harley's fortunes rapidly improved. In 1937, sales exceeded 11,000 for the first time since 1930. The same year brought significant improvements elsewhere in the range: full roller bearing engines, chromolly fork tubes and interchangeable wheels.

As well as these technical advances, the lessons of the Depression had

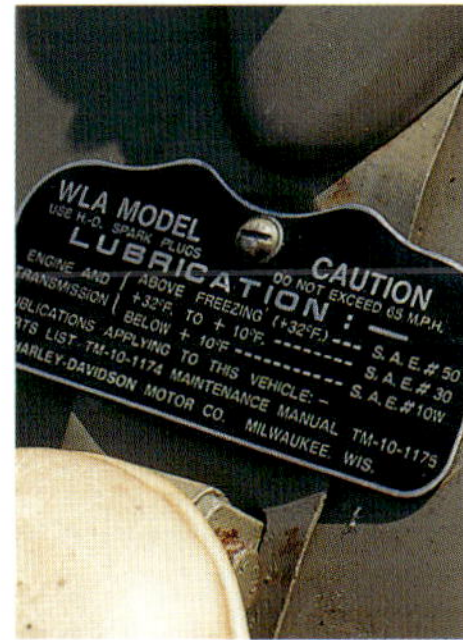

ABOVE AND RIGHT The "A" in WLA stood for army, so naturally military rules came with the machines. Soldiers were warned not to exceed 65mph (104.5kmp).

LEFT AND ABOVE Even soldiers could be customizers: note the "Uncle Sam" on the fuel tank (above) and grenade-box lettering (left).

instilled in the company a faith in styling and cosmetics which stands them in good stead even today. The aftermarket and art-deco innovations of 1932 were continued. Balloon tyres appeared in 1940 (more striking, if less functional, than new aluminium alloy heads for the flathead side-valve models). In 1941, four-speed transmissions became standard across the big twin range. Eleven models were now on the books in four basic engine configurations: side-valves of 45-, 74- and 80-inch (742, 1,216 and 1,293cc), and Knuckleheads of 61-inch Model E (989cc) and 74-inch Model F (1,207cc).

BACK TO WAR

Motorcycle production in Milwaukee rose from a low of 3,703 in 1933 to more than 18,000 in 1941. Harley-Davidson made it through the Depression by the narrowest of squeaks, emerging stronger than ever before. However, not long after this rocky period in Harley-Davidson's history, a catastrophe of an altogether more terrible kind occurred: the world once again went to war. The United States entered the conflict after the bombing of Pearl Harbor on 7 December 1941.

As the country's largest motorcycle producer, it fell to Harley-Davidson to

ABOVE Civilian versions of the humble WL45 could be surprisingly handsome.

LEFT Astonishingly, the WL45 engine survived until the 1970s in the Servi-Car.

ABOVE During the Second World War almost no machines were made for civilian use. This is one of the first post-war WL45 twins, in vibrant red.

ABOVE The noble Knucklehead, Milwaukee's first overhead valve roadster twin.

underpin the bulk of the country's two-wheeled war effort. Throughout the years of America's involvement in the war (1942–45), practically the entire output of the Milwaukee factory was turned over to military production – some 90,000 machines in total.

As with the First World War, the Second was fairly good to Milwaukee. In 1940, sales totalled fewer than 11,000. These soared to 18,000 as the military build-up began in 1941, reaching more than 29,000 in each of the two years that followed before tailing off again as peace approached.

However, since the military favoured Harley Davidson's robust side-valve plodders over the new Model E and Model F, this meant that Knucklehead production was practically zero during the same period.

HARLEY JAPAN

One little-known, highly ironic consequence of Milwaukee's quest for export markets in the 1920s and the economic slump of the 1930s was the creation of a Japanese big twin. During the 1920s, Arthur Davidson had pursued new sales openings with vigour, including the establishment of the Harley-Davidson Sales Company of Japan with a comprehensive network of dealers, agencies and spares distributors. Milwaukee's stock stood so high that Harleys soon became Japan's official police motorcycle.

Less worthily, in 1924 the Murata Iron Works began building copies of the 1922 Model J, but the quality was appalling. Murata would later build the Meguro, a distant precursor of modern Kawasakis. Harley exports to Japan all but ceased in the wake of the 1929 Wall Street crash, as the global economic slump crippled the yen. The story might have stopped there but for Alfred Childs, head of Harley's Japanese operation, who asked: "Why not build Harleys there?"

Juneau Avenue was sceptical at first, but such was Childs' persistence that Harley's first overseas factory soon began production at Shinagawa, near Tokyo. Built with tooling, plans, blueprints and expertise borrowed from Milwaukee, the factory was considered the most modern in the world. By 1935 Shinagawa was manufacturing complete motorcycles, mainly 74-inch V-series flathead twins. In 1930, these had become the official motorcycle of the Japanese Imperial Army. Later, when the army became the effective civil power, it declined the chance to convert production to the new OHV Knucklehead, preferring the proven durability of the side-valve twin. It was at this point that the Sankyo corporation took over control of the factory and began selling Japanese Harleys under the Rikuo name. The "74" twin became the Rikuo Model 97.

As an increasingly truculent Japan readied for war, Harley cut its losses and sold out. As military demand increased (especially after the invasion of China in 1937), Rikuo sub-licensed the product to Nihon Jidosha ("Japan Combustion Equipment Co."). Its "Harleys" were variants of the model 97s, entitled Kuro Hagane ("Black Iron").

Ominously, the factory had only a few more years to run. Nihon Jidosha was located in Hiroshima.

BACK TO PEACE

Although the Second World War ended on 2 September 1945, following the formal surrender of Japan, it would be more than a year before the unveiling of any new revisions from Milwaukee. Even these – theoretically 1947 models – were no more than cosmetic updates of Harley's pre-war machines.

Of all the changes, perhaps the best remembered is Brook Stevens' design for new "streamlined" H-D tank badges. A revamped clothing and accessories catalogue appeared in the same model year, a harbinger of the direction the company would take three decades later.

For the time being, however, motorcycles were scarce as the industry readjusted to civilian production and the loss of military demand. In the aftermath of the War Department's cancellation of orders for over 11,000 machines in 1944, more than 500 Harley-Davidson workers were let go. The rest, limited to a shortened working week, went on strike in late 1945. Paradoxically, limits on civilian production remained in force, and things went from bad to worse when 15,000 war surplus WLs were offered for public sale. It would be two more years before motorcycle production regained its pre-war level.

ABOVE This Harley museum mock-up of an early 1950s showroom features the Model S (left) and Hydra-Glide (right).

There was only one thing that had not changed in the forced interlude of war – Harley-Davidson's winning ways. In 1947, among other successes, seven of the first ten Daytona finishers rode Harleys. Over the next two years, 36 of 47 AMA championship events went to the Milwaukee marque.

Harley-Davidson took up residence in a second factory on Capitol Drive,

BELOW A 1946 FL Knucklehead, as handsome a motor as Milwaukee has ever built.

BELOW Clark Gable, star of *Gone with the Wind,* featured on the cover of *The Enthusiast* magazine in 1942.

RIGHT By 1948 the Knucklehead was history as the era of the Panhead had begun, as with this Hydra-Glide.

ABOVE The Hydra-Glide's telescopic front suspension gave it a striking new look, as well as improved ride quality, starting a new era for Harley.

RIGHT Before the appearance of the Hydra-Glide's telescopic forks, the first Panheads ran with the old girder-fork chassis, as with this magnificently restored 1948 example.

Wauwatosa, in 1947. By 1948, production was at an all-time high and, more important to America's highways, the replacement for the noble Knucklehead made its first public appearance that same year. The Panhead as it became known, was a development of the Knuckle rather than an all-new concept. As well as a revised (and much more oil-tight) lubrication system, the Pan featured aluminium alloy cylinder heads in place of the Knuckle's iron and hydraulic "lifters" rather than solid push-rods. The Pan, so-named because its chrome-plated rocker covers resembled inverted baking pans, was built in both 74cu in (1,200cc) and 61cu in (1,000cc) sizes; the latter was discontinued in 1953. The larger version retained the "traditional" bore and stroke dimensions of $3\frac{7}{16}$ x 4in (87 x 101mm).

The first all-new model powered by the Panhead engine was the Hydra-Glide of 1949, so-called because it was the first Harley to incorporate hydraulically-damped, telescopic front forks. It was also, of course, the first model granted one of the most evocative titles in motorcycling: "Glide". The Panhead engine would do much to get the species on its famous way, propelling not only the Duo-Glide of 1958 but the first of the Electra Glides as well.

Though no-one knew it at the time, this first Glide was to set the visual cues for the "Retro-Tech" Harleys which would appear four decades later. From its deeply-valanced mudguards and its chromed fork shrouds to its stylized rear end, the style of modern Softails owes much to the Hydra-Glide.

INTO THE 1950s

Harley-Davidson styles of the 1950s were in many ways a contradiction of those with which the company is now synonymous. True, 1950s imagery rates high in current Harley design but the decade began under the cloud of the Hollister "riots" of 1947, which tarnished the image of motorcycling and alarmed motorcycle manufacturers. The true creator of the riots, however, was the media (including *Life* magazine) which represented the gathering in Hollister as a major assault on small-town America. The world was just getting over the shock when the Hollister-inspired film *The Wild One* was released in 1953, reopening old

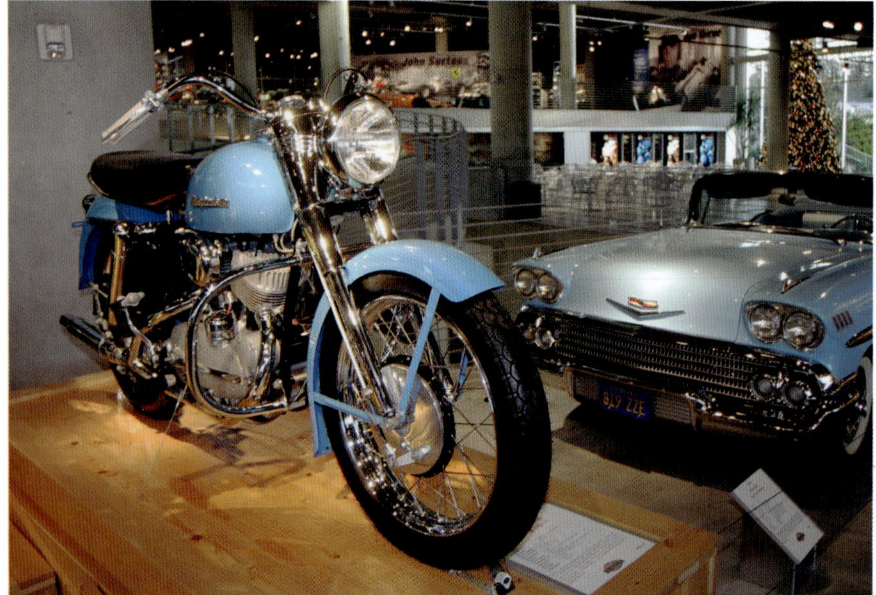

LEFT Matching 1950s style from Harley's Model K and Chevrolet's Bel Air, displayed in the Barber Museum in Birmingham, Alabama.

BELOW The Model K-derived KRTT fared better on the track, whilst on the street, their slowness made them popular with the insurers of Hollywood stars.

ABOVE Millard Reynolds navigates a tricky section on his Duo-Glide at the Jack Pine Enduro in Michigan.

ABOVE Both V-twins and two-stroke singles featured in Harley-Davidson's refreshed range for 1955.

wounds. Although the film's star, Marlon Brando, rode a Triumph Thunderbird on screen, many people swear it was a Harley.

In 1947, the world's foremost manufacturer of big V-twins began the manufacture of two strokes. This seemingly radical departure was an attempt to bring Milwaukee's appeal to a wider market, a move that was applauded at the time by many observers.

The line began with the 125cc Model S, a 1.7 horsepower machine based on the same German DKW RT125 design as the BSA Bantam, the rights to which both companies acquired as part of Germany's war reparations. More than 10,000 were built in the model's debut year, based on the expensive misconception that war veterans would buy almost anything with wheels, before production slipped to a more realistic 4,000 or so per annum. The engine grew to 165cc in 1954, powering the Models ST and Super Ten before increasing to 175cc for the Ranger/Pacer/Scat series in 1962. Perhaps Harley's best-known lightweights were the 125cc Model B Hummer, produced from 1955–59, and the 165cc Topper Scooter of the early 1960s.

Unfortunately, other manufacturers were also intent on broadening their markets. Harley-Davidson had by now introduced dealer demonstrator models and was to lose one competitor with the demise of Indian in 1953, but Triumph's creation of a vibrant new American import network in 1951 was a major alarm.

Isolated by war and supported by military production, Harley had enjoyed easy pickings for too long. Triumph – along with other British marques such as BSA, Norton and

Royal Enfield – had a range of cheaper yet much more exciting and technically sophisticated models than Harley-Davidson (whose flagship model persisted with hand-gear-change until 1952).

Harley's response was heavy-handed and ultimately counter-productive as they attempted to bully dealers into having no business with the British pretenders. Milwaukee also went so far as to apply for federal trade protection in 1952, alleging that the British machines were being subsidized and "dumped" on the American market. They asked for a 40 per cent import tax and quotas on the number of machines that Triumph (and parent company BSA) could import.

Thirty years later, Harley would get the protection that it had wanted, this time against the Japanese. The first time around, however, the Government's Tariff Commission found that Triumph had no case to answer. Worse still, they told Harley to quit its restrictive trading practices – a ruling that was to have devastating echoes for the company in the decades ahead.

OLD, SLOW AND OBSOLETE

No model summed up Harley's problem more than the Model K, introduced in 1952 to replace the WL. The K was a heavy 45.3cu in (742cc) side-valve design compared to the overhead valves, lightweight construction and good suspension offered by British twins (and, in the case of Norton, arguably the finest handling motorcycle in the world). Granted, the K included proper suspension at both ends – a first for Milwaukee – but in virtually every other respect it was woefully outclassed by the British-made bikes.

Harley claimed 30 horsepower for the Model K, which was only a little less than the contemporary Triumph Thunderbird. Whether or not this was true, the 85mph (137kph) V-twin was

RIGHT The Hydra-Glide was special, but something was missing.

BELOW Harley fan Elvis was *The Enthusiast*'s cover star in May 1956.

BELOW RIGHT Chrome and tassels on display at a meeting in 1953.

LEFT The ST165 of the 1950s was a two-stroke single which, like BSA's Bantam and Yamaha's YA-1, was based on German firm DKW's RT125.

BELOW The Shovelhead would replace the Panhead for the 1966 model year, as with this Electra Glide.

no match for the 103mph (166kph) British model, although the KK version, which had hotter cams, was better. Early Model Ks also had serious mechanical problems, although quality and power was improved by a capacity increase to 883cc for the 55-inch KH model in 1954.

Remarkably, Paul Goldsmith took a K-based KR racer to victory by more than two miles (3km) in the Daytona 200 road race of 1953, a victory Harley-Davidsons were to repeat for the remainder of the decade. In 1954, the legendary Joe Leonard became first American national champion on KR and KR-TT racers. Although superficially impressive, these exploits owed much to the now familiar ploy of persuading the authorities to handicap the opposition. In this case, foreign OHV engines competing against 750cc Harley flatheads were limited to 500cc.

The K sold moderately well but overall sales figures show the full extent of Milwaukee's problem. In the wheel-hungry year of 1948, Harley-Davidson produced more than 31,000 machines, the largest figure in its history. Yet by 1955, sales had plummeted to a low of less than 12,000. The problem could not be blamed on public disaffection with motorcycling, either – during the same period sales of imported machines went from strength to strength.

The machine which superseded the Model K in 1957 – the XL Sportster – was better in every way, eventually. The original Sportster's performance was lacklustre but by 1958 it benefited to the tune of 12 horsepower, due to lighter valve-gear, higher compression, larger ports and valves. A legend was born.

Displacing 53.9cu in (883cc), as today, the XL boasted unit construction for the engine and gearbox. Swing-arm rear suspension with car-type dampers allowed early Sportsters to be sold for either on- or off-road use. The XL was an instant hit, accounting for almost 20 per cent of Harley's 1957 production of more than 13,000 machines.

GLIDING INTO THE 1960s

As the 1950s drew to a close, the Hydra-Glide finally got the rear suspension it deserved and the Model F Duo-Glide was born in 1958. The Duo featured a hydraulic rear brake as well as handsome two-tone styling and a swinging-fork rear end.

With a new heavyweight on the block and the Sportster selling moderately well, Harley-Davidson renewed its attention to expanding its market base. One of the more successful measures was a move into glass-fibre moulding – initially boats, but later golf carts and motorcycle accessories. The main goal was still a foothold in the global boom in

ABOVE The Topper scooter was another of Milwaukee's attempts to diversify. At best, these achieved very limited success.

RIGHT Harley-Davidson badged single-cylinder Sprints on the assembly line, at the Aermacchi plant in Varese.

motorcycle sales. At the time, this meant lightweight machines, a demand to which the existing two-strokes were proving unequal. Sales of the ST were roughly similar to those of the Sportster, yet profit margins were much lower. Juneau Avenue's Development Committee decided that collaboration with an overseas company might be the most effective way forward.

AN ITALIAN VENTURE

In 1960 Harley became half-owner of the motorcycle division of Aermacchi, or Aeronautica Macchi SpA, for just under $250,000. Harley anticipated the partnership would generate sales of 6,000 lightweight bikes per year, to be produced in Varese, Italy.

The first Harley-Aermacchi appeared in September 1960, quickly announcing its pedigree with a 1-2-3 result at the Santa Fe AMA short track championship races. The 250 Sprint was based on a spine-framed, horizontal, single-cylinder, four-stroke design similar to that of the famous Aermacchi racers, although most subsequent "joint venture" models would be small two-strokes. The 250 was light, powerful (the company claimed 21 horsepower, growing to 25 by 1964), handled well and spawned a line of superb racing machines.

Yet the Sprint and its fellow 'Macchis – and indeed Milwaukee's home-grown lightweights – all failed to live up to Harley's commercial expectations, for a variety of reasons. Communications between the company's headquarters in the United States and Varese were often poor, causing continuous supply problems with bought-in components and incompatibility with American parts. Later, after the AMF take-over of Harley-Davidson in 1969, specifications were often changed erratically, without appropriate consultation or repricing. Most of all, the products were not wanted by a public being offered Japanese machines of ever-more sophisticated specification at lower prices (Honda had entered the American market in 1959). Nor were they wanted by dealers who had to carry new parts stock, retrain staff and relearn their business – all for a smaller profit margin.

There were high-points, though – not least Walter Villa's consecutive world 250cc road-race titles in 1974 and 1975. The four-strokes got into the act: Roger Reiman took a Sprint-powered streamliner to a new world 250cc speed record of 156mph (251.05kph) in 1964, improved to 177mph (284.85kph) in 1965.

It was an unrewarding marriage and divorce came too late. In June 1978, Harley closed its Italian factory. Juneau Avenue would never again aspire to a true mass market.

BELOW A sparkling new Electra Glide was the ideal all-American lifestyle accessory in the mid 1960s.

THE AMF YEARS

In 1964, Harley-Davidson not only unveiled its first new corporate logo in almost 60 years but also the model bearing possibly the most evocative name in the company's long history: Electra Glide. Yet it was the following year that would be remembered as the more momentous.

According to Harley lore, 1965 represented two climactic events. The first was the unveiling of a new generation of Shovelhead engines, replacing the venerable Panheads. Second, and ultimately more far-reaching, was the decision to list the company on the New York Stock Exchange – after more than 60 years as a family firm, its founding families were now to lose complete control.

More than 1.3 million Harley shares were sold in the four years that followed the original listing. They performed well and investors – and straightforward enthusiasts – felt good. Optimism was short-lived once again, however, as imported Japanese motorcycles made ever-increasing inroads in the American market. Initially, these machines were middleweights – light, fast, affordable and refined – but soon Honda would begin a full-frontal assault with the seminal four-cylinder CB750. The age of the high-performance "superbike" had arrived.

As Harley's fortunes ebbed and its shares dipped, it came under threat of takeover from an industrial conglomerate, Bangor Punta, which was busily accumulating Harley-Davidson stock. In 1968, fearful of the sweeping changes proposed, company president William H. Davidson resumed talks with American Machine and Foundry (AMF).

ABOVE The Sportster gave Harley a smaller, 883cc V-twin family and made a useful all-rounder when fitted with accessories including panniers.

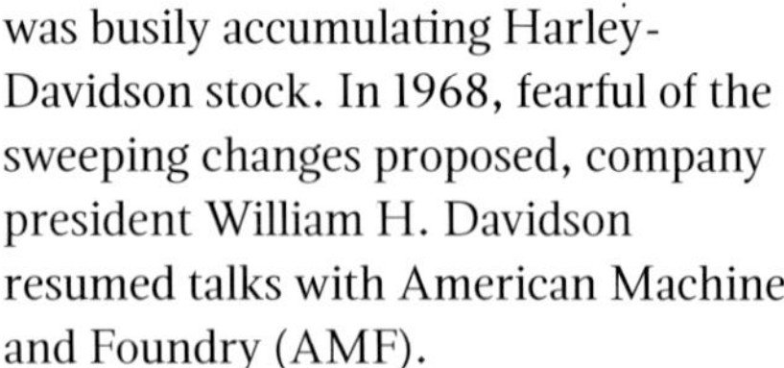

AMF was another industrial giant with designs on Harley but with less of a predatory reputation (chairman Rodney C. Gott was himself a keen motorcyclist). Harley recommended AMF's offer to shareholders, most of whom did well out of the subsequent $21 million deal. So it was that on 18 December 1968, Harley-Davidson voted to merge with AMF, a move ratified by shareholders on 7 January 1969. Thus the American icon became AMF property, with Gott as chairman,

BELOW The simple style of an early Electra Glide makes it easy to understand the V-twin's popularity both in the 1960s and many decades later.

ABOVE Under AMF's ownership, sales improved but quality reputedly suffered, yet the Shovelhead soldiered on.

RIGHT 80-inch (1,340cc) versions of the Shovelhead first appeared in 1978, as with this FLH.

BELOW Harley boosted the Sportster's performance and image in the 1970s with the XLCH-1000.

although it wasn't until 1971 that the new owner's logo would be seen on Harley-Davidson machines.

Today, it is fashionable to believe that AMF starved and milked Milwaukee's finest, that it didn't understand motorcycles or motorcyclists, that quality went to the dogs and that Harley/AMF never built a decent bike. Some of this is probably true, but AMF did sink millions of dollars into its new project. During its first three years in control, total sales more than doubled and, during its 12 years at the helm, sales of American-made machines more than tripled. In addition, the company diversified into such unlikely fields as snowmobiles and desert racers. Sales were reasonably strong but profits, unfortunately, were not.

Difficult labour relations at Capitol Drive were another concern. As a consequence of the tension, the bulk of production was moved to a vacant AMF plant in York, Pennsylvania (where it remains to this day, although Milwaukee has always made engines).

BELOW The OHV Sportster was a vast improvement on the sidevalve Model K.

BELOW More prized still was the tuned XLH Sportster, such as this one from 1972.

ABOVE A 1972 Electra Glide: no other motorcycle could get away with a white leather seat.

More exciting developments were afoot. 1970 brought a whole new kind of iron, the FX1200 Super Glide. This was the first of a string of startling cosmetic innovations from the fertile mind of William G. Davidson. Just as crucial was AMF's marketing and promotion expertise, which certainly rubbed off on the future, independent, Harley-Davidson company.

EXCITING IRON

If the 1970s was a commercially disastrous decade for Harley-Davidson, the hardware it produced at least paved the way for better times to come. Nowhere was this more evident than with the Super Glide, the first major new twin launched by Harley after the takeover by AMF. The Super Glide's hybrid philosophy – a little bit from one model, some from another and more parts from a third – became the essence of all the most memorable Harleys produced since. Despite the splash it made at the time – most road tests praised the Super Glide

RADICAL HOG: THE NOVA PROJECT

Harley's success in concealing its bikes' technical advances has generated accusations of complacency over the years. Much of this has been unjustified, as highlighted by the belated revelation that in the late 1970s the firm developed an advanced 800cc, liquid-cooled V4 called the Nova.

The debut Nova was close to being launched in 1981 as the first of a six-model family, ranging from a 400cc V-twin to a 1500cc V6. But 1981 was also the year of Harley's management buyout, and the rejuvenated firm could not afford both the Nova and the new Evolution V-twin, so the safer option of the Evo went ahead – which history suggests was the correct decision.

BELOW This prototype V4 tourer, pictured in Harley's Museum, would have been just one of many models.

ABOVE Twin filler caps, tank-top speedometer and lashings of chrome: all Harley hallmarks.

ABOVE Italian-built two-strokes, such as the SX125, broadened Harley's range under AMF control in the 1970s but were not a great success.

expansively – early examples were distinctly under-specified for the new "superbike" age. Disc brakes arrived in 1973 and an electric start option, the FXE, in 1974.

By 1977, Willie G. launched another classic derivative: the FXS Low Rider, complete with standard highway pegs, Fat Bob two-piece petrol tank and a seat just 27in (685mm) above the ground. Later the same year, the XLCR Café Racer was launched. This sinister all-black device was too radical a statement to enjoy much sales success at the time, but is a highly-prized collector's piece today.

BELOW Harley celebrated America's Bicentennial in 1976 with Liberty Edition versions of models including the Super Glide and Electra Glide.

The range of options increased further with the introduction of the 80-inch (1,340cc) Shovelhead engine, initially on the Electra Glide in 1978. This led to the FLH one year later, offered as standard with a complete set of touring extras, later to become the long-haul norm: saddlebags, luggage rack, fairing, running boards and additional lights. This in turn led to the FLT Tour Glide of 1980, similar to the full-dress Glide but with better brakes and a larger, twin headlamp touring fairing. More significantly, the FLT featured Harley-Davidsons' first five-speed transmission and, not least, its first use of rubber-mounting to protect the rider from engine vibration.

In fact, 1980 can be viewed as a vintage year all round. The Super Glide cruiser became the FXB Sturgis, named after the famous rally held annually in South Dakota. The "B" represented the first toothed-rubber belt drive – a clean, smooth and trouble-free system now standard across the range. For good measure, there was the FXWG Wide Glide and FXEF Fat Bob.

CHALLENGE FROM JAPAN

Nostalgia tells us that the 1970s produced a stream of classic Harley-Davidson models but, hardware aside, it was all an illusion. Even after shedding its Italian operation, the unpalatable truth was that, at the start of the 1980s, few people gave AMF Harley-Davidson very much chance of survival.

Who was to blame? It is tempting to point the finger at AMF, but whatever the company's shortcomings as custodians of the Milwaukee legend, Harley's biggest problem lay in a quite different direction. After all, it was scarcely AMF's fault that this period coincided so precisely with the rise to global domination of the Japanese motorcycle industry.

It is also a myth that Japan hijacked the American motorcycle market, either from Harley-Davidson or from the Europeans. Even after the British invasion of the mid-1950s, sales of new motorcycles in the United States stood at a paltry 60,000 units per year. By 1973, annual sales had soared to more than two million. This staggering increase was almost solely due to the inventiveness and enterprise of the Japanese, who produced reliable, fast and exciting machines far more advanced than any Harley, at a far lower price. Whatever "image" Harleys possessed was undersold, with few buyers prepared to pay the premium. The AMF years had seen turnover grow from $49 million to over $300 million but profits were going into reverse.

Milwaukee's response was to allege cut-price "dumping" of Japanese models, as with Triumph 20 years earlier. The American International Trade Commission (ITC) agreed that dumping had taken place but that the effective subsidy was almost negligible. It concluded that the practice had not significantly harmed Milwaukee's sales and that the principal cause of Harley's difficulties was self-imposed: its model range was obsolete.

More than a decade earlier, William H. Davidson had remarked that AMF "thought Harley-Davidson could become another Honda. That's ridiculous... we were never meant to be a high production company."

AMF had to some extent attempted to compete head-on with Japan rather than concentrating on the more specialized market that Harley suited best. Production figures for 1982 offer some measure of the hopelessness of such a strategy: Honda built more than

TOP Willie G. Davidson's immortal "factory custom": the trend-setting Super Glide.

ABOVE With its tiny "peanut" fuel tank giving a distinctive silhouette, the XLH Sportster added style if not huge performance to the range in 1979.

LEFT Another Super Glide, this time fitted with optional pillion backrest.

ABOVE Fine-tuning the details: design chief Willie G. looks on as an engine cover is shaped in clay by one of Harley's development team.

ABOVE The American – or is it Harley? – Eagle, proudly displayed in the Visitor Center lobby at Wauwatosa.

3.5 million bikes in the year; Harley built fewer than 50,000.

The situation was desperate. Just six short years after 1973, Harley's share of the rapidly growing American big-bike market had plunged from almost 100 per cent to less than 40 per cent.

Production in the United States plummeted from 75,000 motorcycles in 1975 to 41,000 in 1981. Dire labour relations had brought a 101-day strike in 1974 over cost-of-living wage increases. Some in the company saw this coming, despite an artificial boost in 1978 due to the company's 75th birthday celebrations. Vaughn Beals, company president since 1977, and chief engineer Jeff Bleustein alerted top managers to the unpalatable realities. Beals set up a quality control and inspection programme that began to eliminate the worst of the problems, but all these measures were at a prodigious cost.

New initiatives slowly began to put Harley-Davidson back on track. But what would be the first to give: the problem or the company?

ABOVE The FXEF Fat Bob brought laid-back V-twin cruiser style to Harley's range in 1979; its name would become a long-running favourite.

RIGHT Another symphony in metal from Willie G., the XLCR Café Racer.

"THE EAGLE SOARS ALONE"

The year 1981 brought what was probably the most momentous – and certainly the most audacious – episode in the long history of Harley-Davidson: the management buyout that began the firm's remarkable rise to success.

With AMF losing interest and patience, chairman Vaughn Beals persuaded 12 other Harley executives to join him in an $81.5 million leveraged buyout from AMF control. The group included Charlie Thompson, appointed president the previous year, and Willie G. Davidson. A letter of intent was signed on 26 February and the bid went public five days later at Daytona Beach. The group found a willing lead lender in Citicorp Bank and after several months of tough bargaining with AMF, the newly-independent Harley-Davidson Motor Co. began business on 16 June 1981. The event, not surprisingly, was accompanied by widespread rejoicing and fanfares, under the slogan "The Eagle Soars Alone" – including a symbolic ride-out by the new owners from Milwaukee to York, as well as a solid gold dipstick for the first bike built under the new regime. Harley-Davidson was finally owned and run by real motorcyclists, men who loved the big V-twins, men who really cared. They were heady days, but the euphoria counted for nothing on its own. The American market, and Harley-Davidson's part in particular, was about to cave in even further. The buy-out did not enhance the buyers' fortunes as much as had been hoped – the newly-independent company's share of the shrinking American big-bike cake had dropped to a mere 23 per cent by 1983.

ABOVE The official portrait of the firm's group of 13 new owners, taken in June 1981, includes Jeffrey Bleustein (standing, second left), Willie G. Davidson (standing, far right), company president Charles Thompson (seated, second from right) and chairman Vaughn Beals (seated, far right).

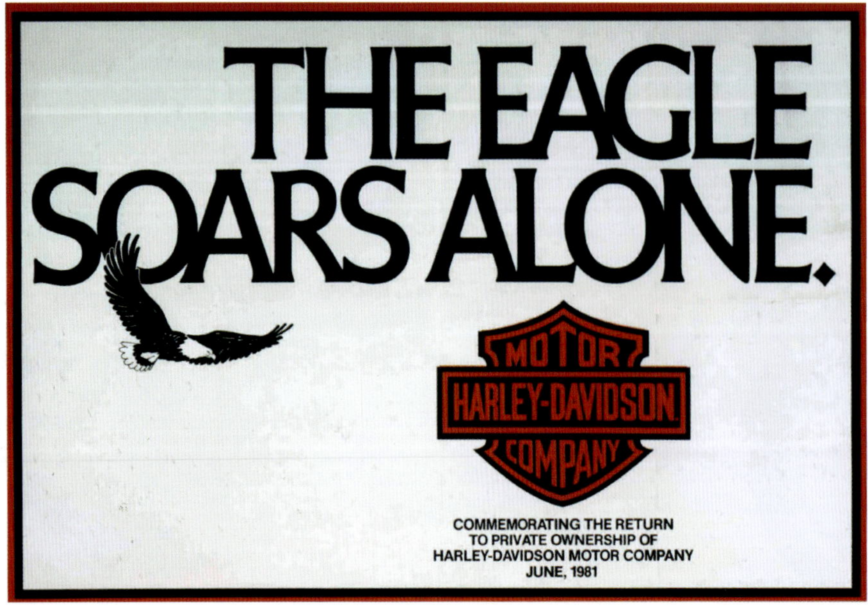

BELOW Harley's advertising celebrated the marque's new-found freedom following the AMF era and reflected a new spirit of optimism in Milwaukee.

Ownership may have changed but one fundamental truth had not: Harley-Davidson's competitors were still producing better bikes at lower cost.

Over-staffing was part of the problem, and almost 200 clerical jobs went almost at once, but there was much more to it. Put bluntly, Harley's – indeed, much of America's – manufacturing culture was antique. Beals and other managers had toured Japanese plants in 1980 but it wasn't

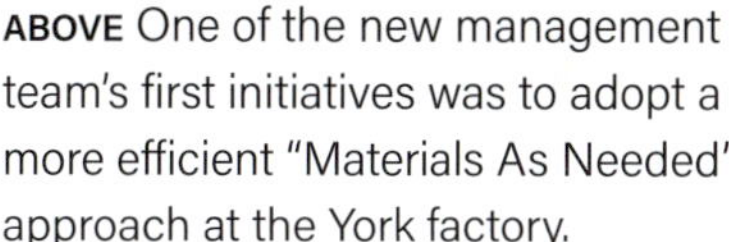

ABOVE One of the new management team's first initiatives was to adopt a more efficient "Materials As Needed" approach at the York factory.

ABOVE The FXS Low Rider, with its kicked-out forks and low bars, became a popular model in the years following its introduction in 1977.

until after the buyout, when they were given the opportunity to inspect the Honda assembly plant in Marysville, Ohio, that they began to fully understand the issues.

As chairman Vaughn Beals remarked: "We found it hard to believe we could be that bad – but we were. We were being wiped out by the Japanese because they were better managers. It wasn't robotics, or culture, or morning callisthenics and company songs – it was professional managers who understood their business and paid attention to detail."

Beals' message wasn't lost on the new team. With help from industrial fixers Andersen Consulting, within four months pilot programmes for "just-in-time" statistical process control (Harley called this "MAN" – Materials As Needed) and other up-to-date production systems were initiated and staff levels were slashed from 3,800 to 2,200. Tom Gelb, in charge of production, explained the situation to Harley-Davidson staff as directly as possible: "We have to play the game the way the Japanese play it or we're dead."

Quality and efficiency was one thing, getting the message across to potential customers quite another. The company shifted its marketing focus, stopped trying to compete against Japanese mainstream motorcycles and threw all of its resources into developing what we now take for granted as its uniquely American big-bike niche. (Along the way, the secret Nova project for a range of liquid-cooled models, from V-twins to V6s, was dropped after several prototypes had been produced.) Was it too little, too late? Despite new models such as the five-speed FXR Super Glide II and a new Sportster, the lone-flying eagle reported a loss of $25 million in 1982. It was going to be a close-run thing.

THE PRESIDENT STEPS IN

In August 1982, another Harley delegation made the trip to Washington, again alleging illegal trading practices by Japanese motorcycle companies. Yet again, the ITC was told that cheap motorcycles were being illegally dumped on the

BELOW The FXB Sturgis of 1980 was based on the Super Glide, and introduced the toothed belt final drive that would become a universal feature.

market and that the Japanese were "virtually copying" Harley models, all of which was seriously undermining their sales. This time Harley had a case, as massive over-supply in declining markets meant that many machines were sold at a loss. As Vaughn Beals put it, "We simply want the US government to restore order to a motorcycle market under siege by Japanese manufacturers who increased production in the face of sharp market decline."

As if to highlight the problem, the local Wisconsin police force bought Kawasaki motorcycles rather than Harleys, prompting a mass ride-out in protest from Capitol Drive.

The Commission duly found in Milwaukee's favour and recommended as much to President Ronald Reagan. On All Fools' Day 1983, the White House confirmed that import tariffs were to be imposed on Japanese machines. The tariffs would apply to all imported models of more than 700cc, at the hefty rate of 45 per cent (in addition to the existing 4.4 per cent duty), decreasing year-by-year to 35, 20, 15 and 10 per cent until April 1988.

LEFT Having persuaded President Ronald Reagan to introduce import tariffs in 1983, Vaughn Beals would score a publicity coup by requesting their early removal four years later.

Although Japanese machines built in the United States, such as Honda Gold Wings, were exempt, the levy was inevitably a major asset to Harley-Davidson's regeneration. In the meantime, they had to continue to improve quality and efficiency. Perhaps most crucial of all, a credible replacement for the aged Shovelhead was long overdue. Short-term fixes such as the digital ignition introduced on the new FXRT in 1983 were no longer enough.

Harley threw $3 million into a "Super Ride" demonstration programme in 1984, to show that the company had solved its notorious quality-control problems. TV commercials invited bikers to visit any of its 600-plus dealers to road test a new Harley. Over three weekends, the

BELOW The aborted Nova project would have included sporty naked models such as this V4 prototype in an attempt to compete with Japanese firms.

RIGHT Honda's Sabre V4 was one of numerous Japanese 750cc models produced in 700cc form for the US market, to beat the import tariffs.

company gave 90,000 rides to 40,000 people, half of whom owned other brands. At first, the venture didn't sell enough bikes to cover its cost, but it made the point.

Then there was HOG – the Harley Owners' Group. This was a major corporate effort to bring customers together in the Harley-Davidson lifestyle. Nothing so ambitious had ever been attempted by any motorcycle manufacturer, yet HOG proved uniquely suited to the Harley image. A runaway success, HOG now boasts roughly a million committed members worldwide and is a model for similar schemes by other motorcycle manufacturers.

The company also began to defend its name, copyrights and trademarks for the first time, and vigorously. In future, if anyone wanted a Harley-Davidson logo, Milwaukee would demand its rightful royalties. Over half a century after pioneering the sale of branded accessories, Harley was at last determined to cash in on the image it had taken eight decades to create. Slowly, Vaughn Beals and his team began to turn the near-disaster around. Thanks to improvements in quality and efficiency, and more aggressive marketing, Harley began steadily to catch up with mighty Honda in the heavyweight division.

At last, this very American company was beginning to make the most of its uniquely American image. 1982's loss became a small surplus in 1983.

A year later, in 1984, Harley reported a profit of $2.9 million on sales of $294 million. Even though there was still a very long way to go, and plenty of stormy weather to navigate, the eagle was on its way.

BELOW The FXWG Wide Glide of the early 1980s had plenty of laid-back Harley style but its build quality did not match that of Japanese models.

EVOLUTION

The anxiously-awaited replacement for the Shovelhead finally arrived in 1984 – and Harley-Davidson's future balanced precariously on a knife's edge. The V2 Evolution engine certainly looked like the answer to everyone's prayers, and it would prove a lasting success.

Despite a bottom-end with origins dating back to the 61E of 1936, the "Evo" was an altogether better power-plant than the Shovelhead it replaced.

As the name suggested, it was a development of the Shovel rather than a totally new design, yet almost every component was different and improved. Its cylinders, splayed at the "classic" 45 degrees, displaced 81.8cu in or 1,340cc (though badges rounded this down to 80in). Scaling 20lbs (9kgs) less but producing 15 per cent more torque than its predecessor, the Evo would prove to be all it was cracked up to be.

In 1983, Harley-Davidson made sure its new baby created an impact with a publicity stunt to mark the company's 80th birthday celebrations: 8,000 miles (12,875 km) at an average of 80mph (128.7kph) with none of the routine servicing a customer's machine would receive on standard FLT Tour Glides. At Talladega Speedway in July 1983, the Evolution-engined Tour Glides thundered through the designated 8,000 miles, but slightly off the scheduled pace: allowing for mishaps that never occurred, they averaged 85mph (136.8kph).

A brand-new engine was cause enough for celebration (helped perhaps by the new H-D brand beer), but the first model powered by the Evo engine was a landmark in its own right. This was the 1984 FXST Softail, and with it came a whole new concept in motorcycle style and design. With its fake "hardtail" rear end, gleaming chrome and low, rounded lines, the Softail was a strident echo of motorcycles of the 1950s: the age of Retro-Tech had dawned. Sportsters still cut a dash, especially with the launching of the new XR750-inspired XR1000. A year later, the Heritage Softail followed the basic FXST.

Almost overnight – or so it seemed

ABOVE One of the first Evo engines in one of the first Softails: a big advance for both powerplant and chassis.

RIGHT Retro-Tech: the hardtail look of this Heritage Softail is clear. The system uses twin shock absorbers hidden beneath the engine.

ABOVE The Springer Softail adopted a traditional girder-style front end.

ABOVE As well as being lighter and more powerful than its Shovelhead predecessor, the Evo unit would also prove more oil-tight and reliable.

RIGHT The "basic" Softail models retained telescopic front forks.

– Harley-Davidson had a credible range and, after the gremlins of the Shovelhead years, a reputation for the dependability that had once been its hallmark. Again it had a product capable of meeting the demands of the California Highway Patrol (CHiPs) who, after a decade mounted on Kawasakis and Moto Guzzis, in 1984 ordered 155 FXRP Police Specials.

To Harley insiders, however, the "Evo year" was probably far more memorable for the financial strife which continued to undermine them. In 1984, Citicorp Bank, underwriter of the original buy-out, was becoming concerned that Harley's future might not be so rosy once the tariff on foreign competitors ended in 1988. Reasoning that the best time to get a good price for the company was when sales were still on the rise, they moved quickly, hitting Harley's directors with the bombshell: all credit facilities would be severely restricted from the following year.

This was a major blow to Harley's ambitious plans and the survival of the entire buy-out. Harley-Davidson was broke.

TURNING BACK THE TIDE

"Hawking begging bowls around Wall Street" was how Vaughn Beals described his desperate response. Over the summer of 1985, Beals and chief financial officer Richard Teerlink (later to succeed Beals as H-D's head), chased in vain after new lenders. Then, with the situation looking hopeless and lawyers drafting bankruptcy plans, Dean Witter Reynolds put Beals and Teerlink in touch with the Heller Financial Corporation. Luckily for Beals, Heller's second-in-command, Bob Koe, was a long-time Harley buff and willing to listen. He was impressed by what he heard, and on 23 December 1985 a financial package was agreed – the best Christmas present for which Harley could have wished.

The rescue package turned out to be a good deal for everyone but Citicorp, who had badly underestimated the outlook for this vibrant new Harley-D. Including credits, the bank received $49 million for the deal, $2 million less than it had poured in. Harley received $49.5 million of working capital. In a supreme irony, Harley recovered the Number One spot from Honda a year after being abandoned by Citicorp, with 33 per cent of the over-850cc American market. The long struggle to

improve production and marketing, and regenerate the model range was beginning to pay dividends. 1986 profits were $4.3 million on sales of $295 million.

Harley's financial base was secured in July 1987 by floating the company on the New York Stock Exchange. The offer raised more than £30 million, allowing the company to reschedule its debts and buy the Holiday Rambler Corporation, a leading manufacturer of recreational vehicles. In October, the manufacturing rights to the military MT500 motorcycle were acquired from the British Armstrong company. Less comforting was the closure of the competition department, though it made sound financial sense. Production of XR750 dirt-track engines was

ABOVE The FLS Electra Glide Sport of 1988 combined Evo performance with style and all-round ability.

ABOVE The round air filter cover was a distinctive Evolution engine feature.

LEFT Electra Glides and Tour Glides evolved ever-more luxury features such as cruise control, CB radio and intercoms.

ABOVE Executives Tim Hoelter, Vaughn Beals and Rich Teerlink celebrate Harley's Wall Street flotation, July 1987.

unaffected, and racing continued in the famous livery through independent dealer teams.

The most impressive news of all came on 17 March. In what turned out to be a public-relations triumph, Harley had taken the unprecedented step of asking that trade protection be removed a year ahead of schedule. As Vaughn Beals explained at the time, Harley-Davidson "no longer need tariff relief to compete with the Japanese". The chairman highlighted "the strong message... to the international community: US workers... can become competitive in world markets." Harley was again "the pride of America".

This was brought home best of all by President Ronald Reagan. After touring the York factory in Pennsylvania in May 1987, he hailed the turnaround in Harley-Davidson's fortunes as "an American success story". And how right he was.

A major contribution to future success was tied up with the XLH 883 Sportster. With a price tag of just under $4,000 when introduced, the 883 was the type of entry-level machine so conspicuously absent from the Milwaukee stable in the past. In 1987, 883 owners got an even better deal with the announcement of Harley's innovative buy-back scheme: "Trade in your XLH against an FX or FL within two years and we'll guarantee $3,995 on your old machine."

Major new models included the stunning Heritage Softail Classic, Electra Glide Sport and Low Rider Custom. By the end of 1987, Harley had 47 per cent of the American "super-heavyweight" market, a figure which would rise to 54 per cent just one year later. At last, Harley-Davidson was truly starting to soar.

SPRINGING AHEAD

1988 saw the debut of the largest-capacity Sportster ever – the 1100 grew to the full 1200cc of the XLH 1200. 1988 also brought a revamped FXRS Low Rider with improved forks and twin-cap Fat Bob fuel tank. Most

ABOVE In stark contrast to the Electra Glide's luxury features was the Sportster series, of which this 1984 XR-1000 is surely the best looking and most prized.

RIGHT In Europe, as well as the United States, Evo Harley sales began to boom. This Heritage Softail Classic thunders across the Belgian Ardennes.

LEFT In places such as Florida's Daytona Beach, Harleys inspire crowds of fans of American iron. Fittingly, this is the famous Iron Horse Saloon.

striking of all was the model chosen to mark Harley-Davidson's 85th birthday, the FXTS Springer Softail. The Springer was a radical step both forward and back. Looking like a 1950 classic, it dispensed with the telescopic front end in favour of gleaming, chromed, lookalike girders. For the first time, a Harley had Retro-Tech at both ends and, almost overnight, became the style king of the Milwaukee range.

Within a year, the Springer and new Low Rider were joined by "Ultra Classic" versions of the all-conquering Tour Glide and Electra Glide models. These luxurious machines came equipped with a host of extras as standard, including cruise control, cigar lighter, intercom, CB radio and a sophisticated stereo hi-fi system. These were the best-equipped and most expensive models in the range. The high prices did not prevent them from becoming popular.

Ironically, as standard equipment became even more comprehensive, there was counter-demand for a model more like the stripped-down Glides of the 1970s, such as the handsome FLHS Electra Glide Sport introduced two

LEFT International Harley: an Electra Glide Classic in the damp Welsh mountains.

BELOW A big twin in the heat of New Mexico, south-west USA.

RIGHT The Sportster family followed the big twins in being given a substantial boost with new Evolution engines, here with a 1200 model from 1990.

RIGHT Jackets and other branded clothing have long been a lucrative part of Harley's business.

BELOW During the 1990s, Dyna Glides evolved from Low Riders to become one of the core elements of the Milwaukee line-up.

years earlier. In 1989, a revamped clothing division – "MotorClothes" – was launched. MotorClothes, allied with Harley-Davidson's flourishing aftermarket hardware accessories, accounts for a substantial portion of overall annual profits. It is now possible to buy anything from bowie knives to toiletries bearing the celebrated H-D motif. Since the early 1990s there have been "Harley" shops that sell no motorcycles at all.

With this priceless image came a turnaround in overall fortunes, from near-broke leviathan to glorious sales success. The foundations were varied: much-improved manufacturing of a broader, better model range allied to shrewd financial management, as well as inspired marketing. Production methods had witnessed a revolution, with each worker both a vital part of the quality-control process and a partner in Harley-Davidson's affairs. The Evolution engine earned a deserved reputation for rugged durability, oil-tightness and general user-friendliness. Not least was Harley-Davidson's good fortune in being located in the world's largest market for big-inch touring machines.

BOOM TIME

As the traditional style-improving quality and enduring charm of Harley's V-twin cruisers and tourers attracted riders, including affluent professionals and movie stars, the Milwaukee firm began a golden age – three decades of spectacular growth in both production levels and profitability.

By the early 1990s, the tide had well and truly turned – indeed the boot was on the other foot. Annual production had reached more than 62,000 units, with 20 models accounting for 61 per cent of the American heavyweight market and more than 30 per cent of output exported to Milwaukee fans worldwide, double the figure of four years earlier. At the same time, sales of Japanese motorcycles were in steep decline, their dealers cutting margins or going out of business altogether.

Having not so long ago been regarded by the general public as the transport of hooligans, Hell's Angels and other undesirables, Harley-Davidsons had somehow become aspirational leisure vehicles. Countless newspaper and magazine articles detailed how, behind their facade of black leather and tattoos, the new breed of "rich urban bikers" or RUBs were lawyers, medics and other affluent professionals.

Harley tapped into this, with promotional events at upmarket venues including Bloomingdale's department store that reinforced the image of the motorcycle as "yuppie" status symbol. Forbes reported that in 1990 the typical Harley customer was a 35-year-old

ABOVE The moody Road King was a stylish attempt to return to the leaner, cleaner lines of the earliest Electra Glides.

BELOW The Fat Boy's clean lines, monotone finish and disc wheels made the big V-twin a unique style statement.

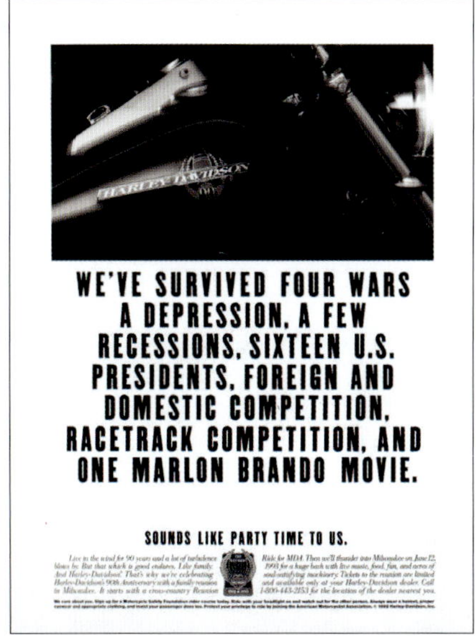

ABOVE By the mid-1990s, top of the range Glides had added fuel injection to their extensive repertoire of "goodies".

ABOVE RIGHT In 1993, Harley-Davidson's 90th anniversary presented plenty of reasons for celebration.

RIGHT Top of the range for 1995 was the freshly fuel-injected Electra Glide Ultra Classic.

male with a household income of $45,000, far above the national average, and 60 per cent were college graduates.

Those who had invested in the company also had plenty to be cheerful about. As Harley's earnings rose at an average of 57 per cent annually from 1986 to 1990, the stock price followed suit. By June 1990 the stock had risen tenfold from its initial $11 per share price of a few years earlier. Management teams from other firms, Forbes reported, were "flocking to Milwaukee and York to witness first-hand the healthy vital signs of what ten years before had been a basket case".

NEW DESIGNS

New hardware continued to stream out of the York factory. Many Harley fans rated the star of the 1990 catalogue as one of the most beautiful Harley-Davidsons ever created. "Fat Boy" was its unprepossessing and controversial title (Harley firmly denied rumours that the name was inspired by the "Fat Man" and "Little Boy" bombs dropped on Japanese cities in 1945), yet the original FLSTF was an understated symphony in silver-grey.

Harley's new aspirational status was reflected by Hollywood, most memorably by Arnold Schwarzenegger, the Fat Boy-riding, shotgun-wielding star of *Terminator 2: Judgement Day* – 1991's highest grossing movie. In the same year, Mickey Rourke starred in *Harley Davidson and the Marlboro Man*, which made less impact but put the spotlight on Milwaukee again.

If Harley had any problems during the 1990s, one was encroaching noise and emissions regulations; the other the sheer difficulty of meeting soaring demand as customers waited up to a year for their bikes. A major victory for environmental concerns was the first fuel-injected Harley roadster, the Ultra Classic Electra Glide, in 1995. Injection made the twin smoother and cleaner-running than any previous V-twin.

INVESTMENT SUCCESS

Solving the supply problem involved a whirlwind programme of capital investment. The spending had begun with the opening of a huge new automated paint plant at York in 1992. This $23 million facility finally broke York's crippling production bottleneck, taking manufacturing capacity beyond 110,000 machines per year.

Accompanying this was a hard-nosed commercial edge which began with the defence of trademarks – even including attempts to copyright the "Harley sound". To many diehard fans, Harley's corporate clout sat uneasily alongside the image of easy-going, down-home virtues the company was at pains to present.

Before long, Harleys were being conceived and developed in an environment as implacably space-age as the bikes themselves were defiantly old-fashioned. The Willie G. Davidson Product Development Center was completed in 1997, at a cost of $40 million. Standing just a stone's throw from the Capitol Drive engine factory, it boasted a floor area of 213,000sq ft (20,000sq metres) under a graceful arc of concrete and glass, a structure befitting 21st-century ambitions.

A new Big Twin power train plant was also opened in 1997, located at nearby Menomonee Falls. The following year Harley opened an $85 million Sportster plant at Kansas City. Sales topped $2 billion for the first time, with output totalling 150,818 bikes.

In 1998 Harley also took a majority holding in Buell, which had been founded by former racer and Harley engineer Erik Buell five years earlier,

ABOVE Arnold Schwarzenegger gave the recently released Fat Boy useful publicity when starring in *Terminator 2: Judgement Day* in 1991.

BELOW The Heritage Springer Softail was a stylish way to combine girder-style front forks, whitewall tyres and fringed leather panniers in 1997.

ABOVE For 1999, 15 years after the arrival of the redoubtable Evo, a new generation of Twin Cam 88 big twins hit the Harley scene.

and was assembling bikes in nearby East Troy. The acquisition was intended to boost performance and broaden appeal. Harley supplied Sportster engines to Buell, whose team added horsepower with tuning modifications, as well as bolting the V-twins into radical chassis featuring an anti-vibration mounting system and under-slung rear shock unit.

The benefits of this were illustrated in 1998 by the differences between the Harley-badged Sportster 1200S and Buell's S1 White Lightning, which was 7bhp more powerful and had sharper handling – albeit without the Sportster's traditional appeal.

Buell had also aimed to attract younger and novice riders with the Blast, a 492cc, single-cylinder lightweight that Harley boss Jeff Bleustein had envisaged as an ideal training and entry-level model. But although the Blast's engine was based on half of a Sportster V-twin unit, the bike was relatively expensive to produce, and failed to sell in the hoped-for numbers.

DESIGN INNOVATION

Harley's model range received a major boost in 1999 with the introduction of the Twin Cam 88 powerplant, which had been developed to increase both performance and reliability,

ABOVE For 1999, models including the Dyna Wide Glide and the Road King were fitted with the more powerful and reliable Twin Cam 88 engine.

BELOW Buell's White Lightning offered more power and handling ability than the 1200 Sportster on whose engine its 93bhp unit was based.

particularly when tuned. But as Earl Werner, the firm's Vice President of Engineering, emphasised, this was no radical step.

"We had three main aims: it had to look like a Harley engine, it had to sound like a Harley engine, and it had to feel like a Harley engine," Werner said. "We have the technology to produce a smooth, vibration-free motor, but our customers everywhere tell us that's not what they want. This motor was engineered to have roughly the same amount of vibration although it has a larger capacity."

The Twin Cam 88 got its name from its twin camshafts – which still operated pushrods – and capacity of 88 cubic inches, or 1450cc, up from the 1340cc, 80-cube Evolution engine. The importance of the Twin Cam's arrival to Harley could be judged from the fact that this was the firm's first new motor for 15 years, and only the sixth major redesign since the first V-twin's introduction in 1909.

Besides the revised cam system and extra capacity, the motor was strengthened throughout with larger bearings and better lubrication, to the extent that very few Evo components remained. Initially, seven models were fitted with the 88 motor: the Dyna range of cruisers, including the new Dyna Super Glide Sport; and the Tourers including the Road Glide.

A year later, for the 2000 model year, the Softail family, whose engines were solidly- rather than rubber-mounted, received a similar update with the Twin Cam 88B, the B standing for balancer – a pair of contra-rotating balancer shafts. These were the first Harley had ever used, and were situated low down on the right of the engine. "Six new bikes with new engines, in the most important sector of our range, makes this the largest product introduction in the 96-year history of Harley-Davidson," claimed Werner.

Not that most motorcyclists, even most Harley riders, would have appreciated the engineers' efforts just by looking at the bikes. The firm's stated aim had been to "change everything, without changing a thing". They had succeeded, too, making the machines faster, more comfortable, easier and more pleasant to ride while barely altering their style or character at all.

By contrast the V-Rod, launched in 2001, began a bold new era for Harley with its 1,130cc liquid-cooled, DOHC eight-valve V-twin engine, whose cylinders were set at 60 degrees apart, instead of the familiar 45. With its

ABOVE Jeffrey Bleustein, one of the 13 managers involved in Harley's buyout in 1981, took over as CEO in 1997.

BELOW The Deuce, introduced for the year 2000, sports the latest balance-shafted Twin Cam 88B engine.

aluminium finish the V-Rod looked stunning, and its 115bhp output gave it performance to match, backed up by very respectable handling and braking.

Any disappointment in Milwaukee that the V-Rod did not make the sales impact that its style and performance arguably merited was surely tempered by the sight of aircooled V-twins continuing to roar out of showrooms as fast as the factory could build them. The firm had motored into the new millennium on the back of more record production, which in 2000 had topped 200,000 for the first time.

In 2003 Harley celebrated its centenary, and was well able to afford a huge party in Milwaukee, as sales reached 291,000. Just three years after that, in 2006, the firm shipped 349,196 bikes – close to ten times the 1986 total. Profit topped $1 billion, an equally remarkable figure. It had been a wildly successful 30-year ride. But there were some big bumps in the road up ahead...

ABOVE The V-Rod added liquid-cooled V-twin performance and dramatic style in 1999 but did not make the sales impact that Harley had hoped.

BELOW An estimated 200,000 riders attended Harley's centenary celebrations in Milwaukee in 2003, as sales continued to rise.

SURVIVING THE STORM

Harley-Davidson's three decades of continuous growth came to an abrupt halt in 2007 with the financial crisis that rocked many industries around the world. Most motorcycle manufacturers were hit hard, with demand for Harley's high-end bikes especially badly affected.

Sales plunged from an all-time high of 344,000 in 2006 to 222,000 in 2010 – a loss of 35 per cent in four years. Having made a profit of a billion dollars in 2006, by 2009 Harley was posting a loss of $55 million. In the first three quarters of 2009 the firm's Finance division, specializing in loans to buy new bikes, lost over $100 million, having made a similar amount in the same period a year earlier.

The credit crunch was the trigger, but the bubble had been threatening to burst for years. Harley's traditional market was ageing rapidly and was not being refreshed by young riders. In 1985, the median age of a Harley owner had been 27. By 2008, when the firm stopped disclosing the figures, it was 48 – and still going up.

LEFT The Night Rod Special of 2008 was powerful but no more successful than others in Harley's liquid-cooled V-twin line.

The company was also a victim of its own success. The huge sales over many years had created a pool of high-quality used machines, with many enthusiasts owning several bikes. Continued technical improvements ensured that new Harleys remained attractive, but the incentive to invest in a visually little-changed model had waned.

Broadening the brand's appeal had also proved difficult. Acquiring Buell had been part of that strategy, especially with a view to increasing sales in Europe. But despite much effort and investment, Buell production had increased slowly, the high point of 13,000 in 2008 being just a few per cent of the company total.

BELOW The Softail Rocker was stylish and cleverly designed but arrived too late to catch the chopper craze.

ABOVE MV Agusta's 1078 Brutale and sporty F4 were glamorous but the firm's affair with Harley was short.

In that same year Harley made a more spectacular attempt to diversify, paying over $100 million to buy MV Agusta, the historic Italian firm renowned for its racing history, glamorous sports bikes and frequent financial crises. Several tens of millions more were then spent on debt repayment, new production machinery and model development.

BELOW Erik Buell's enthusiasm for innovative engineering could not make the Buell marque a lasting success.

BELOW MV's Claudio Castiglioni (left) with Harley CEO Jim Ziemer and new MV boss Matt Levatich in 2008.

CHANGING STRATEGY

With financial pressures mounting however, this was not the time for expansion. Harley made a dramatic change of direction following the arrival as CEO in May 2009 of Keith Wandell, who was a controversial appointment: he was the first boss from outside the company, having previously headed a Milwaukee-based auto parts supplier, and didn't ride a motorcycle.

Wandell acted fast, closing the Capitol Drive plant and a distribution centre in Franklin, and cutting 25 per cent of the workforce. Many jobs were lost at the York plant, which had been hit by a long strike in 2007. Wandell modernized the factory and negotiated union contracts to allow more temporary workers, meaning production could be more easily adjusted to suit demand.

Two dramatic changes were announced in October 2009: MV Agusta was to be sold, and Buell was to close with immediate effect. Buell was deemed to be too closely allied to Harley for it to be sold off so that production could continue, even though axing it cost over $100 million.

The similarly huge amount that had been spent on MV was also lost; the firm was eventually sold in 2010, to long-time president Claudio Castiglioni, for just €1. "We were allocating our limited resources to different brands, and starving the Harley-Davidson brand," Wandell later explained.

Those losses and the costs of updating Harley's factories were estimated at close to half a billion dollars, but they were vital in reducing long-term expenditure. Wandell's medicine proved effective. Sales began to recover, reaching 270,000 in 2014. By this time the firm was back in profit and its stock price had risen six-fold since the low of 2009.

ABOVE Buell's 1125R sportster failed to impress on its launch in 2008 but it was a shock when Harley closed down the firm a year later.

CONTINUING IMPROVEMENTS

Harley had at least managed to continue improving its bikes through the financially tough times. In 2007, the Twin Cam 96 powerplant had increased the Big Twin models'

BELOW While Harley negotiated turbulent financial times in 2009, the Road King Classic was updated and rumbled on contentedly.

BELOW The Street 750 offered respectable performance and a relatively low price but lacked the character of Harley's aircooled V-twins.

ABOVE The Forty-Eight's raw, simple style and abundance of aircooled V-twin character tempted plenty of riders to ignore its poor fuel range.

capacity to 1584cc, also adding a six-speed gearbox and lighter clutch. Two years later, the Touring family was updated with new chassis incorporating firmer suspension and stiffer frames and swing-arms.

Another big step came in 2014, when the Touring models were updated following a program called Project Rushmore. This incorporated changes in more than 100 areas, including engine performance and heat control, handling, braking, wind protection, pillion accommodation, luggage, lighting, sound system and navigation.

There was a new and more powerful Twin Cam 103 motor, which for models including the flagship Electra Glide Ultra Limited was liquid-cooled for the first time. The Street Glide, which had led the "bagger" movement and become Harley's most popular model, also received most of the updates, although not the liquid-cooling, which required fairing lowers.

The Sportster family remained successful, not least in its entry-level 883cc capacity. In 2004 the family had been improved by the adoption of rubber-mounted engines. The Sportster's appeal was highlighted in 2010 by the Forty-Eight, featuring a tiny "peanut" gas tank above its 1200cc engine. It wasn't fast or light, and its fuel range was feeble... but it was seriously cool, and very popular.

For 2015, the Forty-Eight and its 883cc sidekick the Iron were updated with new graphics, retaining their simple aircooled engines and timeless retro charm. The year's more significant arrivals were very different: the Street 750 and 500, powered by the new "Revolution X" engine, featuring liquid-cooling, SOHC valve operation, and cylinders angled at 60 degrees rather than the usual 45.

Harley hoped the Street models would attract a new generation of riders to replace the ageing "baby boomers" who remained the marque's customer base, especially in the US. They were priced well below the Sportster models and had been developed partly to satisfy many Asian markets' growing demand for premium brands.

The Street models had the Harley-Davidson name and a look reminiscent of the XLCR Café Racer of 1977. Their performance was good if not exceptional. But they couldn't match the character of aircooled models including the Sportsters, and sold slowly almost everywhere.

MARKET DIVERSIFICATION

Harley's move to build bikes in India was a continuation of a policy that had begun with a factory in Manaus, Brazil, in 1998. Milwaukee's ambition of increasing export sales had been hampered by high import duty in countries including India. By 2018 Harley also had a factory in Thailand.

BELOW The 2014 Ultra Limited was one of the Touring family models comprehensively revamped under the program named Project Rushmore.

LEFT The LiveWire was stylish and quick, but the electric bike's high price and limited range marred its appeal.

BELOW New CEO Jochen Zeitz was encouraged by the response to the Pan America, following the adventure V-twin's launch in 2020.

But foreign production brought difficulties, not least when President Donald Trump set tariffs on imported steel, which increased costs – and which were followed by retaliatory European tariffs on motorcycles. CEO Matt Levatich reacted by aiming to move more production abroad, triggering criticism from Trump. Harley's problems with tariffs were ironic given the way the firm had benefitted from Ronald Reagan's protection of its home market decades earlier.

If foreign expansion was one possible route to growing sales, discovering new market sectors was another. Harley's most ambitious attempt at this was LiveWire, the electric bike that the firm had unveiled in prototype form in 2014, with a bold programme of public demo rides across the US. The bike was powerful, strikingly styled and neatly engineered.

Response to the demo rides was positive, and Harley became the first mainstream manufacturer with a high-performance electric model when the LiveWire went on sale five years later. But the firm's ambition to become the two-wheeled equivalent of

LEFT The Sportster S of 2021 began a new, powerful liquid-cooled generation that had little in common with the aircooled Sportsters of old.

RIGHT The 2024-model Hydra-Glide Revival was another example of Milwaukee's ability to create models inspired by those of the past.

Tesla swiftly foundered on the drawbacks of high price and limited range that had made rival bike manufacturers more cautious. Sales started slowly and declined; in 2021 fewer than 400 units were sold worldwide.

In the same year Harley spun off LiveWire into a separate company and floated it on the Stock Exchange, with the aim that growth would be easier as a start-up firm. New CEO Jochen Zeitz announced a second, less powerful and expensive model, the Del Mar; and set a hugely ambitious goal of increasing LiveWire sales to over 100,000 by 2026. But sales of the rebranded LiveWire One model remained flat, investors pulled out, and Harley was forced to invest more heavily.

At least sales of Milwaukee's familiar V-twins had rallied, after Covid 19 had dragged 2020's total sales to barely 180,000, a level not seen since the turn of the millennium. And if Harley's bold gamble on electric bikes had yet to come good, its belated arrival in another, much more established market sector – adventure bikes – proved successful.

The Pan America was launched in 2020, combining distinctive, snub-nosed styling with a 1252cc, liquid-cooled, 60-degree V-twin engine, long-travel suspension and advanced electronics. It was powerful, handled well both on- and off-road, and was appealing both to existing Harley riders and owners of rival models.

Versions of the Pan America's Revolution Max V-twin engine were also used to power the Sportster S and the Nightster, the latter with smaller 975cc capacity. These naked roadsters were intended to take over from the old aircooled Sporter models, which disappeared from European showrooms for emissions reasons before production finally ended in 2023.

In the same year, Harley announced a partnership with Indian giant Hero MotoCorp. This involved local production of premium models for the Indian market and also development of new entry-level models, starting with the X440, a 27bhp aircooled single. A similar partnership with Chinese firm Qianjiang had led to a 338cc single, also developed mainly for Asian markets.

Harley-Davidson had clearly come a long way since the early Nineties, when the recently reborn firm's focus had been on its new generation of Evolution V-twins, and on growing its production and profit. Back then, CEO Rich Teerlink had warned that "Change is here to stay. It's never going to go away. Get used to it." Several decades later, his words seemed more true than ever.

RIGHT Harley created a new entry-level model in 2024 with the Nightster, whose 975cc, liquid-cooled V-twin engine produced 89bhp.

CYCLES

FACES AND PLACES

Harley-Davidson was founded on friendships, family and youthful enthusiasm. The single Harley (William S.) and the three Davidson brothers (Arthur, Walter and William) were practical men who would transform some garden-shed engineering into an enduring motorcycle legend.

Although Harley-Davidson ceased to be a family company in the 1960s, the Davidson name has remained involved through the highly revered Willie G. Davidson and more recently his son Bill, who joined the company in 1984 and is the great grandson of co-founder William A.

Harley's facilities have come a long way since the small wooden shed that was used in the early years, but for more than 120 years the company has remained true to the ideal of building the ultimate motorcycle.

LEFT Willie G. Davidson at the factory Museum in Milwaukee with the bronze sculpture of a hill-climber that his family donated on its opening in 2008.

FOUNDING FAMILIES

Harley-Davidson was created in 1903 by a Harley and three Davidsons and was owned by those families for more than half a century. Family ties held through a third and fourth generation, adding meaning to the famous double-barrelled name on every fuel tank.

ABOVE The founders, left to right: William A. Davidson, Walter Davidson, Arthur Davidson and William S. Harley.

WILLIAM S. HARLEY

"Young Bill" began work at the age of 15 in a Milwaukee bicycle factory, and even as an enthusiastic dabbler soon showed engineering skills. As able in the saddle as he was in the workshop, he later became Harley-Davidson's chief engineer and treasurer, positions he held until his death from heart failure on 18 September 1943.

On graduating from university in 1908, he had set about designing Harley's first successful V-twin, which appeared the following year, although it was 1911 before the design became as dependable as earlier singles.

Bill was later responsible for a host of classic Harleys, not to mention the first clutch, kick start and many other developments. In 1914, he established the factory's race shop, which scored 26 major wins in its first season. During both world wars, his contacts with the military were vital to the company's (and the nation's) success. Active in the governing body of American bike racing, the American Motorcycle Association (AMA), he was also a keen wildlife photographer in private life.

ARTHUR DAVIDSON

A pattern-maker by trade, Arthur had the reputation of being the most outgoing of the founders, his energetic temperament making him particularly suited to sales. Arthur became the company's secretary and general sales manager, roles he discharged with distinction until his death in a car accident on 30 December 1950, at the age of 69. His own son, James, and James' wife, were also to die in a road accident 16 years later.

Perhaps Arthur's most lasting legacy was the establishment of Harley-Davidson's nationwide and international dealer networks. Beginning in 1910, he had no fewer than 200 American outlets by 1912, later expanding to include official Harley-Davidson dealerships as far away as Australia and New Zealand. In the early years he practically ran the AMA "because there was no-one else around". After the Second World War, he spent an increasing amount of time at his farm in Waukesha County where he raised prize-winning Guernsey cattle.

WALTER S. DAVIDSON

Trained as a mechanic and machinist, Walter was a naturally gifted rider who brought the emergent Harley-Davidson company its first competition success. In June 1908, he entered a Harley-Davidson single in a two-day endurance run in New York's Catskill Mountains. The sole Harley in a field of 61, he scored a "perfect" 1,000 points, outstripping all of the preferred bikes. One month later, Walter was at it again, winning a Long Island economy run at no less than 188mpg (66km/litre) over 50 miles (80.5 kilometres).

Walter is best remembered, however, as Harley-Davidson's first president. Generous and scrupulously honest, he also became a director of First Wisconsin, the state's biggest bank. Walter died on 7 February 1942, still in charge at Juneau Avenue.

WILLIAM A. DAVIDSON

If Walter was the head of the company, "Old Bill" Davidson was regarded as its heart and driving force. Perhaps the least able rider of the foursome, Bill quickly found his niche as works manager, a vital position in a company

BELOW Harley-Davidson's first "factory", a 15 x 10ft wooden shed.

RIGHT Co-founder and star rider Walter Davidson with a robust single in 1908, the year of his and the firm's first competition success.

expanding as quickly as Harley-Davidson. A big, burly character equally at home hunting and fishing as on the factory floor, he had a generous but paternalistic attitude to Harley's employees. Despite his bitter opposition, the factory first became unionized in April 1937. Within two years, Old Bill was gone, the victim of diabetic complications and the first of the founders to die. His son, William H., believed the stress of losing the battle to the unions hastened his father's death.

SECOND GENERATION

In the late 1920s, the founders' sons began to join the company. William H. Davidson joined in 1928, although he had worked on the shop floor while a student at the University of Wisconsin. A year later, he was joined by Gordon and Walter C. (both sons of Walter S. Davidson), William J. Harley and, later, John E. Harley. Of the other sons, Allan Davidson, son of William A., worked only briefly for the company and died young; Arthur Davidson Jr. made a successful business career in his own right. Four of these "first generation founders" were to make major contributions to the American icon the company would become.

William J. Harley succeeded his father as the company's chief engineer. He became vice president in charge of engineering in 1957, a position he held until his death in 1971. A connoisseur of fine wines and cheeses, he evidently needed little encouragement to visit the Harley-Davidson factory in Varese, Italy, after the take-over of Aermacchi.

John E. Harley, younger brother to William J., was elected to the board in 1949 and ran the Harley parts and accessories business, today one of Milwaukee's major profit centres. He rose to the rank of major during the Second World War, including a spell instructing army motorcyclists.

Walter C. Davidson ultimately followed his uncle Arthur as vice president of sales, earning a reputation during the Second World War as the man who could somehow get materials other companies could not. After the war he fought Harley's increasingly rebellious dealer network, as Triumph and BSA in particular began offering

BELOW Just four years after building their first bike, the four founders line up with their staff at their Milwaukee factory in 1907.

LEFT The famous Juneau Avenue factory, which was a large step up from the wooden shed.

BELOW The Founders inspect the first Knucklehead to roll off the Juneau Avenue production line for the 1936 model year.

cheaper and faster products in the American market. Harley's efforts to hold the fort not only backfired at the time but were to lead to legislation which would later open the door for the Japanese. When AMF took over the company in 1968, Walter saw the writing on the wall and took early retirement.

William H. Davidson, the son of William A., made the most lasting mark of all. A skilled rider (he won the prestigious Jack Pine Enduro in 1930 riding a Model 30DLD), he was later described as "the mortar that cemented the company". He joined Harley-Davidson full-time in 1928, was elected to the board in 1931 and became vice president six years later. For the next five years, he was the driving force behind Harley-Davidson's vital government contract work. When Walter S. died, William H. was the obvious candidate to lead the company, becoming president "by common consent" on 23 February 1942.

RIGHT The co-founders cut a cake to celebrate the company's 50th anniversary at Capitol Drive in August 1953.

William H. had no doubts about where the company's future lay: "We tried for a long time to convince people that motorcycles had some utility value," he once presciently observed, "[but they] have never been anything but pleasure." In 1971, three years after the AMF takeover, he was appointed chairman of Harley-Davidson, but felt that the new company had "pulled my teeth" and soon resigned. Nor did he fully share AMF's ambitions, observing with typical foresight that AMF "thought Harley-Davidson could become another Honda. That's ridiculous... we were never meant to be a high production company."

RIGHT Willie G., wearing his signature beret, with the distinctive Springer Softail in a photo to mark his retirement from the firm in 2012.

WILLIE G. DAVIDSON

The remarkable Willie G., son of second president William H. and grandson of co-founder William A., began his working life not with Harley-Davidson, but with Ford and Excalibur cars. By the time he joined his grandpa's company in 1963, he had a broad schooling in industrial design – although he had also found time to design a new Harley-Davidson tank logo in 1957. He spent most of his career as vice president of styling – arguably the single most important role in such an image-conscious company.

The bike that made Willie G.'s name, the FX Super Glide of 1971, was the first major new model produced by the much maligned AMF. A decade later, Willie G. was one of the prime movers of the buy-out from AMF orchestrated by chairman Vaughn Beals. AMF's hold on Harley-Davidson may not have lasted but Willie G.'s did. As one Harley historian put it, "When we admire, lust after or buy a Sturgis or Softail... we do so only because Willie G. had some parts and some fibreglass and the guts to do something outrageous with them."

His huge contribution was recognized by the naming of the Willie G. Davidson Product Development Center on Capitol Drive, but to the biking world he remained the man in the trademark black beret at gatherings such as Sturgis and Daytona Bike Week, ogling hardware just like any other Harley fan. Willie G. retired in 2012, aged 78, after almost half a century at Milwaukee, ending one of the longest and most important careers the motorcycle industry has ever seen. Son Bill, who joined the firm in 1984, ran HOG before taking charge of the Museum; and daughter Karen ran the MotorClothes division for many years, continuing Harley-Davidson's status as a family affair.

BELOW The man himself in front of a display of fuel tank designs inside the Willie G. Davidson Development Centre in Milwaukee.

BELOW Bill Davidson, son of Willie G. and great grandson of co-founder William A., was head of Harley's Museum following its opening in 2008.

HARLEY-DAVIDSON FACTORIES

William S. Harley and the Davidson brothers first went into production in 1904 in a shed hastily thrown up in the Davidson's Milwaukee backyard. A century and more later the firm would be building motorcycles and engines in several States in the US plus other countries including Brazil and Thailand.

That first shed bore the grand legend "Harley Davidson Motor Co." on its humble wooden door. These days its location, on 38th and Highland Boulevard, is owned by a firm producing something else for which Milwaukee is famous – the huge Molson Coors brewing company.

ABOVE 3700 W. Juneau Avenue, possibly the most famous address in motorcycling.

JUNEAU AVENUE

The founders took on their first employee in 1905, and moved into their first building on the present Juneau Avenue site 12 months later (although the road was then called Chestnut Street). In that year another five workers joined the Harley bandwagon as production soared to 50 motorcycles. Progress was relentless – and punishing. Walter Davidson later described how "we worked every day, Sunday included, until at least 10pm. I remember it was an event when we quit work on Christmas night at 8pm to attend a family reunion."

So it continued: 1907 – around 150 machines built, including the first police Harleys; 1908 – 18 employees and production tripled again to 450 units. By this time, manufacturing was in Harley-Davidson's first brick building, with a floor area of 2,380sq ft (2,20sq metres). From 1907 to 1914, the Harley facility at least doubled in size every year.

At the outbreak of war in Europe, 1,574 employees built more than 16,000 machines in a factory of almost 300,000sq ft (28,000sq metres). With no exaggeration, the Milwaukee Journal described the company's breakneck progress as a "modern miracle".

Wartime pressure for space became so intense that the company once threw up a 220sq metre (2,400sq ft) brick building, only to tear it down and build something even bigger six months later. Even Prohibition came to the company's aid, in a manner far more benign than Al Capone's. When breweries became idle, Harley stepped in to rent the Pabst Brewing Company as storage space for motorcycle parts.

LEFT The Juneau Avenue factory, pictured here with scaffolding in 1914, was continually expanded to allow a rapid increase in production.

The post-war boom helped Harley-Davidson become, briefly at least, the largest motorcycle manufacturer in the world, pumping machines out of its huge, six-storey plant on Juneau Avenue, offering more than 500,000sq ft (50,000sq metres) of floor space on its completion in April 1919. The distinction lasted only until the Depression of 1920, when annual sales collapsed from more than 28,000 to just 10,202. America's economy recovered from this slump but motorcycle sales did not. It was 1942 before Harley sales again exceeded 1920 levels.

Since its conversion to offices and warehousing in 1973, there has been no manufacturing at Harley's most evocative address: 3700 West Juneau Avenue, Milwaukee. Instead, the old site – and the grand old building – houses H-D's corporate headquarters and training departments.

RIGHT Harley-Davidson workers assemble a row of Model W bikes behind the big windows of the Juneau Avenue factory in 1919.

ABOVE On Juneau Avenue, even the water is branded Harley-Davidson.

RIGHT Now more than a century old, the former main factory is a protected historical site.

ABOVE The building that Harley had occupied at Chestnut Street in 1906 seemed tiny as the firm continued its rapid growth.

LEFT A group of Harley-Davidson workers getting to grips with some heavy machinery inside the Capitol Drive factory in 1947.

CAPITOL DRIVE

Harley looked to increase production after the Second World War. In 1948 Capitol Drive, a single-story former aircraft propellor plant located in the Milwaukee suburb of Wauwatosa, became the firm's second manufacturing centre. But Harley sales were continually outstripped by British imports during the 1950s and 1960s, so it was decades before the factory's potential was fully realized.

Engine assembly moved to Capitol Drive from Juneau Avenue in 1971, although the original site continued to undertake engine painting and the assembly of XR race engines for some years. The Capitol Drive plant built "small powertrain" V-twins before closing in 2011, when production moved to York.

YORK, PENNSYLVANIA

In 1972, AMF's massive plant in York lay almost idle. This coincided with Harley-Davidson's urgent need for more manufacturing capacity. The factory was refurbished and motorcycle final assembly took over. The first "York" Harley rolled off the lines in February 1973, leaving Capitol Drive to build only engines and transmissions. York remains Harley's largest production facility, although its days of manufacturing military hardware – the casings on some of the bombs dropped over Iraq during the Gulf War were made at York – are long gone. The factory has received much investment over the years, and accounts for the bulk of Harley's production, including the Softail and Touring models.

MENOMONEE FALLS, WISCONSIN

The factory on Pilgrim Road in Menomonee Falls, 15 miles (24km) north-west of Milwaukee, was built by engine firm Briggs and Stratton in 1979, and bought by Harley in 1996. Known by the firm as the "home of the Big Twin", it is the base for Powertrain Operations,

LEFT The Harley "bar and shield" is as recognizable in Morocco as here in Milwaukee.

RIGHT Sportster engines awaiting shipment from Capitol Drive to Kansas.

LEFT For finishing items such as mudguards, no machine can match a craftsman, as here at the factory in York, Pennsylvania.

RIGHT A technician on the York, Pennsylvania assembly line uses a hydraulic wrench to tighten a bike's rear wheel nut.

LEFT A Dyna passes down the line at the York factory, which is much changed but remains by far Harley's largest facility.

producing the engines that are then transported to York for bike assembly.

TOMAHAWK, WISCONSIN

About 250 miles (400km) north-west of Milwaukee lies the old Tomahawk boat company plant. Harley bought a 60 per cent share in 1962, principally to make Servi-car three-wheeler and golf-cart bodies. In recent years the factory has manufactured fairings, saddlebags, windshields and sidecars.

KANSAS CITY, MISSOURI

The brand-new $85 million plant in Kansas City was billed as the jewel in Harley's manufacturing crown when it opened in 1998. Kansas built all Sportster models, and also produced Street, Dyna and V-Rod family machines. It was the nearest a Hog-building came to state-of-the art, but it closed in 2018 as Harley opted to use more overseas facilities for manufacturing.

OVERSEAS PRODUCTION

In 1998, the first Harley-Davidson factory outside the USA opened in Manaus, Brazil, taking advantage of the free economic zone there. Harley produced bikes at Bawal in India from 2014, starting with the Street 750 and 500, but closed the factory in 2020. The firm opened a new facility in Thailand in 2018, following increased import tax on steel and aluminium coming to the US.

LEFT "Heavy powertrains" – Evo engines – awaiting shipment to York.

RIGHT Heavyweight engines are now made at Pilgrim Road before shipment to York for their final assembly.

PRODUCT DEVELOPMENT CENTER

Harley-Davidson's most significant innovation of recent decades is arguably not a motorcycle but the Willie G. Davidson Product Development Center, or PDC for short. It is in this state-of-the-art facility in Milwaukee that the models of the future are shaped.

LEFT The PDC is located to the rear of the former "small powertrains" plant on Capitol Drive.

Located near the site of the old Capitol Drive factory in the north-west of the city, the PDC was opened in 1997, named to honour Harley's long-serving Vice President of Styling.

The high-security building, built at a reported cost over $30 million, contains a series of laboratories in which the main processes of designing and testing new models are carried out. There's an Acoustics/NVH (Noise, Vibration and Harshness) lab whose anechoic chambers eliminate sound reflection, allowing engineers to measure power train sound during riding simulations. The ability to pinpoint and reduce unwanted engine noise allows more of the "right" sound – notably the signature "potato-

BELOW Stylists and designers at the PDC have plenty of old models and tank designs to use for inspiration.

BELOW Prototypes are subjected to endurance testing by machines that can simulate demanding conditions.

ABOVE Willie G. with a Springer Softail outside the Product Development Center on the opening of the building bearing his name in 1997.

potato" exhaust note – to be retained.

In the Structures Laboratory, machines recreate the road conditions that motorcycles experience over their lifetimes: working the suspension of a complete bike; producing the vibration that electrical components must withstand; flexing a frame to create the effect of heavy braking; or simply operating a sidestand mechanism thousands of times. Over at the Electrical Systems Lab, components or complete bikes are tested with high-frequency radio emissions, or put through 24-hour rain tests in the "Hog Wash" to check moisture resistance.

There's a sophisticated dynamometer room (to test power output) and emissions testing facility, and a Materials/Finishes Lab where all paints, resins and other materials can be analyzed. The Vehicle Build and Machine Shop Lab contains sophisticated computer-controlled machinery that can measure components precisely, duplicate them and produce prototype parts using Computer Aided Design (CAD) technology.

The Product Development Center is a high-security area throughout, with the most closely guarded zone the Mock Up Area at its centre. Here, prototypes of future bikes and parts are displayed throughout their development cycle, allowing Harley's designers and engineers to see and touch them as they work. Visitors are rarely admitted to the PDC. Any non-employees who are allowed in will find this area cleared.

BELOW The anechoic chamber's walls eliminate sound reflection, allowing engineers to measure and fine-tune the sound produced by an engine.

HARLEY-DAVIDSON MUSEUM

Harley had been in existence for 105 years before opening its Museum in Milwaukee in 2008. As well as showcasing more than a century of two-wheeled history, the Museum now acts as a focal point for marque enthusiasts from around the world.

One reason the Museum project hadn't happened earlier became clear on its opening: the company had such a huge number and variety of potential exhibits that choosing, preparing and arranging them – in a large, purpose-built building that cost about $75 million – had been a daunting undertaking.

Many of the 150-plus bikes on display had not required restoring, because they had been in Harley's ownership, unridden, since being taken off the production line immediately after being assembled. Back in 1915, the four co-founders decided to set aside at least one bike from each year's production. A few years later, they bought up some of the bikes they'd sold

ABOVE The Museum's striking architecture incorporates spectacular steel girders and wall logos created using thousands of hand-cut bricks.

LEFT A police-issue Servi-Car three-wheeler and an Italian-built 250cc Grand Prix racer lead the way in the Museum's display of 1970s machines.

RIGHT Single-cylinder models from 1911 (left) and 1909 help tell the story of Harley's early production.

since starting out in 1903. Until the Museum's opening, the growing collection had been stored at Juneau Avenue and seen by few people, most of them Harley employees.

The Museum built to showcase them them is spectacular, combining external steel girders with gigantic "Harley" and "1903" wall logos made from thousands of hand-cut bricks. Outside is a larger-than-life bronze sculpture of a hill-climber in action, donated by Willie G. Davidson and his family. Nearby is a "rivet wall" displaying messages left by visitors on chromed buttons.

Inside, the appeal of those largely unrestored bikes and other exhibits is enhanced by comprehensive labelling, and by imaginative and high-tech features. Pressing various buttons makes engines roar, or starts a short film about Harley's board-track racers, the company's role in the Second World War, or the management buy-out of the early 1980s.

Mostly it's all about the bikes – starting with a line of grey-painted singles from Harley's opening decade; the robust machines whose quiet running earned the nickname "Silent Grey Fellow". Nearby in a room by itself is Serial Number One, the only surviving example of the first, 1903-model single – so valuable that it sits behind glass in a climate-controlled environment.

The lines of bikes lead in chronological order, moving from early, grey-painted V-twins to the more colourful machines of the 1930s. Several three-wheeled Servi-cars are on display, along with a police bike as built for the California Highway Patrol. Another area is devoted to military machines, notably the famous WLA of the Second World War.

The Museum's 1956-model KH is the bike owned by Elvis, who was pictured on the cover of Harley's magazine, *Enthusiast*, with the headline: "Who is Elvis Presley?" Across this large display hall, another line of production bikes is led by the 1949-model FL Hydra-Glide. With its big fenders and fat tyres, it looks strikingly similar to more modern machines such as the Fat Boy from further down the line.

Racebikes include the streamlined blue V-twin on which Joe Petrali broke the US speed record in 1936, and an early 1970s example of the XR750 that dominated dirt-track racing for decades. The only surviving Model T racer from 1914 is displayed on a section of board-track alongside other bikes ridden by the legendary factory team that became known as the Wrecking Crew. Trophies, photos, posters and racers' clothing – woollen jumpers in various colours – bring the story to life, along with snatches of period film.

It's easy to understand why the Museum has become a popular tour destination and location for functions since its opening, attracting hundreds of thousands of visitors each year. More than a century in the making, it is set to document Harley-Davidson's rich history for many more decades.

BELOW A bronze sculpture captures the movement of an early hill-climber.

BELOW A vivid display of bikes and posters from the 1940s and 1950s.

1948
1949
1949 FL HYDRA-GLIDE
OHV V-TWIN

THE HARDWARE

Wild innovation has not usually been the Milwaukee way. Neither young Bill Harley nor the Davidsons had a taste for the radical or the extreme. From the outset, their target was dependability.

That's not to say that Juneau Avenue was opposed to progress. Bill Harley was quick to understand the importance of heat-treatment and metallurgy, and to employ this new technology in his designs. By 1915, Harley models offered advanced features including three-speed transmission and an internally expanding rear drum brake.

This tradition of rugged strength and steady improvement was maintained from early inlet-over-exhaust and side-valve designs, through the Knucklehead, Panhead, Shovelhead and Evolution V-twin motors. Twin Cam and Milwaukee-Eight V-twins then took the classical 45-degree powerplant to new heights.

In recent decades Harley has also added liquid-cooled sophistication to the V-twin format with the Revolution and Revolution Max engines. The firm has found adventure with the Pan America and taken a bold leap towards an electric future with LiveWire. Much of its finest technology remains deliberately well hidden, but Harley-Davidson continues to evolve and to deliver a magical riding experience.

LEFT The distinctive style of 1940s Harley-Davidson models, such as these in the factory Museum, has been echoed in countless machines produced in more recent years.

F-HEADS AND FLATHEADS, 1903 & 1926

Harley-Davidson soon established a reputation for robust four-stroke powerplants. By 1909 the firm was producing both singles and V-twins, and another difference between models was their valve arrangement, with both the "F-head" and side-valve or "Flathead" layouts proving popular.

F-HEADS

A halfway house between flathead and overhead valve design was the inlet-over-exhaust (ioe) layout. Also called the "F-head", as the name suggests, this configuration combined an overhead inlet valve with a side exhaust valve.

All early Harleys followed this design, with one important additional characteristic. For reasons of simplicity, the inlet valve was of the "automatic" or induction type, in which the descending piston simply "sucks" the valve open only for it to be returned to its seat by a conventional spring. This spring was of necessity light, which precluded high engine revs. One major advantage of the system was that by removing the inlet valve housing, both valves could be removed easily for servicing – a considerable advantage on these relatively primitive engines. It was also found that since the valves directly faced each other, the incoming fuel charge helped cool the exhaust valve, extending its life.

LEFT The F-head. The long push-rods to the overhead inlet valves and the "under head" exhaust valves are clear on the 1915 twin shown here.

As well as the early singles, the first V-engines adopted the same layout – to their cost, for it proved an untimely failure with the twin cylinder design.

Both the revised twin and the 5–35 series singles of 1913–18 moved to a far more positive ioe arrangement with a conventional, mechanically-operated overhead inlet valve. The same design was grafted on to the 74-inch Model J of 1922, also known as the "Super-powered Twin". This 18 horsepower engine was also the first Milwaukee twin to feature lightweight aluminium pistons.

LEFT Inlet-over-exhaust layout was the norm on singles, such as this 1914 example.

ABOVE Harley's 45cu in (742cc) side-valve Model K engine of the 1950s could not match the performance of British overhead valve parallel twins.

ABOVE By the late 1920s, side-valve engines were the norm.

FLATHEADS

"Flathead" was the unflattering generic title given to any side-valve engine, whether made by Harley-Davidson or not. The reason for the nickname is obvious: with all the valve gear, including the valves themselves, located below the level of the piston at the top of its stroke, the heads were flat. The first side-valve Harleys were the Series A and B singles of 1926. All roadster twins from the end of the 1920s until the arrival of the Knucklehead in 1936 were flatheads as well. Milwaukee's catalogues continued to feature side-valve models until 1951 and even into the 1970s.

Side-valve engines were popular because they were relatively cheap to make and maintain, as well as much more compact than F-head and overhead valve designs. Although valve control was usually quite good – the camshaft and valves were in close proximity – the side-valve layout inevitably produced an elongated combustion chamber with tortuous gas-flow characteristics and poor valve cooling. This placed a severe limitation on the power such designs could produce. Side-valvers were renowned as dependable plodders, such as the seemingly unstoppable WL45.

The flathead layout was less successful when used for a model intended for high performance. Most notably, the Model K of 1952 lacked the horsepower to compete with British rivals that featured overhead valves. Harley claimed a maximum output of 30bhp from the 45cu in (742cc) V-twin, which was good for about 80mph (130kph). But Triumph's 650cc Thunderbird, launched two years earlier in 1950, was much faster, despite being rated only slightly more powerful at 34bhp. The parallel twin's better breathing allowed it to cruise at 90mph (145kph) and even record a top speed of 100mph (161kph).

Harley's side-valve years threw up one notable exception – the overhead valve 21-inch (346cc) single, produced from 1926 until the eve of the Knuckle in 1935. Designed with the help of British engineer Harry Ricardo, this single was not only successful in its own right but gave rise to the celebrated "Peashooter" racer. Five years earlier, Ricardo created the Model R, Triumph's first four-valve engine. His company contributed to the development of the latest Triumph triples and Aprilia's new V-twin, the RSV Mille.

BELOW Side-valve engines formed the backbone of the Harley range into the 1950s, as with this WL45.

KNUCKLEHEAD, 1936

The Knucklehead's chunky looks make it the quintessential Harley-Davidson. To many motorcyclists its debut in 1936 announced the end of years of crippling economic depression survived by only two American motorcycle manufacturers – Harley and Indian.

In 1935, sales were so poor that Harley's entire range comprised just two models. With the new model – formally designated the Model E – as its flagship, Harley's fortunes rapidly improved. Sales in 1937 exceeded 11,000 for the first time in the decade.

Development of what would become the Knuckle effectively began in the late 1920s, first with specials comprising single-cylinder Peashooter top-ends grafted on to existing V-twin JDH crankcases, then with the factory DAH racers. Although substantially new, the DAH utilized heads derived from the Peashooter's. Board approval for the "official" Knuckle project was granted in 1931 – a bold move at a time when the factory was running at just ten per cent capacity. The engine would probably have been in production by 1934 but for government restrictions intended to reduce unemployment, which effectively barred overtime in the engine development shop. It was a long haul but certainly worth the wait.

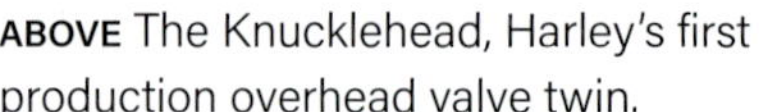
ABOVE The Knucklehead, Harley's first production overhead valve twin.

The Knuckle was a Juneau Avenue "first" in many respects – the first four (forward) speeder, the first engine with hemispherical (hemi) heads and the first overhead valve roadster twin. The engine was heavily influenced by the competition experience of the legendary Joe Petrali, Harley-Davidson development rider and near-unbeatable racer. The Knuckle announced its arrival with a resounding flourish by posting 136.183mph (218.8kph) on the sands of Daytona Beach, Florida.

The 61-inch – actually 60.32cu in (989cc) – Knuckle was initially available in three specifications: E (standard), ES (sidecar) and EL (high compression sport, with 6.5:1 pistons). Petrali's influence was clear. With more than 40 horsepower at 4,800rpm, the EL in particular offered a huge increase in performance over the sluggish side-valvers. Despite its leisurely route to production – and not for the first time – there were initial reliability problems.

The worst of these concerned its new dry-sump lubrication. Some parts got too little oil while others – including

BELOW Developed from the OHV Peashooter single, the Knuckle was a direct ancestor to the Evo engine of 1984.

ABOVE But for the Depression, the Knucklehead would almost certainly have reached production before 1937.

RIGHT The Knucklehead's distinctive cylinder head shapes and air filter cover helped the overhead valve unit stand out from its side-valve predecessor.

the road underneath – got too much. A partial fix came in 1937 but the problem was not solved fully until the arrival of the 73.7cu in (1,207cc) Model F Knuckle in 1941, with its centrifugally-controlled oil pump by-pass. Although notorious for oil leaks through its many external seals and separate primary drive oiling, in very hot conditions many riders would prefer the big Knuckle's oil system to that of the later, "improved" Panhead.

BELOW LEFT AND RIGHT The numbers of Knucklehead models built were severely curtailed by the Second World War, three years after which it was succeeded by the Panhead.

The bigger Knucklehead had come about largely in response to competition from large-capacity Indian V-twins. The larger engine's extra torque demanded a new seven-plate clutch in place of the old five-plate device, giving 65 per cent greater friction area. In addition, there was a bigger rear brake, an "airplane-style" speedometer and a larger, more efficient air-cleaner.

For a variety of reasons, the Knuckle never quite made the impact it deserved. It would certainly have reached production earlier, but for the Depression. No sooner had the Model F reached the street than the Japanese attacked Pearl Harbor in December 1941. The outbreak of war obliged the factory to divert most of its attention to military production.

Milwaukee lore has it that the best of the big Knuckles were those built in that final pre-war year, but hostilities meant that relatively few 74-inch (1,207cc) Knuckles reached the road until 1947.

By 1948, a new boss at Harley meant that the Knuckle was consigned to the annals of company history.

PANHEAD, 1948

In 1945, Harley resumed civilian motorcycle production, although sales would not return to pre-war levels (partly due to industrial action) until 1947. In 1948 the replacement for the noble Knucklehead made its first public appearance, with aluminium heads and redesigned valve gear.

In the Milwaukee tradition of steady evolution, the "Panhead", as it was dubbed, was a development of the Knuckle rather than an all-new concept. So-named because its chromed steel rocker covers (stainless steel from 1949) resembled inverted baking pans, the Pan was built in both 74-inch – actually 73.66cu in or 1,207cc – and 61-inch (989cc) sizes, although the latter was discontinued in 1953. The larger version retained the "traditional" bore and stroke dimensions of $3\frac{7}{16}$ x $3\frac{31}{32}$in (or 87.3 x 100.8mm).

The Pan featured aluminium alloy cylinder heads in place of the Knuckle's cast iron ones, new rocker gear and hydraulic tappets (or "lifters" as they're known in the United States) rather than noisier solid push-rods, as well as a revised and less leaky lubrication system. The camshaft was also new. Although the bottom-end was substantially like the Knuckle's, the oil system benefited from a larger capacity oil pump and the main oil feeds were now internal rather than untidy external lines.

The new aluminium heads not only improved engine cooling but contributed to an engine weight 8lbs (3.6kg) lighter than before. To ensure durability, the spark plugs and cylinder bolts threaded into steel inserts rather than the relatively soft aluminium of the head itself. Despite these improvements, the power output of early Pans was about the same as the Knuckle's – around 50bhp at 4,800rpm for the 74-inch motor. The valve lifters were relocated from the top of the push-rods in 1953, to lie between cam lobe and push-rod in the timing case. At the same time, both crankcase halves were heavily modified, with

ABOVE From above it's easy to understand why the Panhead unit was so-named. The rocker covers were among several updates including hydraulic tappets and improved lubrication.

BELOW Since 1948 Pans have powered everything from the first Glide, the Hydra-Glide...

BELOW ...to crazy competition machines, as pictured here.

ABOVE The Duo-Glide had also been Panhead-powered.

RIGHT The very first Electra Glide was Panhead-powered.

particular emphasis on oil control. In 1956, Harley-Davidson introduced even more of the same. By now, a freer-breathing air cleaner and high-lift "Victory" camshaft had brought a gain of around 5bhp on the Pan's original power output. Near the end of its life in 1963, the Panhead reverted to the Knucklehead's external top-end oil feeds to prevent overheating, a particular problem in the scorching deserts of the American south-west.

At least as enduring as the Panhead itself was the name given to the first new model to bear such an engine. The Hydra-Glide of 1949 was the first Harley-Davidson to employ hydraulically-damped telescopic front forks. It was also the first model granted one of the enduring names in motorcycling: "Glide".

The Panhead engine would do much to get the famous species on its way, propelling not only the Duo-Glide of 1958 but the very first of the Electra Glides as well. The Duo-Glide's plush ride and the Electra Glide's easy starting were key features, but it was the Panhead unit on which Harley's progress was based.

BELOW One of the first Panhead Harleys, a 1948 girder-forked Model F.

SHOVELHEAD, 1966

According to Harley-Davidson lore, 1965 is notable for two things. The first was the decision to list the company on the stock market. The second was the unveiling of a new generation of Shovelhead V-twin engines, replacing the venerable Pans.

The Shovelhead's impact would be adversely affected by that momentous decision to go for the stock market listing. What no doubt seemed a good idea at the time would ultimately lead to takeover by American Machine and Foundry (AMF).

Popular opinion now says that AMF neglected the company, that it didn't understand motorcycles and that quality went rapidly downhill. Much of this criticism has an element of truth to it but AMF actually sank millions of dollars into its new project and actually tripled annual sales.

If Harley had a problem it was probably as much to do with being part of America as being part of AMF for, like many other sectors of American industry, it was overwhelmed by the tidal wave of sophisticated new products pouring in from Japan. As the British motorcycle industry learned to even greater cost, the 1960s and 1970s were no place for leisurely updates of a 1930s design. Put simply, the Shovelhead never had a chance.

First seen on the 1966 Electra Glide, the Shovelhead followed the usual Harley practice of bolting a new top-end on to the tried-and-tested crankcases developed during the course of the previous generation of engines. There were minor revisions to the right crankcase half and a fin-less timing cover, but the bottom-end was essentially that of a 1965 Panhead, including the external oil feeds reintroduced in 1964.

An all-new top-end included aluminium alloy cylinder heads and iron cylinder barrels. Light alloy was also used for the rocker boxes in place of the Panhead's pressed steel. These were derived from the XL Sportster engine and enclosed redesigned rockers and exhaust valves. Although this rendered the Shovel top-end slightly reminiscent of the Sportster range, the latter was a quite separate family of unit-construction engines. Equally striking was the Shovel's "Ham-can" air cleaner cover, mated to a constant velocity Tillotson diaphragm carb from late 1966 onwards. The "Power Pac" head design gave around 60bhp in FLH specification, 5bhp more than an equivalent Panhead. The standard FL developed 54bhp. Observers described the new heads as resembling the backs of coal shovels, hence the nickname.

Like all Harley Vs, the OHV engine runs forked con-rods with both

LEFT This is a "generator" Shovelhead, produced up to 1970.

ABOVE The view from above shows the cylinder head shape, resembling the back of a coal shovel, that earned the Shovelhead its name.

ABOVE "Alternator" Shovelheads are recognizable by the conical housing on the end of the crankshaft, here marked with AMF's Number One logo.

cylinders in the same plane to eliminate rocking couple. Primary drive is via chain to a four-speed box (with a sidecar option up to 1980, of three forward and one reverse). The Shovel received its new bottom-end in 1970, in which a crankshaft-mounted alternator replaced the previous generator (and made the engine even wider) – hence "generator" and "alternator" Shovels. The later type, also called "cone motors", are recognized by their cone-shaped, right-side engine cover. The ignition points assembly was moved from its original external position inside the timing case and the timing gears simplified.

Originally produced in 74cu in (1,207cc) form, Shovels grew to 80cu in (1,340cc) with the FLH-80 of 1978, when electronic ignition was added. Two years later, the first five-speed gearbox appeared, initially on the FLT Tour Glide, and was also the first of Harley's rubber-mounted engines.

RIGHT Harleys managed to be both practical and stylish.

V2 EVOLUTION, 1984

Perhaps the biggest fault of the next in Milwaukee's noble line of big twins was the lack of an attractive nickname. Its official title was "V2 Evolution" which, in common with most Milwaukee monikers, became a registered trademark.

Like the Shovel and Panhead before it, the Evo engine evolved from its predecessor rather than representing an all-new design.

Appropriate as the name might have been, it was not evocative at all. After decades of Flatheads, Knuckles, Pans and Shovels, it had to be said that "Evo" lacked the same gritty authentic ring. Happily for its creators, an unkind early suggestion of "Blockhead" failed to stick.

It's a curious Milwaukee fact that so many major Harley-Davidson OHV engines were born in the midst of strife. The Knuckle had been a child of the Depression, the Pan had arrived surrounded by strikes and post-war rebuilding, and the Shovel had heralded years of decline. As the long-awaited replacement for the Shovel arrived in 1984, Harley-Davidson was effectively broke. The story of how the company got out of perhaps the biggest crisis in its history is related elsewhere, but never had Milwaukee been in greater need of an engine that would deliver the goods for them.

RIGHT The Evo unit not only performed notably better and weighed less, it was an elegant piece of design, with its aluminium cylinder barrels' efficient cooling fins on display.

Fortunately for Harley-Davidson fans everywhere, the Evo was everything they and Milwaukee had hoped for. Compared to the venerable Shovel that had begun life 18 years before, the Evo was 20lbs (9kgs) lighter and generated 10 per cent more horsepower and 15 per cent more torque. Its cylinders retained the "classic" dimensions of 3$\frac{7}{16}$ x 4$\frac{1}{4}$in (88.8 x 108mm), giving an actual displacement of 81.8cu in or 1,340cc (not 80in as it was nominally called). As with the evolution of Pan to Shovel, the Evo used a bottom-end derived from its (alternator-type) predecessor but with improved con-rods and a new all-alloy top end. Efforts were made to improve oil-tightness and reliability, and decrease maintenance chores, with great success.

The extra power (around 70bhp at 5,000rpm) came mainly from steeper, straighter ports feeding into redesigned combustion chambers, a new ignition, revised valve timing and higher compression ratios. During the seven years of the new engine's development, much effort had also gone into redesigning the lubrication system to prevent the Shovel's notoriously leaky nature. All but a handful of Evos sported five-speed transmission and, from later 1984, a much-improved diaphragm clutch. By 1986, the 1340 Evo had been joined by V2 Sportster cousins offering 883cc and 1100cc, the

LEFT By 1985, Evolution engines powered the entire big twin range, with Sportsters getting similar treatment one year later. It eventually gave way to the Twin Cam.

ABOVE The Fat Boy was one of the most stylish models of the Softail family, and a notable Evo-engined success.

BELOW The Electra Glide Ultra Classic introduced the Evolution-engined V-twin family to fuel-injection in 1995.

latter growing to become the first 1200cc Sportster two years later. Unlike the 1340s, Sportster Evos were of unit construction in which the crankcases and gearbox formed a single unit. Like the Big Twin engines, the new Sportster lumps were more powerful and reliable, cooler running and generally superior.

So much for metal. As far as the vibrant, imaginative management team running the newly-independent company was concerned, the Evo had one other priceless asset the much-derided Shovelhead had lacked. Milwaukee now seemed to have its finger on the pulse of motorcycle culture, and most importantly, seemed to understand its market.

Those at the helm now reached out to their customers in a way that the remote, faceless AMF never could, in stark contrast to the Shovelhead era. They sold their new product as if Harley's life depended on it – which, make no mistake, it did.

TWIN CAM 88, 1999

The Twin Cam 88 got its name from its twin camshafts – which still operated pushrods – and capacity of 88 cubic inches, or 1,450cc, up from the 1,340cc, 80-cube Evo unit. Harley's first new engine for 15 years offered retained V-twin character plus additional power and strength.

The Twin Cam was unveiled in 1998 and billed as "the biggest change in engine design since the Knuckle". First seen on the 1999 Super Glides, Dyna Glides, Road Kings, Road Glide and Electra Glide, the Twin Cam offered more power and torque in a smoother, more refined package. Yet despite the name, this was still an overhead valve engine – the cams in question were downstairs. Unlike the gear-driven camshafts of previous big twins, these were chain-driven and far less costly to produce. Considerable savings were also made in crankcase machining, which required 37 distinct operations on the Evo but only three on the Twin Cam.

One area which received particular attention was the oil circulation. Surprising though it may seem, as they set out to create the Twin Cam, Milwaukee's engineers had very little idea what the lubricating oil in the Evo engine actually did – except that it didn't always go where it ought and that pressure could fall dangerously under very hot conditions. After 18 months of painstaking work on engines littered with Plexiglass "windows", the engineers believed they had the new engine figured out at last. In fact, the actual hardware – a high-capacity "gerotor" pump and two distinct scavenge systems – was less crucial than the engine's internal detailing. This was simple compared to the project's biggest problem, which had nothing to do with hardware, but with people. After the lay-offs of the 1980s, Harley simply didn't have a team capable of developing a new engine. One had to be created almost from scratch before work on the Twin Cam could begin. Depending on the state of tune, Harley claimed a 14–22 per cent power increase (to 87bhp on the Dyna Glides) compared to the previous Evolution design. This was achieved partly through higher compression ratios, improved combustion-chamber shape and induction plumbing, as well as a new ignition pack.

Last but not least was a ten per cent increase in capacity to 88.4cu in (1,449cc),

ABOVE Known as plain P22 during its development, the Twin Cam did not attract a pet name, despite unkind suggestions that "Fat head" might have fitted the bill.

BELOW The Twin Cam brought a new dimension of power and refinement, first to heavyweight Glides, then to the Softail range.

ABOVE Twin Cam power reached the Softail range with the balance-shafted Twin Cam 88B for year-2000 models.

making this the largest stock engine Milwaukee had ever built. To achieve the extra volume, the stroke had decreased from $4\frac{1}{4}$ to 4in (108 to 101.6mm) while the bore had risen substantially from $3\frac{7}{16}$ to $3\frac{13}{16}$in (88.8 to 95.3mm). Some traditionalists may have bemoaned the departure from the hallowed 88.8 x 108mm ($3\frac{7}{16}$ x $4\frac{1}{4}$in) dimensions that had endured since the Shovel.

They certainly did not bemoan, however, the Twin Cam's prodigious peak torque: 86lb/ft (116Nm) at a mere 3,500rpm. Riders needing more could take heart: the Twin Cam had been designed to allow an increase in displacement as high as 1550cc, adding another six to eight horsepower.

Compared to the bolted-up crankshafts of previous OHV twins, the Twin Cam had a pressed-up crankshaft. With its shorter stroke, it was capable of higher revs. Although the 5,500rpm redline was only 300rpm higher than before, development engines had been safely tested at up to 7,000rpm.

Harley surprised everyone by dropping the Evo and unveiling the Twin Cam 88B for the year 2000, a unit-construction engine specifically tailored for the Softail range.

It represented another Harley first – twin balance-shafts to smooth out engine vibrations. Softails were no longer able to lay claim to being the "judderers" of the range. The shafts, driven by chain from the crank, neutralised the remaining 50 per cent of primary vibration, the flywheel having taken out the rest, and dramatically improved the Softail family's comfort.

BELOW Faster, cleaner, easier to service – any Harley rider's delight.

REVOLUTION, 1999

The word "revolution" is over-used in the automotive world, but it rang true as the name of the powerplant with which Harley accelerated into the new millennium. The liquid-cooled, 60-degree, DOHC engine was like nothing before from Milwaukee.

The V-Rod was a stunning looking machine. And its 1130cc, liquid-cooled V-twin engine, developed from that of Harley's V1000 racebike, which had been competing with little success since the mid-1990s, took the firm in a radical new direction.

Much of the work in developing the VR engine into the new Revolution unit had been done at the Stuttgart base of Porsche Engineering, where key Harley engineers had been frequent visitors for several years. Milwaukee's links with the German firm dated back to the late 1970s, when Porsche had helped develop a family of liquid-cooled, 60-degree V-twin, V4 and V6 engines for the Nova project, which had not reached production.

Two decades later, a similar format derived from the VR1000 was used for the Revolution engine: liquid cooling, 60-degree cylinder angle, and twin overhead cams opening four valves per cylinder. Over-square cylinder dimensions helped the engine rev, and deliver a peak power output of 115bhp at 8500rpm. That was almost double the figure of a typical Twin Cam unit, and made the V-Rod by far Harley's most powerful cruiser yet. By contrast the Revolution motor made slightly less peak torque, delivered at twice the revs.

ABOVE The V-Rod's long, low look had a hint of dragster and its 115bhp engine gave strong acceleration.

BELOW LEFT AND RIGHT The cleanly styled 60-degree V-twin engine featured a downdraft fuel-injection system fed from the dummy tank, with fuel held under the seat.

ABOVE Its large-diameter steel frame and aluminium parts included disc wheels and gave the V-Rod a striking finish.

Unlike Harley's pushrod engines, the new unit had side-by-side conrods (instead of a forked conrod design) and a wet sump. It also featured forged pistons, a single balancer shaft, hydraulic clutch and five-speed gearbox. Cam drive was by chain to a central shaft, on the other end of which was the water pump; and from there by a further chain to each pair of cams.

A large airbox in the conventional fuel tank position fed the fuel-injection system via a downdraft intake; fuel lived under the seat. The exhaust was a 2-1-2 system, with a large collector box leading to the twin silencers. The radiator and oil cooler were hidden by a curvaceous shroud that ducted air onto them in a swirling motion to improve efficiency.

The rest of the V-Rod was suitably special. Its use of aluminium gave a gleaming silver finish. The centrepiece of the chassis was a large and very visible tubular steel frame, created using a hydroforming process (involving high-pressure water) to give smooth bends. The front forks were kicked out. Wheels were solid aluminium discs, the rear holding a fat, 180-section tyre.

That 115bhp output gave thrilling acceleration off the line, pushing its rider back into the stepped seat. The bike was long, low and heavy but handled better than most cruisers. It also had powerful disc brakes and Harley's normal excellent finish.

The V-Rod didn't sell particularly well, especially in the US, where any bike without pushrods was far too revolutionary for most folk. But its descendants the V-Rod Muscle and Street Rod kept the line going for more than a decade, so Harley's bold leap to liquid cooling can be considered at least a partial success.

BELOW The 2006-model Street Rod's engine was mechanically unchanged but a new "shotgun" exhaust increased maximum output to 120bhp.

MILWAUKEE-EIGHT, 2017

If the V-Rod's Revolution engine had been a bold leap into the unknown, the Milwaukee-Eight engine with which Harley updated the Touring family in 2017 was the opposite. This new V-twin was aimed squarely at the firm's existing customers.

The Eight, named to highlight its doubled number of valves compared to Milwaukee's traditional aircooled V-twin unit, was a return to the process of gradual evolution that had been taking place for over a century.

Harley's familiar 45-degree cylinder angle and pushrod valve operation remained. Changes included a move from twin to single camshaft, made possible by the smaller valves' reduced spring pressure. These developments had largely been dictated by feedback from existing Harley riders, who had been asking not only for more power and cooler running but also for reduced vibration and engine width.

The Milwaukee-Eight design delivered all that, with the four-valve layout's improved flow being most responsible for the extra performance

LEFT A more angular air filter cover was the Milwaukee-Eight engine's most obvious new feature; inside it had a single camshaft instead of two.

BELOW The Street Glide used the basic, 1745cc Milwaukee-Eight 107 engine; CVO models had the bigger, more powerful 114cu in unit.

ABOVE The half-faired Road Glide was powered by the standard, aircooled Milwaukee-Eight 107 engine.

RIGHT Radiators in the Ultra Classic's fairing lowers allowed it to incorporate liquid-cooled cylinder heads.

(just as the Japanese manufacturers had said about their 16-valve fours in the early 1980s). There was roughly ten per cent more torque through much of the rev range, with the peak delivered at a lowly 3250rpm.

The reduced vibration came from a new balancer shaft, located low down at the front, that had been carefully designed to give the right compromise between increased comfort and retained character. According to Harley, that meant 75 per cent less vibration at idle.

The Eight came in three varieties. The basic Milwaukee-Eight 107 – used by the Street Glide, Road Glide and Road King models – had enlarged capacity of 1745cc, or 107 cubic inches (up from the previous Twin Cam 103 unit's 1690cc), and featured new oil-cooled cylinder heads. A version of the 107 with liquid-cooled heads powered the full-dress Ultra Classic; and there was also a bigger, 1868cc unit, the Milwaukee-Eight 114, for the exotic Custom Vehicle Operations models.

The big tourers' natural habitat was the American Midwest, but Harley's updates made sense wherever they were ridden. Some were obvious even before pulling away: the new counter-balancer reduced vibration dramatically, so there was much less of the traditional jiggling about at tickover.

Idle speed was reduced from 1,000 to 850rpm, which contributed, along with the new oil-cooled heads (and re-routed rear exhaust, which benefitted a pillion), to cooler running. The reduced mechanical noise had allowed Harley to make the exhaust's "potato-potato" thump slightly sharper, adding to the bikes' character.

The main benefit came when the throttle was cracked open. The increased torque meant a gain of two to three bike lengths from zero to 60mph (96kph), and a significant boost to top-gear roll-on performance. That extra shove added to the entertainment, made overtaking easier, and was especially welcome with a pillion and luggage on board.

They say competition improves the breed, and in the case of these V-twins the phrase rang true. Old rival Indian's recent rebirth had given Harley-Davidson a serious US adversary for the first time in decades. The Milwaukee-Eight engined models – more powerful, smoother and more refined – were a timely and much-needed response.

BELOW The Street Glide's batwing fairing retained its unmistakable look, but straight-line performance was improved.

REVOLUTION MAX, 2021

When the Pan America 1250 was launched in 2021, powered by a new-generation liquid-cooled, 60-degree V-twin engine called Revolution Max, it quickly made an impact in a market sector that was completely new for Harley-Davidson.

LEFT The Pan America had a different look to any previous Harley – and every other firm's adventure models.

The introduction of the Pan America model was not a smooth one. The 1252cc adventure model had been unveiled in 2019 alongside a naked streetbike called the Bronx, which was powered by a smaller, 975cc version of the DOHC, eight-valve Revolution Max unit. CEO Matt Levatich had intended both models to lead the firm's "More Roads Lead to Harley" attempt to diversify the range. But poor financial results in early 2020 led to Levatich departing, even before the firm was rocked further by the Covid-19 virus. New boss Jochen Zeitz arrived with a cost-cutting programme called Rewire, followed by an even tougher initiative named Hardwire – which killed off the Bronx.

The Pan America survived, and entered production the following year – when it soon became clear that this distinctively styled Harley was good enough to make its considerable presence felt. Its Max motor made a competitive 150bhp and featured variable valve timing, plus two balancer shafts that kept it respectably smooth.

The PanAm was very much a Harley-Davidson for the 21st century, featuring modern electronic systems including ride-by-wire throttle, multiple riding modes and traction

BELOW LEFT AND RIGHT Cutaways of the Revolution Max engine show the chain-driven DOHC valve arrangement that contributed to its 150bhp output.

RIGHT Softer cams and smaller valves boosted the Revolution Max powered Sportster S's midrange output and reduced its maximum to 120bhp.

control. Alongside the basic 1250 model, the higher-specification Special even had semi-active suspension that automatically lowered the bike as it came to a halt – a feature that its established class rivals did not offer. All-round performance was excellent. The Harley also proved robust, and its bold and distinctive style helped earn it a strong following.

Later in 2021 the Pan America was joined by the Sportster S, powered by a Revolution Max motor that combined unchanged 1252cc capacity with softer camshafts and smaller valves, giving more midrange torque and a lower peak output of 120bhp. This Sportster was more of a successor to the V-Rod than to previous aircooled Sportsters, which were being phased out due largely to tightening emissions regulations. It offered thrilling acceleration, good chassis performance and plenty of sophistication.

The following year it was joined by a smaller-capacity, 975cc naked sibling – called not the Bronx but the Nightster, and intended as Harley's new entry-level V-twin. The Nightster made 89bhp and handled well but lacked the traditional charm of the aircooled Sportster models, and was considerably more expensive.

REVOLUTION X - THE STREET 750 AND 500

Harley had introduced another liquid-cooled V-twin family in 2014 with the Street models, middleweights which for many markets were produced at Harley's plant in India, and were intended for relatively young riders, including those in developing markets.

The Revolution X engine shared the liquid-cooling and 60-degree V-twin angle of the V-Rod's Revolution unit (and the later Revolution Max powerplant) but differed in having single instead of twin overhead camshafts. It made about 50bhp in its larger capacity; good for a top speed of about 100mph (161kph).

The Streets combined café racer style with respectable performance and prices that were low by Harley standards. But they failed to match Harley's sales targets, and production lasted only a few years.

BELOW The Street 750's 749cc Revolution X engine featured liquid cooling and a 60 degree angle but had a SOHC valve layout.

ODDBALLS

Harley-Davidson began as a company with lofty aspirations, but some developments must have surprised even the founders. In 1924, a Harley-engined (18hp) plane built by Harvey Mummert won the speed and efficiency contest at an air race at Dayton, Ohio.

In 1928, Flying and Glider Manual published plans for crafting a propeller for a 74-inch Harley twin. By the mid-1930s, several hundred light planes were powered by Harlequin engines, using Harley-Davidson cylinders on special, horizontally-opposed crankcases. The resulting boxer twin produced 30 horsepower and could be built for less than $100. At the opposite end of the spectrum was the bicycle built for Harley by the Davis Sewing Machine Co. from 1918–24 – a "Hog" with no engine at all.

Milwaukee twins have also been used in boats and as all manner of stationary engines. Contrary to popular belief, it has not been a single, seamless tide of thundering big twins from almost the dawn of the 20th century into the 21st. Other than the early singles, perhaps the best-known variation from the V-twin theme was the Sport Twin of 1919–22, using a 37in (584cc) horizontally-opposed engine, similar to contemporary Douglas motorcycles. A generation later, the military XA appeared during the Second World War, powered by a transverse, horizontally-opposed, flathead twin.

Even the oddball XA might not have made it had other military prototypes reached production. These included a three-wheeler for use over rough ground, an armoured machine-gun carrier and a small tank powerplant consisting of a linked pair of Shovelheads. By then, one Milwaukee three-wheeler was an everyday part of American civilian life.

They called it "Servi-Car" when introduced in 1932. Although the front

LEFT Harley-Davidson golf clubs?

RIGHT Well, Milwaukee did make golf carts for a while.

ABOVE Another variation on Harley wheels, this time used as paddock transport by the factory race squad.

BELOW Riders and sidecar passengers are dressed for the occasion in a 1920s shot entitled "Sidecar Beach Party".

BELOW The Tour Glide certainly wasn't strange, but for a while motorcycles towing trailers were. Now they are commonplace.

TOP Odd, but the Servi-Car worked, from 1932 until the 1970s.

ABOVE This Evo-engined prototype of a Servi-Car successor failed to reach production.

end – "borrowed" from the Model D side-valve V-twin – was fairly conventional, what lay behind caused surprise. Above a two-wheel rear axle sat a metal-framed "boot" (trunk): this ungainly-looking device was a cheap delivery vehicle which found a ready market in Depression-torn America. For many Harley fans worse was to come, beginning with the 1947 Model S and ending with the Topper Scooter.

One of the strangest ventures was a Harley two-stroke manufactured in the United States – without wheels. The Harley Snowmobile, powered by either 400 or 430cc engines, was built for four years until 1975. Another quest for diversity saw the company branching out to build military bomb casings, computer circuit boards and "Holiday Rambler" recreational vehicles.

More recent oddball models have been much closer to Harley's roots. The Tri Glide Ultra and Freewheeler, powered by Big Twin engines, are

ABOVE One American icon mutates into another: the Harley hamburger.

luxurious and upmarket three-wheelers. Especially popular with older riders, they are very different to their humble Servi-Car predecessors. If nothing else, this demonstrates just how far the company had strayed from what it now regards as its essential roots. Until recently some observers thought that all future Harleys would be aircooled, 45-degree V-twins with cylinders in line. The electric LiveWire's launch confirms that, on the contrary, we ain't seen nothing yet...

RIGHT Trikes such as the Tri Glide Ultra have become popular with older riders graduating from heavy two-wheeled Touring bikes.

BUELL

The Buell company began in the early 1980s as a young Harley-Davidson engineer's dream of building sporty bikes and became a successful manufacturer and then a part of Harley itself, before being abruptly terminated in 2009.

Erik Buell's creation gave Milwaukee a valuable high-performance division, and produced more than 100,000 bikes – many of them both technically advanced and exciting to ride.

LEFT The RS1200 of 1989 was a landmark model for Buell – mainly because, unlike the fully faired RR1200, it put its Harley V-twin engine on display.

BEGINNINGS

Erik Buell grew up in Pittsburgh and worked in local motorcycle shops while earning an engineering degree at night school. He landed a job as test engineer at Harley and became a leading national class road-racer on bikes including a Yamaha TZ750. He also started building motorbikes in his spare time, firstly a racebike called the RW750 with a 750cc Barton two-stroke engine. The RW was sufficiently promising for Erik to quit his Harley job to produce it, working out of a barn on his farm near Milwaukee – only for the AMA to close the Formula One class it was designed for, killing demand at a stroke.

Buell did not give up. Instead, he turned to his former employer for an XR1000 Sportster engine, and created the RR1000 Battletwin, the first Harley-engined Buell motorcycle. It featured Erik's patented Uniplanar chassis design, which used a system of rods and joints to restrict engine vibration to the vertical plane, allowing rubber mounting while employing the V-twin unit as a stressed member of the chassis.

The RR made the most of its power by enveloping the bike in wind-cheating bodywork, incorporating a big front mudguard plus integrated fairing and single seat. It was a success, despite the high prices dictated by its hand-built construction. Buell's small team

ABOVE The Buell's raw lines and radical engineering are abundantly clear with body-work removed.

LEFT The Buell assembly line in East Troy, an hour from Milwaukee, shown before Harley bought in.

ABOVE Erik Buell, here with an S2 Thunderbolt in 1995, was a talented racer as well as an innovative engineer.

ABOVE Buell's publicity material emphasized the naked Cyclone's raw appeal.

built 50 in 1987 and 1988, before stocks of the XR1000 motor ran out. Erik's Harley contacts then helped him to find supplies of the 1,203cc V-twin from the Sportster. In 1989 he released the similarly styled RR1200, and also the RS1200, featuring a half-fairing that revealed the Harley motor for the first time.

HARLEY-DAVIDSON STEPS IN

The Buell Motor Co – slogan "America's Faaast Motorcycle" – was on its way. Further models and development led to increased production in the next few years. In 1993 Harley, looking for a relatively inexpensive way to get into the sports bike market, bought a 49 per cent stake in Buell. The firm was renamed the Buell Motorcycle Company and moved into bigger premises nearby at East Troy.

Harley brought finance, marketing skills, development facilities and the opportunity to increase production from 100 bikes per year to 600 or 800. A year later Buell began building the S2 Thunderbolt, with fresh styling and a power increase due to improved breathing. This was followed in 1996 by the S1 Lightning, a stripped-down roadster, and by the more basic M2 Cyclone.

By this time Buell had begun exporting, initially to Europe and Japan. In 1998 came an even bigger move, when Harley bought a further 49 per cent of the company, taking overall control with 98 per cent. The search for more performance from Harley's V-twin motor led later that year to the S1 White Lightning, whose new Thunderstorm cylinder heads helped increase output to 101bhp. The X1 took the evolution process a stage further, with fuel-injection and other changes.

Part of Buell's appeal for Harley-Davidson was as an entry-level marque that would attract young and female riders. In 2000, Buell introduced the Blast, a single-cylinder roadster whose 492cc, aircooled engine was essentially half a Sportster 883 unit. The Blast was

BELOW The Thunderbolt of 1994 was the first Buell built under Harley control.

ABOVE The Firebolt XB9R featured aggressive styling, a radical aluminium-framed chassis and a 984cc, Sportster-based engine producing 92bhp.

LEFT The Lightning X1 of 1998 took Buell's naked V-twin line to a new level with fuel injection, new cylinder heads and a more rigid steel frame.

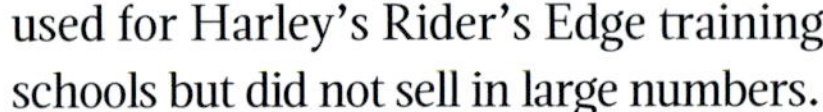

used for Harley's Rider's Edge training schools but did not sell in large numbers.

Buell's advertising phrase "different in every sense" was summed-up by the Firebolt XB9R, a sports bike that was launched in 2002 featuring a twin-spar aluminium frame that also held the fuel. This rigid and compact design allowed the airbox to be positioned in the conventional fuel tank position, instead of alongside the engine. Other innovative features included the swing-arm, which doubled as the oil tank, and the large-diameter perimeter front brake disc.

The Firebolt, powered by a new short-stroke, 984cc V-twin that produced 92bhp, was not fast by sports bike standards but it was stylish, light and agile. A year later it was joined by the Lightning XB9S, a naked streetfighter that combined a similar chassis with a more upright riding

BELOW Buell began its 1,203cc family in 2004 with the faired Firebolt XB12R (left) and naked Lightning XB12S.

position and an aggressive twin-headlight look.

In 2004, Buell added performance with Firebolt XB12R and Lightning XB12S derivatives, powered by a 1203cc V-twin that produced 100bhp with strong midrange output. The following year's Ulysses XB12X was an adventure sport model, holding a slightly detuned, 94bhp engine in a new chassis featuring long-travel suspension. The trio helped take production to an all-time high of just over 13,000 bikes in 2008.

But Buell's attempts to move forward with a new family of more advanced models, powered by a DOHC, liquid-cooled, 72-degree V-twin developed by Rotax of Austria, hit trouble. The 1125R sports bike was belatedly introduced in 2008. It produced 146bhp but was marred by mechanical problems, quirky handling and controversial styling. The closely related 1125CR cafe racer that followed a year later also failed to make an impact.

THE END OF THE ROAD

This left Buell vulnerable, because Harley was struggling through the global financial crisis. In October 2009, new Milwaukee boss Keith

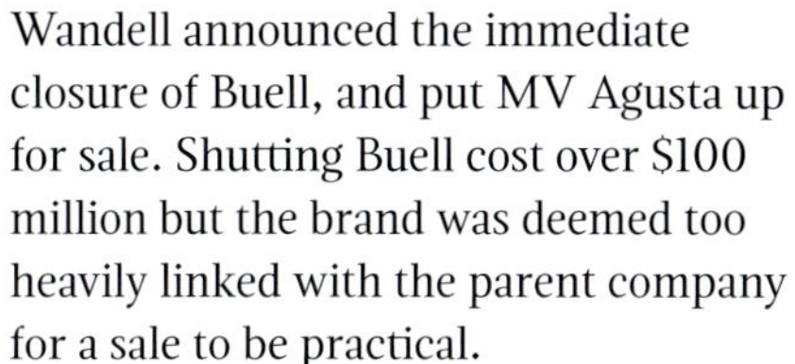

Wandell announced the immediate closure of Buell, and put MV Agusta up for sale. Shutting Buell cost over $100 million but the brand was deemed too heavily linked with the parent company for a sale to be practical.

Erik Buell had always seemed the ultimate survivor, dating right back to the adversity he had overcome with his first ever bike. But the recession that had hit Harley harder than most had claimed a notable scalp at East Troy. Harley would recover, and Erik would attempt low-volume production as an independent firm, but Buell's time in the spotlight was over.

ABOVE The 1,203cc XB12 engine's long-stroke dimensions helped give it plenty of midrange performance.

RIGHT Handling quirks and mechanical issues plagued the 1125R's launch in 2008 and hastened Buell's demise.

BELOW Buell's XB models held fuel in the frame, oil in the swing-arm, and featured a perimeter disc front brake.

LIVEWIRE

Harley-Davidson, famed for many decades for its retro-styled machines and rumbling V-twin engines, shocked the two-wheeled industry in 2019 by becoming the first major manufacturer to embrace the brave new world of electric motorcycles.

ABOVE Aggressive naked styling and Harley's traditional orange-and-black paintwork give the LiveWire a deceptively conventional appearance.

The spectacular LiveWire's launch, years ahead of battery-powered high-performance models from any other big firm, confirmed that for all Harley's emphasis on tradition, it was also looking to the future.

Part of Milwaukee's motivation for instigating the LiveWire project was the need to rejuvenate its ageing customer base. Fellow American firm Tesla's success doubtless provided inspiration, too, although the market for electric motorcycles was years behind that of its four-wheeled equivalents.

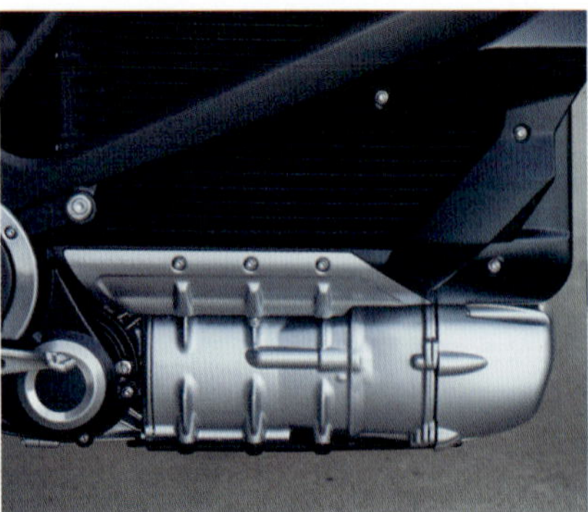

LEFT AND ABOVE The dummy fuel tank's cap opens to allow recharging. An aluminium frame holds the large battery pack with the electric motor below it.

Harley could not be accused of failing to consult potential customers. In 2014, the firm introduced the LiveWire project by unveiling a prototype and inviting thousands of motorcyclists to test ride it, initially in the US and later all around the world. The feedback was sufficiently positive for the bike to be put into production.

Harley's designers had done a good job with the LiveWire's styling, which was distinctive yet relatively conventional. The compact naked bike was aggressively styled and neatly detailed, with low handlebars, a dummy fuel tank above an aluminium perimeter frame, and a single rear suspension unit.

RIGHT Sporty geometry and firm suspension helped make the LiveWire exciting to ride on a twisty road.

Instead of an internal combustion engine it was powered by a liquid-cooled, permanent magnet electric motor that turned on a longitudinal axis and was held low, below the ribbed aluminium battery casing. Maximum output was 78kW or 105bhp, with huge torque from zero revs. Final drive was by toothed belt, with no gearbox.

Performance was in many respects excellent. The LiveWire was quick, accelerating fiercely to a top speed of about 110mph (177kph), with a jet-like scream adding to the thrill. Although no lightweight, at 249kg (549lb), it was fairly agile, and despite sportily firm suspension it was respectably comfortable.

But Harley's engineers had been unable to overcome several drawbacks inherent to electric bikes. Although the LiveWire could be ridden gently for 100 miles (161km) on a full charge, hard use almost halved its range. Recharging with a fast-charger took little more than an hour, but those were rare almost everywhere, and home charging was slow.

The other drawback was price: the LiveWire cost more than an Electra Glide. Sales were below 400 worldwide in 2021, and barely higher the following year. In 2021, LiveWire was "spun off" to create a separate all-electric bike brand, which was floated on the stock exchange, to help attract investment. The debut model was rebranded LiveWire ONE and relaunched with a reduced but still high price.

Harley optimistically projected that LiveWire sales would top 100,000 by 2026. Harley-Davidson itself would become an all-electric company, CEO Jochen Zeitz said, "in a long-term transition... that would take decades". LiveWire launched a second model, the flat-track styled S2 Del Mar, that was lighter and less expensive. Meanwhile, most of the motorcycle industry continued to watch and wait.

BELOW The S2 Del Mar roadster offered flat-track styling, reduced weight and a more competitive price.

BELOW The new LiveWire firm's debut model, the ONE, was essentially Harley's LiveWire with fresh paint.

Harley-Davidson

BIKES FOR WORK AND WAR

Almost as soon as the first model rolled off the Milwaukee production lines, Harley-Davidsons have been involved in all kinds of work.

In 1909, Harley provided motorcycles for the fledgling Rural Mail Carriers of America, but it is their association with police forces across the United States that is most well-known. 1908 was the year when the first Harley became involved with law enforcement; since then they have gone on to be an integral part of police forces' transportation worldwide.

Fire engines, delivery vans, golf carts: Milwaukee-built engines have driven them all. And if they were indispensable as civilian workhorses, as a tool for the military they were unsurpassed. The First World War was the first time a Harley had been used in a major conflict and, having established themselves as "Uncle Sam's choice", they went on to be invaluable during the Second World War.

Whether with a side-valve V-twin Model D for the police, a Servi-Car for deliveries or military 45-inch WLA, Harley-Davidson has always been able to come up with the goods.

LEFT Harley has been supplying police and rescue forces for many decades, often with special Electra Glides equipped with extras including lights, sirens and radios.

WORK AND WAR

Through more than a century of civilian production and two World Wars, Harley has built bikes, trikes and sidecars that have delivered news and supplies, assisted police departments, fought fires and engaged in battle. Police and rescue models continue to be a valuable part of the Milwaukee range.

WORK

Throughout the 1920s and 1930s, the words "Harley-Davidson" and "workhorse" were almost synonymous. Much of America's road network scarcely existed until President Roosevelt's job-creation programmes of the Depression years; even the celebrated Route 66 dates from only 1926. Any affordable, rugged machine able to cope with rough terrain had something going for it, and Milwaukee's finest certainly met that bill. Harleys have offered mobility in every walk of American life, from painters to policemen. The company saw this potential early – Arthur Davidson attended the annual meeting of the Rural Mail Carriers of America in 1909, coming away with a pocketful of sales.

It is with the police, however, that Milwaukee twins are best associated. Literally thousands of Harleys have joined America's police forces since they first went into uniform, in Detroit in 1908. Indeed, Harley-Davidsons have been popular across the globe, and Milwaukee twins have often been prominent in newsreel footage of presidential cavalcades in countries as far flung as Burma (now Myanmar) and Guatemala. By 1915, Juneau Avenue was also producing "rapid response" sidecar outfits equipped with fire extinguishers and first-aid kits. A decade later, Harley motorcycles were in use by more than 2,500 American

ABOVE Police officers on 1944 UL models patrol Minneapolis, Minnesota. Harleys have been involved in law enforcement since 1908.

BELOW The Servi-Car three-wheeler did much to allow Harley to endure the Depression.

BELOW A police Panhead, one of thousands of machines to have served US law-enforcement.

ABOVE An impressive line-up of police Harleys outside the Juneau Avenue factory.

RIGHT AND BELOW This immaculately restored Flathead served with the Daytona Beach Fire Department.

police forces, some of which quickly saw the public-relations benefits of organizing their riders into display teams. By the 1930s, police-model special equipment included radios (initially only one-way; two-way arrived in 1948), although some squads made riders buy their own police lights and sirens.

The same period also welcomed two definitive Harley-Davidson workhorses. The archetypal side-valve V-twin Model D, introduced in 1929, became the Model W in 1937 and continued in production until 1951. Although crude and slow – its 22-or-so-bhp, 45-inch engine generated around 65mph (105kph) – it was rugged, dependable and easy to fix, ideal for cash-strapped Depression America. The American military version, known as the WLA – the "A" stood for "Army" – represented the bulk of Milwaukee's contribution to

ABOVE Fancy being paid to ride a Harley at Sturgis: a local cop.

the Second World War. Though the majority of WL production during the war years was earmarked for military use, some also went to police forces and other strategic or security operations.

The Servi-Car, introduced for 1932, was the Model D's three-wheeled sister ship, and enjoyed an even longer production run, until 1974. The model's

ABOVE An Evo serving with Volusia County Police, one of several forces in the Daytona Beach area.

capacious boot (trunk) made it as popular with trade and delivery riders as it was with local police forces. This unique three-wheeler remained in service, even in metropolitan San Francisco, into the 1990s. One user-friendly Servi-Car touch was the adoption of the same 42in (1,070mm) wheel track as the typical car, so riders would not need to forge their own ruts in mud and snow.

The later Shovelhead years were not happy ones for Harley-Davidson's law-enforcing pretensions. Quality-control problems and general performance issues caused many forces to look elsewhere. For around a decade, even the California Highway Patrol (CHiPs) found itself powered by Italian Moto Guzzi V-twin and Japanese Kawasaki four-cylinder machines. The arrival of the Evolution engine in 1984 meant that Harley could again supply machinery that met the force's requirements, with police models including the FLHT-P Electra Glide and FXRP Pursuit Glide.

Recently, Harley has offered Electra Glide and Road King models developed for both the police and rescue services. After extensive evaluation, a Police Road Glide was added to the range for the 2024 model year. Some US police forces also tested versions of the Pan America and LiveWire, with both bikes looking set for important roles. In 2022, the Milwaukee Police Department became one of the first to use a Pan America for law enforcement duty.

ABOVE Daytona: Sun, sea and Harleys.

LEFT The job of a Daytona Beach motorcycle cop includes posing on a Harley in shades and short-sleeved shirt, and chatting to passing pedestrians.

THE FIRST WORLD WAR

By the time the United States entered the First World War in 1917, H-D machines had already seen action in skirmishes against the forces of Pancho Villa, the Mexican revolutionary. Under General "Black Jack" Pershing, machine-gun toting Harley-Davidsons proved themselves ideal for border patrols in rough terrain.

In the process, Juneau Avenue proved itself adept at meeting military demands. An order for additional machines was placed by a War Department telegraph on 16 March 1916. A dozen motorcycles equipped with William Harley's design for a sidecar gun carriage duly arrived at the border – more than 1,000 miles (1,610km) distance – two days later. Nine days later still, a second order for six machines reached Milwaukee. This one was filled in just 33 hours. Needless to say, the factory was not slow to advertise its efficiency in meeting "Uncle Sam's Choice".

Harley was just as quick to recognize the contribution it might make to the war in Europe. Within four months of the United States' entry into the war, Arthur Davidson was telling a sales meeting where the country's – and perhaps the company's – destiny lay: "The time is coming when no man can be in the middle of the road. He must be either for America or against America, and the sooner we get together on this question, the better able we will be to win the war."

During the first year of America's war, roughly half of all motorcycle production went to military service. By the end of the conflict, every motorcycle Milwaukee made was built for Uncle Sam. Along the way, William Harley, a member of the Motorcycle War Service Board, was instrumental in giving motorcycles a "B-4" classification, which gave them essential production status with priority for raw materials. Some 312 Harley-Davidson employees also enlisted, of whom all but three survived.

ABOVE The day after First World War Armistice in November 1918, Roy Holtz and his bike were "The first Yank and Harley to enter Germany".

RIGHT William Harley oversees the testing of specially equipped Harley twins during the early years of the First World War.

LEFT The horizontally-opposed XA twin looked more like a German BMW or Zundapp, but served in small numbers during the Second World War.

As to hardware, in all some 20,000 motorcycles became American "conscripts" in the First World War, the vast majority of which were Harley-Davidsons. This success finally leapfrogged Harley ahead of its main rival, Indian, a position it was never to relinquish. Military Harleys were mainly 61-inch (989cc) twins of conventional F-head design, producing almost nine horsepower. They were employed mainly for dispatch and scout duty.

BELOW A handful of the near 90,000 WLA V-twins that Harley produced during the Second World War, riders ready with goggles and weapons.

One became a cause célèbre. Its rider was Corporal Roy Holtz of Chippewa Falls, Wisconsin. On 8 November 1918, with the German army in chaotic retreat, Holtz was assigned to take his company captain on a reconnaissance mission. At night and in foul weather, the captain became disorientated and, over Holtz's objections, directed him across enemy lines where the duo stumbled across a German field headquarters at which Holtz was instructed to ask directions. They were taken prisoner but released with the Armistice three days later. Holtz – and his Harley V-twin – thus became the first American serviceman on German soil.

THE SECOND WORLD WAR

Harley-Davidson began planning in anticipation of military needs in autumn 1939, shortly after the outbreak of war in Europe and more than two years before the US entered the conflict. Early work focused on a flat twin Servi-Car to meet army proposals for a three-wheeler for rough terrain. Other unfinished projects were even stranger, including an armoured machine-gun carrier and a prototype powerplant for a small tank comprising paired overhead-valve engines.

BELOW The robust WLA in normal use with its rider's gun stowed in the scabbard alongside the front wheel.

RIGHT There are no weapons in sight on these WLAs as they take part in a parade in 1945 to celebrate the end of the Second World War.

With civilian motorcycle production suspended, by far the bulk of the firm's war effort was the production of military versions of the WL side-valve V-twins, the WLA. The equivalent 74-inch (1,207cc) military UA and USA (sidecar) models were built in much smaller numbers. Of almost 90,000 military Harleys, around 88,000 were 45-inch WLAs, of which one third served with Soviet forces. The same attributes of rugged simplicity that had brought the side-valve twin such a dependable peacetime reputation made it ideally suited to the harsher demands of war.

With very few Knuckleheads "enlisting" (although a special ELC model was built for the Canadian army), Milwaukee's other major contribution was the oddball Model XA, powered by a horizontally-opposed flathead twin displacing 45cu in (739cc). The XA was expressly designed for use in the North African desert, with its shaft final drive and plunger rear suspension, but proved ill equipped for the sandy conditions. There was also an XS variant, with sidecar.

Harley-Davidson's contribution was not confined to hardware. John E. Harley, later in charge of the parts and accessories division, rose to the rank of major. Among his tasks was the training of army motorcyclists at Fort Knox, Kentucky.

From late 1941 until the armistice in 1945, Juneau Avenue burned the midnight oil to meet the demands of the forces as almost the whole of American industry was turned over to the war effort. The firm's contribution was recognized by the award of three coveted Army-Navy "E" awards for excellence in wartime production.

Milwaukee's military models did not end with the Second World War. In 1987 Harley bought rights to the NATO-approved MT500 motorcycle from the British Armstrong company. This was developed to create the MT350E, with smaller-capacity Rotax engine, electric starter and disc brakes. It made 30bhp, featured large front panniers plus a rear gun case and sturdy rear carrier, and was produced from 1993 to 2000.

BELOW Although intended primarily for service in the North African desert – hence this colour scheme – the XA suffered badly from all the sand which would collect in its wheel bearings.

LIVE TO RIDE ... RIDE TO LIVE

To aficionados, a Harley-Davidson is as much an emotion as a lump of metal, and certainly much more than a mere motorcycle. Precisely what the "more" constitutes isn't easy to explain, except that Milwaukee iron can be almost anything you want it to be: wheels, plaything, lifestyle accessory, fashion statement, membership card or any of a hundred other things. To many owners, their Hog is almost as crucial as life itself. Transport is often the last thing on a Harley owner's mind.

LEFT Blue sky above, a road stretching out ahead, and a big Harley-Davidson V-twin engine beating lazily below... for many riders it's the perfect combination.

STYLE

The image forged from steel in the American Midwest travels across frontiers and media, and retains a uniquely powerful allure. It's as instantly recognizable in Bangkok as it is in Brooklyn, as rich with associations in Clackmannanshire as it is in Cincinnati.

For decades advertisers have taken advantage of Harley's image and used it as shorthand for youth, freedom, rebellion and freewheeling affluence. It is almost impossible to watch a commercial for anything from cars and pensions to jeans and toiletries without a Harley-Davidson cropping up sooner or later. In other words, Harleys may be motorcycles – but they're also stars.

Some of this rubs off on the people who ride them. Owning a Harley isn't about speed or performance, or about imitating your favourite racer or impressing friends. It's about individuality but also brotherhood, retro-cool and happening places, latter-day cowboys or folk who just want to get away from it all.

When they move, most Harley-Davidsons cruise. To the ear, they also thunder rather than rev. You can cruise around the block, along the beach or down to the bar; equally you can cruise from New York to San Francisco if that's your thing. They work equally well on the long-haul because of where they evolved – in a land of empty spaces and almost no corners at all.

"God rides a Harley", according to some. The King certainly rode one. As well as Elvis Presley, celebrity hoggers have included Cher, Whoopi Goldberg, Arnold Schwarzenegger, Tina Turner, Brad Pitt, George Clooney, Justin Tiimberlake and dozens more. You're as likely to see a film star in Hollywood riding a Harley-Davidson today as lounging in a stretch limousine. Often,

ABOVE Poster of Peter Fonda and Dennis Hopper cruising to New Orleans in *Easy Rider*.

ABOVE Christian Slater and Harley in the 1989 movie *Heathers*.

BELOW "Captain America" and helmet, as ridden by Peter Fonda.

BELOW "Harley-Davidstones" – one Stones fan wears his heart on his Harley.

ABOVE Nothing else out there: just you, your Harley and the open road.

the stars want something out of the ordinary. Custom builders can easily charge $100,000 for bespoke machines and, in the process, become minor celebrities themselves.

The phenomenon is far from new. Photographs from Hollywood's golden years show everyone from *Gone with the Wind*'s Clark Gable to Marlene Dietrich astride Milwaukee machines. Some pictures were pure publicity stunts, but even Roy Rogers rode a Harley when he wasn't riding Trigger. Hollywood even had its own Harley group once – the Three Point Motorcycle Club.

Harleys themselves have become film stars, notably Robert Blake's mount in *Electra Glide in Blue* and, of course, in the hugely successful *Easy Rider* starring Peter Fonda and Dennis Hopper. A Fat Boy starred with Schwarzenegger in *Terminator 2: Judgement Day*, and with John Travolta in *Wild Hogs*.

ABOVE You will find Hogs everywhere!

RIGHT Mickey Rourke cuts loose on a Harley in *The Marlboro Man*.

BELOW "Born in the USA" – long before Springsteen sang it.

RALLIES: STURGIS

Sturgis is an unremarkable farming community in South Dakota. For most of the year very little happens until, in mid-August, this sleepy hamlet goes motorcycle crazy as tens of thousands of riders arrive and the famous Sturgis Rally lets rip.

The monster that Sturgis has become was born way back in 1938 when the Jackpine Gypsies Motorcycle Club organized the first Black Hills Rally and Races, with a $300 purse to the winner. Almost every year since, bikers by the thousand have cruised in along Interstates 85 and 90 to renew old friendships or make new ones. Being conveniently located in middle America – if 900 miles (1,450 km) from Chicago and 1,500 miles (2,410 km) from San Francisco can be considered convenient – attendance tends to be huge. Any old Sturgis Rally attracts several hundred thousand of the faithful. For the 75th anniversary in 2015, over 700,000 turned up.

Sturgis is not specifically a Harley event, and reborn rival Indian has made its presence felt in recent years, but Milwaukee metal very much dominates. It lasts for ten days – of swap meets, drag-bike racing, tours, gawking at fancy Harley hardware and generally having a good time. Bikers hang out at joints like the Bear Butte Café. Main Street is air-cleaner to wheel-spindle full of Hogs. If you need a break, there are tours to the nearby Dakota Badlands, Devil's Tower (featured in the movie *Close Encounters of the Third Kind*) or Mount Rushmore.

There's strangeness, as well. One year, a guy rode a buffalo into town, moseyed down Main Street and hung a left on to Junction Avenue. Another year, the nearby US Air Force base reputedly laid on a rather special kind of fireworks display when a couple of their jets dipped low over town, hit their afterburners and drowned out even the noise of a thousand V-twins.

The whole town joins in (Sturgis is usually quite lucrative, estimated to bring over $800 milion to South Dakota every year), from the women of the United Presbyterian to the Grace

ABOVE Harley's magazine *The Enthusiast* covered the inaugural Black Hills Rally and Races in its May 1938 edition – and in many others since.

ABOVE And some people say all Harley owners are alike.

LEFT This photos is from 2012, but Sturgis has hardly changed in decades.

ABOVE Main Street in Sturgis, as can be seen, is a car-free zone.

Lutherans. There have been occasional troubles with biker gangs, but on the whole Sturgis is comparatively peaceful (if far from tranquil). These gangs are actively encouraged by the Sturgis city fathers, who clearly know a good deal when they see one.

According to Jackpine founder, former Indian dealer J.C. "Pappy" Hoel, there's never been a serious problem with outlaw biker groups: "We have their co-operation as long as we don't hassle them."

Mostly, it's one long biker party. Behaviour has been known to be on the excessive side, but it's usually harmless and only takes place once a year. Besides, it's legendary.

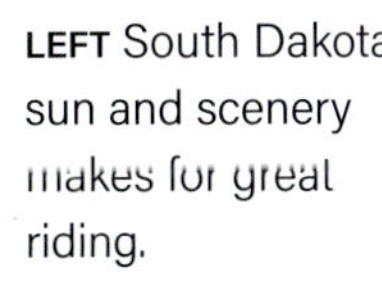

LEFT South Dakota sun and scenery makes for great riding.

RIGHT Buffalo are common but few make it to Main Street.

DAYTONA BIKE WEEK

Outside the Rat's Hole custom shop, Main Street reverberates to the rumble of big-bore Vs on open pipes. Heavy-looking bikers in wraparound shades stand beergut-to-beergut, shoulder-to-tattooed-shoulder on every inch of sidewalk.

It's March and almost 200,000 bikers have Daytona Beach under siege.

Like Sturgis, this is one long party that runs over two weeekends. For the most part, the siege is friendly. As the barmaid at La Playa Hotel put it, "Bike Week's the best because they're all really nice. You don't see manners like this any other time. Wannanother beer?"

Like Sturgis, Daytona's Bike Week is one of those mammoth events that didn't begin as a celebration of all that is Harley-Davidson but somehow became one. Bike Week takes place every March in the Florida coastal city of Daytona Beach. Its focal point is ostensibly the races at nearby Daytona International Speedway, a spectacular banked oval which also hosts the famous Daytona Nascar races.

It's yet another of those Harley enigmas that, as the factory's interest

RIGHT Like it says: "Daytona Beach Welcomes Bikers".

BELOW Spot the Honda.

BELOW RIGHT If you can find a standard bike, you can keep it.

ABOVE Cruising down Main Street feels best with high bars, thick forks, fat front tyre and a big V-twin engine.

ABOVE The rider's patches say he's a Special Forces Veteran; the career of his sidecar passenger is unknown.

BELOW According to some of its numerous stickers, this Road Glide rolled off Harley's assembly line in 1981.

ABOVE If you can't paint your Hog, paint your clothes...

in the races declined, the firm's profile in Bike Week as a whole rose dramatically. Milwaukee's official XR750 road racer last competed at the Speedway in 1973, and its last win was by Cal Rayborn in 1969, but this didn't spoil the party one bit. Even Harley's recent victories in the King of the Baggers race failed to draw a big crowd. Not having to ride the few miles out to the Speedway leaves more time for downtown fun. Daytona has become pure festival.

Sturgis, a relatively small town, is understandably overwhelmed by bikes. Daytona Beach is big, yet the effect is much the same. The scene centres on the junction of Atlantic and Main Street, where bikes and bodies are crammed sidewalk to sidewalk. Harley-Davidson – wise to the public relations coup Daytona has handed them – takes over the city's Hilton Hotel to strut its corporate stuff and show the latest models. However most Daytona life goes on in the street, in the bars, on the beach and in nearby campgrounds.

Bike Week has custom shows and impromptu drag races. During the day, bikes cruise along Daytona's beaches. There's official racing at the Daytona Supercross, the oval quarter-mile flat track and the main event at the International Speedway. There are swap meets in which enthusiasts sell or search for bike parts, notably at the Volusia County Fairgrounds.

Mainly it's lots of partyin', posin' and cruisin', and if you can't wait 12 months for your next Daytona fix, you can return for the smaller but similar Biketoberfest in October.

RALLIES AND HOMECOMING RIDES

Harley-Davidson has a long and imaginative tradition of embracing the interests of its customers, whether with rallies, rides, publications or through HOG, the Harley Owners Group – now over 40 years old, and motorcycling's largest owners' organization.

As early as 1916, Juneau Avenue was producing its own magazine to encourage fellowship among Harley owners. *The Enthusiast* carried tales of racing, travels and other daring Harley deeds. Within three years it was selling 50,000 copies.

During the 1930s Depression, Harley instigated the "medal system" in which bonuses were offered to owners generating a motorcycle sale. In 1951 the firm introduced the Harley-Davidson Mileage Club, which offered recognition for riding achievements. Members could earn a pin badge and membership card for clocking up 25,000, 50,000 and 100,000 miles. By the end of 1954, more than 70 had logged 100,000 miles (160,930km).

Harley's enthusiasm for anniversaries dates back to its 50th, in 1953, when the company held a small ceremony outside the Capitol Drive

ABOVE A rider flies the Austrian flag during European Bike Week at Faaker See in 2002, by which time the festival was already hugely popular.

BELOW The Street Glide's distinctive batwing fairing is prominent in this shot of riders at the 2023 edition of European Bike Week.

ABOVE Ape-hangers, springer forks and a large-diameter front wheel help if you want to stand out at a HOG rally.

RIGHT Sun, sea, sand and a big bunch of Harley-Davidsons: HOG Rally heaven at Cascais in Portugal in 2019.

factory during the annual sales conference. The concept of homecoming rides was sparked 25 years later, with the 75th anniversary in 1978. Groups of Harley executives and guests rode from seven points across America to Louisville, Kentucky, then on to Milwaukee, visiting many dealerships along the way.

A key moment of inspiration came in 1983 with the formation of HOG, the Harley Owners' Group. The manufacturer-backed organisation anticipated the way motorcycling was going before any rival bike firm took note. HOG now boasts over a million members in more than 1400 chapters worldwide. On almost any summer weekend it offers a choice of rallies in the United States, plus others as far-flung as Tunis, Darwin or Argentina.

HOG has been integral to Harley's increasing popularity, as reflected by the anniversary rides. For the 85th, in 1988, an estimated 60,000 riders converged on Milwaukee, raising more than half a million dollars for the Muscular Dystrophy Association, a long-time beneficiary. Ten years later the attendance had more than doubled to over 130,000; by 2008 the number was up to 250,000 riders, and the celebrations had expanded to include musical events, tours and visits to Harley's factories around Wisconsin.

Meanwhile HOG had gone international, starting in 1991 with a European rally at Cheltenham in England, and soon spreading to Asian countries including Singapore and Malaysia. Harley's centenary in 2003 was a truly global celebration, beginning a year earlier in Atlanta, Georgia with the Open Road Tour, which visited eight cities around the world before ending the following September in Milwaukee.

September also sees the annual European Bike Week at Faaker See in Austria, which began as a small Harley anniversary event in 1998. By 2018 it had grown to become a huge festival, attracting more than 200,000 people including thousands who rode in a parade around the picturesque Lake Faak. Bike Week's attendance exceeds even that of the annual European HOG rally, which takes place in a different country each year, and drew more than 100,000 to Budapest in Hungary in 2023 to celebrate the 120th anniversary.

BELOW Almost every type of Harley and rider came to Milwaukee for the 120th anniversary celebration in 2023.

BAD BOYS

Several decades ago, mentioning the name Harley-Davidson to someone in the street would typically have triggered a comment about Hell's Angels. Those days are long gone but a hint of outlaw image remains – and the biker gangs still make occasional headlines.

The Angels were formed in California by Second World War veterans. Shocking and antisocial, they became a role model for outlaw biker gangs across the world. They were immortalized in movies, and in books including Hunter S. Thompson's *The Hell's Angels: a Strange and Terrible Saga.*

But although a few stereotypes about Harley riders persisted, the negative image largely faded as the marque's owners became older, wealthier and better educated. Indeed, the stereotype has long been not a grime-ridden outlaw but a well-off professional cruising a city's more fashionable streets. Harleys are the weekend wheels of lawyers and bankers: respectability with an edge.

Hell's Angels and other self-styled "one per centers" still exist, though, albeit only on the fringes of Harley-Davidson and general motorcycling culture. Occasionally they hit the headlines. A wave of bombings and shootings between rival Canadian gangs in the early 1990s left around 40 dead.

Shortly afterwards, Scandinavian countries witnessed a spate of murders and even anti-tank missile attacks arising from a long-standing feud between the Angels and Bandidos for control of drugs interests. In 2008, seven members of Outlaws motorcycle club in the UK were jailed for life after gunning down a Hell's Angels member on the motorway as he rode his custom Harley home from a rally.

ABOVE The original Hell's Angels were a group of Californian war veterans. Note Willie G., standing, facing the camera, second from the left.

ABOVE Imitators of the original Angels have since evolved as far apart as New Zealand...

BELOW ...and Germany.

BELOW "Many are called... few are chosen" and even fewer care.

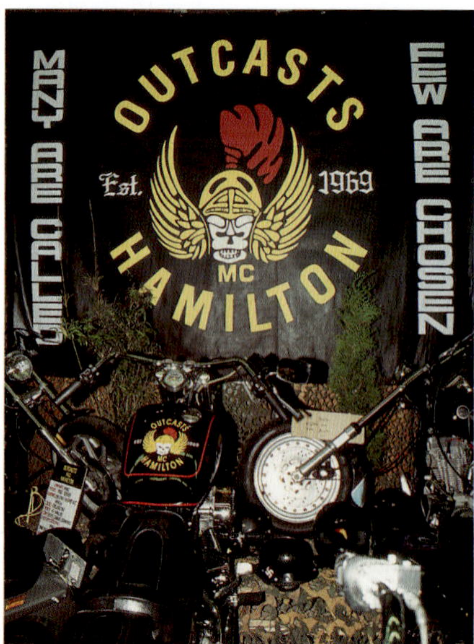

RIGHT Satans Slaves is a group of affiliated biker gangs, mostly in Britain.

In the States, the Outlaws were involved in a fatal shooting with the rival Sidewinders in Massachusetts in 2019. Three years later, seven bikers were reportedly stabbed as the Hell's Angels and Pagans clubs fought in the same state. Public interest remains high. Outlaw biker clubs starred in the popular US television series *Sons of Anarchy* and its follow-up *Mayans MC*, set in fictional Californian towns.

Ironically, much of the Harley Owners Group's paraphernalia – its insignia, colours and organisation into "chapters" – echoes the ways of the outlaw gangs. Beards, badges and leather are part of many everyday Harley riders' uniforms, although the trappings say little about the person underneath. Sometimes the observer in the street must be hard-pressed to tell the difference. Perhaps Milwaukee likes it that way.

LEFT Austin Butler starred as Benny, a member of the Vandals, in director Jeff Nichols' 2024 movie *The Bikeriders*, based on the genuine Chicago Outlaws club from the Midwest in the 1960s.

A DAY OF INFAMY

One of the most notorious episodes in American motorcycling history concerned the so-called Hollister riots of 1947. Events unfolded around the first Hollister Memorial Day races to be held since the Second World War, a focal point for recently demobbed biking GIs. The races were welcomed by residents of the Californian town for the business and prosperity they brought.

Thousands arrived for the races, including bike clubs such as the "Booze Fighters" from Los Angeles and San Francisco. Main Street was crowded and undoubtedly rowdy. "Riots... Cyclists Take Over Town" and "Havoc in Hollister," cried the San Francisco Chronicle. Other papers and magazines quickly jumped on to exploit the bandwagon.

Six years later, the "riots" were commemorated on celluloid in *The Wild One*, starring Marlon Brando and Lee Marvin. In the film, Johnny – angrily and effectively played by Brando – is asked what it is he's rebelling against. "Whaddya got?" he replies, one of Hollywood's most memorable lines. Although Harley-Davidsons feature heavily in the film, Brando is actually portrayed riding a Triumph. Nonetheless, the American Motorcycle Association saw fit to picket the movie on its release.

It was one thing for the movie to portray fiction, quite another for the contemporary press to do the same. For the truth was that the Hollister riots were largely fabricated. Some people were arrested for drunkenness but this was certainly nothing resembling a riot. As local hotelier Catherine Dabo later recalled to journalist Mark Gardiner, "I didn't even know anything had happened until I read the San Francisco papers."

According to one witness, cinema projectionist Gus Deserpa, the famous *Life* magazine photograph of a drunken biker sitting on his Harley, surrounded by bottles, was faked. The drunk was real but the bike wasn't his and the bottles had been gathered to "improve" the picture. Yes, Hollister was a weekend of infamy: for the media.

LOOKING FOR ADVENTURE

Harley-Davidsons are owned, ridden and cherished in every corner of the globe, by a diverse community of people and in a wide variety of situations. Whatever type of ride appeals, you can find it from the seat of a Harley.

Since the *Easy Rider* era of the 1960s, looking for adventure has typically meant heading out on the highway behind a pair of high handlebars, or the screen of an Electra Glide. These days it can equally involve off-road exploration aboard a Pan America, possibly with a group of like-minded riders and on any of six continents.

For many Harley enthusiasts, cruising a Hog across the good ol' US of A remains the ultimate fantasy – or for those fortunate enough to experience it, the thrilling reality. Epic American journeys are the stuff of Milwaukee dreams: thundering across the wide-open Midwest prairies or the baking deserts of the south-west; soaring over the Rocky Mountains or gliding down California's Highway 1. There is simply nowhere else where Harleys feel so resolutely, resoundingly right.

Harleys suit the United States perfectly because they're part of the cultural landscape you find yourself riding through. In the States, Harleys open doors, start conversations and bring smiles to passing faces, but best of all is the way they glide over the staggering panoply of scenery that is the American West.

ABOVE Author Mac McDiarmid heading north on Route 95 in Utah, with the Colorado River in the background.

LEFT Dream come true: a group on a Harley package tour cruises through Baja, Mexico.

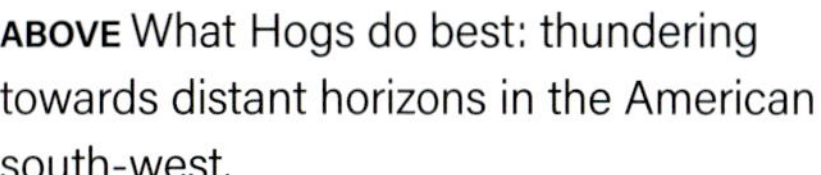

ABOVE What Hogs do best: thundering towards distant horizons in the American south-west.

ABOVE RIGHT A group of German riders on hired Harleys near Monument Valley on the Arizona/Utah border.

RIGHT A Fat Boy swings through the bends under the towering cliffs of Zion National Park, Utah, USA.

CRUISING

From the saddle of a Glide or Low Rider, America passes by at a pace your senses can get a hook on; horizons rise in waves, roll in like a gentle swell and gently recede under your wheels. It demands a different sort of tempo – more relaxed, less preoccupied with destinations – than riding in Europe. As the big, lazy V-twin thumps over hills and plains, it seems attuned to the environment in a way that other machines never could be.

Then, with a jolt, you encounter somewhere like Utah – scenic America at its most extraordinary. Utah is Mother Nature under hallucinogenic influence. It has National Parks in profusion, all with something spectacular and different: Arches, Canyonlands, Bryce, Capitol Reef and glorious Zion, to name but a few. Next door are Arizona and the Grand Canyon, Colorado and the Rockies,

ABOVE Baja California, the sea of Cortez beyond, and what better way to enjoy them?

LEFT Hoggers on a traditional ride-out from the Sturgis Rally to Dakota's Devil's Tower.

BELOW A group of Pan America riders on tour, here on a well-surfaced road but with some spectacular scenery waiting to be ridden through.

Nevada's sweeping high desert basins and the red rocks and white sands of New Mexico.

From magical, mystical Moab, it's just a short ride up Highway 191 to Canyonlands. Hang a left and let the Harley thunder up the endless grades until suddenly the road stops and the world simply disappears. Gone. In its place, space – a void as big as the Alps. Half a mile (800 metres) below, the Colorado River surges noiselessly, framed by a rocky never-never-land that might be awe-inspiring if it were real. It takes a while to get your head around the fact that it is.

If the landscape is dramatic, the sheer scale is extraordinary. Take Route 41 – cresting a rise north of Montezuma Creek, a view 200 miles (320km) leaps into sight. Seventy-five miles (120km) away in Arizona, the

ABOVE A heavily loaded Pan America makes light of a dirt road.

LEFT Whatever type of adventure you want, it's out there somewhere.

orange spires of Monument Valley guard the western horizon; to the east, the snowcapped Colorado Rockies are fully 125 miles (200km) distant. For experiencing the great, mythic emptiness of the United States there is no better place to be than the seat of a Harley-Davidson V-twin.

And these days there's no need to stick to the road – or to ride alone if you prefer company. The Pan America's arrival has opened up even more possibilities for adventure, as have the growing numbers of organized tours and expeditions, both in the States and all over the world. Whether your dream adventure is a solo dirt-road trek across Australia, a two-up tour in Europe or Asia, or a guided group ride in Africa or South America, there is a Harley-Davidson ideally suited to the trip, and someone who can help make it happen.

BELOW Many tour operators can supply riding kit as well as a bike.

HARLEY·DAVIDSON

THE CUSTOM SCENE

The identity of the first Harley-Davidson custom isn't recorded but it's surely almost as old as the company itself. It's in the nature of motorcycles that owners seek to "improve" them – not because there's necessarily anything wrong with the way they came out of the crate, but to add that extra touch of individuality.

Over the years, this "extra touch" turned from a trend into a craze and finally into a phenomenon. Today you'd be hard-pressed to find a Harley that has not been altered in some manner from the original that Milwaukee intended. Indeed, to judge by the amount of customizing that goes on, a Harley certainly isn't finished when it leaves the factory, if ever. Far from being discouraged by this slight on its judgement, the company actively encourages it, notably by promoting shows and events, and commissioning hand-built bikes. Custom Hogs are booming.

LEFT Custom paint and a free-breathing intake are among the features of this Harley that was on display at the European Bike Week at Faaker See in Austria in 2023.

RISE OF THE CUSTOMS

A customized Harley today can be anything from a Softail pared down to the barest essentials to a Glide decked out with almost anything you'd expect to find in a deluxe motorhome. Things were very different when riders began modifying Milwaukee-built machines.

In the very early days, most changes were functional: one carburettor worked better than another; this mudguard kept you cleaner than that. America's love affair with horsepower soon meant that engine tuning became a growth industry: in almost every state of the union, someone was willing to sell you "hot" camshafts, high-compression pistons or other goodies to make an engine stronger.

More than with any other make of motorcycle, Harley-Davidson customizing is an oddly circular process. Many owners of early Harleys modified them, and some of these creations were very attractive. This was noted in Milwaukee. Styling ideas that had first appeared as owners' one-offs fed back into the melting pot of Juneau Avenue design. As far as graphics and paint are concerned, early examples included the art-deco designs that Harley introduced in the 1930s.

The true custom scene arrived in California in the 1950s, with pioneers including Von Dutch and Ed Roth. Often, 1930s art-deco was their

TOP Bob Lowe's streamlined custom creation "Evil Twin".

ABOVE Not surprisingly, this one goes by the name of "Full Metal Jacket".

LEFT AND BELOW In 1999 the California Motorcycle Company built replicas of Peter Fonda's famous Captain America chopper from *Easy Rider*.

ABOVE Custom legend Arlen Ness with son Cory, whose own son Zach also became a leading bike builder.

BELOW A typically long, low and intricately detailed Ness creation.

ABOVE Light-Ness (closest), Antique-Ness and Smooth-Ness, three of Arlen Ness' most famous creations.

RIGHT Sometimes, Milwaukee must wonder why it bothers at all.

inspiration in creating "blend" bikes – machines built from parts of several different models, as well as one-off components. The 1960s and 1970s saw the arrival of the chopper, an unmissable form of expression with its radically extended forks and often spectacular paintwork and chrome, highlighted by the bikes ridden by Captain America and Billy in *Easy Rider*.

THE CUSTOM ARTISTS

The same period was also notable for a different breed of customizers whose creations were more art than motorcycle. Celebrated custom artists included Dave Perewitz, Ricki Battistini, Donnie Smith and the most revered of all – Arlen Ness. From his base in California's Bay Area, Ness began modifying bikes as a hobby, before people took note and asked him to craft something equally extraordinary for them.

Beginning in 1967 with an old Knucklehead he had bought for a few hundred dollars, Ness designed and manufactured everything down to the tiniest, most exquisite chrome-plated details. He forged a string of unique bikes, often with a long, drag-racer influenced look that became known as the Bay Area style.

Among his best-known bikes was the silver "Light-Ness", which held Ness's own "light weight" V-twin motor in a special aluminium frame. Its tank, fenders and other parts were crafted from the same, highly polished metal. Another unique aluminium creation was "Smooth-Ness", whose all-enveloping body was inspired by the flowing lines of a classic Bugatti car.

The yellow "Antique-Ness" was a sidecar outfit powered by a 1200cc Sportster engine, inspired by Harleys of the 1920s. It was created in partnership with two other leading customizers, Mun and Jimmy Rose, and was built for Arlen's wife Beverly. The Ness operation was very much a family concern. Arlen's son Cory and grandson Zach also became leading custom builders, continuing the business after Arlen passed away in 2019, aged 79.

SPECIALS AND CAFÉ RACERS

If the typical American custom bike from the 1970s onwards was a rangy chopper or low-slung Bay Area cruiser, elsewhere the focus of modified motorcycles was sportier – and there was still plenty of potential for Harley-Davidson involvement.

LEFT The Stuttgart-based Schwarz brothers created the stunning AMC Harley by housing a hotted-up 1,340cc V-twin in a steel ladder frame.

BELOW Fritz Egli's café racer, named Lucifer's Hammer after the famed Twins racer, featured the Swiss engineer's trademark steel spine frame.

European enthusiasm for road-racing and the British tradition of hard-riding Rockers inspired hand-built specials that mostly featured British twin-cylinder engines or Japanese fours, but also led to some spectacular Harley-powered machines.

Given that the starting point in each case was a Milwaukee-built, 45-degree V-twin, the variety was striking – ranging from faired café racers powered by bored-out Big Twins, to high-handlebarred Sportster-based specials, some inspired by Harley's all-conquering XR750 flat-track racer.

Several of Europe's leading fabricators rose to the challenge of housing a big-inch Harley V-twin in a bespoke chassis. Famed Swiss engineer Fritz Egli bolted a 1,607cc motor into one of his trademark spine frames. Dutch race-frame specialist Nico Bakker's 1,705cc, Softail-based motor was held in a comprehensively reworked chassis complete with single-sided swing-arm. In Germany, brothers Eberhard and Richard Schwarz of AMC, near Stuttgart, created a stunning red café racer by bolting a tuned, 1,340cc engine into a lightweight frame welded from Reynolds 531 steel tubing.

Fast Company co-founders Hal Baxter and Michael MacDowel lived amid the twisting roads of South Carolina, which inspired their creation of an agile Sportster special featuring a swoopy tank-seat unit. Even closer to Harley's home, Wisconsin-based Erik

ABOVE Dutch engineer Nico Bakker with his Softail special, featuring spine frame and single-sided swing-arm.

ABOVE Jim Feuling's outrageous W3 was a 2,458cc triple that made 156bhp and accelerated like a drag bike.

Buell began by building small numbers of the RR1000, essentially a Harley-engined special, in the 1980s before growing his business into a full-blown manufacturer that he eventually sold to Harley-Davidson.

The Sportster engine has been used by many builders from outside the States, including English engineer Simon Goodman, from the family that founded Velocette. His Goodman HDS, short for Harley-Davidson Special, was another to feature a frame of Reynolds 531 tubing. By contrast Brian Udall, boss of Harley tuning and spares firm Hogbitz, used a modified standard frame for his alloy-tanked café racer, inspired by the Triton he'd ridden when frequenting London's Ace Café as a youth.

The XR750 flat-tracker inspired numerous specials in the 1990s, the best-known being built by Steve Storz, who had worked as a Milwaukee factory race mechanic before relocating to California. Bartels, a Harley dealership in nearby Los Angeles, also built a stylish XR replica, the XLR1200. Across the Atlantic, Bristol-based Adrian Pavey's Métisse Harley held an iron-barrelled XR1000 engine in a frame which, in Métisse tradition, was made from nickel-plated steel tubes.

Those street trackers combined outstanding design and engineering, but arguably the most remarkable custom Harley was very different. Jim Feuling, who like Storz was based in Ventura, was a leading engineer, tuner and inventor who had been commissioned by Harley to help develop the Twin Cam 88 engine. His W3 special, based on that engine, was so-named because it had three cylinders in a W shape – the brilliant Feuling having added an extra pot, held at a similar 45-degree angle, to raise capacity to 2,458cc, or 150 cubic inches.

ABOVE The British-built Hogbitz Café Racer featured a tuned Sportster engine and Triton inspired alloy tank.

RIGHT Former Harley flat-track mechanic Steve Storz's Sportster specials resembled the mighty XR750.

CHOPPERS AND THE NEW WAVE

The new millennium began with a chopper craze in the United States, largely caused by Harley-Davidson although the company was not the main beneficiary. Instead, a host of new firms built radical and spectacular bikes before quickly fading away.

Harley's surge in popularity through the 1990s, and its inability to meet demand, led to long waiting lists for new bikes – and to riders desperate to make theirs stand out from the crowd, inspired by television shows including *American Chopper* and *Biker Build-off*.

Harley did benefit, of course, with sales of bikes and custom parts. But many of the new breed of choppers were built by specialist firms such as Pure Steel and Big Dog, around "Harley clone" V-twin engines from tuning firm S&S. Harley developed a chopper model, the Softail Rocker, but by the time it reached production in 2008 the global financial crisis had ended the craze and put most of the new manufacturers out of business.

Custom culture then shifted towards down-to-earth, shed-built bikes, often with Japanese engines. But while many builders embraced humble parallel twins, others created imaginative and brilliant Harley customs. In 2021, leading website *Bike EXIF*'s Top Ten Customs list featured three Harleys that could hardly have been more different – a turbocharged Panhead chopper, a Sportster-engined flat-tracker, and Rule Breaker – a LiveWire-based electric creation from Dutch firm Moto Adonis.

Leading European professional builders including Wrenchmonkees from Denmark have fashioned striking Harley-engined V-twins. Blitz of France produced a lean flat-track style Sportster titled Venice Beach Vibes. Spanish firm El Solitario built a trio of rugged Desert Wolves V-twins based on the Roadster 1200.

TOP Los Angeles dealer Laidlaw's won the 2019 Battle of the Kings contest with its elegant Coast Glide bagger.

ABOVE One of the trio of dual-purpose Desert Wolves built by El Solitario of Spain for the Wheels & Waves rally in 2017.

LEFT Choppers for sale at the Daytona Speedway in 2005. A few years later most of the firms had ceased trading.

RIGHT Italian firm Gallery Motorcycles' hardtail custom, inspired by board-track racers, was voted Best of Show at European Bike Week in 2023.

Californian-based craftsman Shinya Kimura – who raced a Harley WL in Japan before moving to the States – used his trademark hand-formed aluminium panels to create sculptural bikes, notably the Knucklehead-engined Junkyard Phantom and Spike. DP Customs of Arizona fashioned Harleys including American Graffiti, inspired by a 1955 Chevy.

Deus Ex Machina's workshop in Sydney produced a classy café racer, the XV-Twin 1200. Taiwanese firm Rough Crafts' builds include Stealth Bullet, Asphalt Glider, Tarmac Raven and Mighty Guerilla – each a fresh take on founder Winston Yea's blacked-out signature style.

Harley has contributed by commissioning custom bikes and promoting events, notably the annual Battle of the Kings contest. Dealerships worldwide have joined in, notably Thunderbike of Germany, Bangkok Harley – whose Street Bob, named The Prince, took the crown in 2018 – and Laidlaw's of Los Angeles, whose Coast Glide bagger won in 2019. More than 50,000 people voted in the following year's contest for Sportster-based customs, won by Oscar Peralta from Mexico with Apex Preditor.

Custom shows continue to highlight spectacular and ingenious hand-built creations, many of them powered by Harley V-twins of every age and type. Prize winners have ranged from Gallery Motorcycles' vintage-style flat-head to Custom Creations' radical bagger Touring Absurd; from fellow Slovenian firm VK Customs' rangy chopper to Custom Thom's squat V-Rod Muscle.

ABOVE Celebrity tattoo artist Dr Woo aboard the vintage themed Silent Dancer, his LiveWire-based custom.

RIGHT Mexican builder Oscar Peralta's sporty Apex Preditor won the Battle of the Kings contest in 2020.

CUSTOM VEHICLE OPERATIONS

The term "factory custom" is an oxymoron; a custom bike is one that has been changed since leaving the factory. But the phrase has come to mean a production model that resembles customized bikes or is in some way special – and Harley-Davidson has long been expert at using this to its advantage.

Even before the Second World War, some Harley riders modified or beautified their bikes, which was noticed in Milwaukee. Designers at the factory began to incorporate owners' details and styling touches in models for future production. In 1970 the wheel came full circle when Willie G. Davidson's team fashioned the FX1200 Super Glide, often referred to as the first factory custom.

Harley also mined a lucrative seam with tuning parts and accessories, under the name Screamin' Eagle. This was stepped up in the 1990s, following the end of a contract to supply military bikes. A Milwaukee building in which these had been assembled was used to create a pair of FX derivatives with special paint and extra glitz. The 1999-model FXR2 and FXR3 were built in limited numbers of 900 each, beginning Harley's Custom Vehicle Operation programme.

The CVO initiative was a success,

ABOVE Flame-effect paintwork and free-breathing Screamin' Eagle intake are typical CVO model features.

TOP For 2022 the CVO Street Glide featured paint by Gunslinger and a Milwaukee-Eight 117 powerplant.

ABOVE This CVO Road Glide from 2022 combines the 117cu in engine with classical orange and black paint.

BELOW Along with its special paint scheme, the 2009 CVO Road Glide had a bigger Twin Cam 110 engine.

RIGHT The Road Glide Special Anniversary was Harley's choice for the Icons series in 2023, the firm's 120th year.

BELOW This Road Glide's orange-and-black tank features bar-and-shield logos, under the Apex Factory Custom Paint program.

BOTTOM The laid-back Seventy-Two was available with 1970s-inspired Hard Candy Custom Metal-flake paint.

and the following year Harley followed up with another variant, the FXR4, plus a Screamin' Eagle Road Glide that combined touring ability with additional performance. In 2001 the programme was expanded with an assembly line at the York factory. Alongside another special Road Glide was the FXDWG2 Switchblade, a Wide Glide featuring scarlet paintwork with 23 carat gold-leaf flames.

Each year since then, the factory has picked between two and five models for special treatment, calling them Screamin' Eagle bikes until 2009, when the name was changed to CVO. They have ranged from Softail Springers and Electra Glides to V-Rods and even the Tri Glide trike. Paint and badging are exclusive to the CVO bikes, with proof of ownership required before parts can be replaced. This helps maintain exclusivity, even with annual CVO production of over 10,000 units.

Harley has often introduced new engines with CVO models, starting in 2000, when the Screamin' Eagle Road Glide debuted the 95ci (1,556cc) Twin Cam 88 unit. By 2023, the CVO Street Glide and Road Glide were showcasing the 121ci Milwaukee-Eight engine, with 1,977cc capacity and variable valve timing.

The CVO models are no longer the only limited-edition Harleys. In 2021 the factory introduced the Icons programme, choosing one model for retro treatment. That year's Electra Glide Revival invoked the 1969 original with blue-and-white paintwork. For 2022 the Icon was the Low Rider El Diablo, also limited to 1,500 units, featuring red paint with a 1980s Southern California vibe.

Harley has also given bikes a lift with special paintwork, notably the Hard Candy Custom metalflake used on models including the Forty-Eight and Seventy-Two. More recently the Apex Factory Custom Paint programme, an option on touring models, offered orange-and-black schemes inspired by factory flat-track racers. Harley enthusiasts desiring something special have never been so spoiled for choice.

PARTS
UNLIMITE
HARLEY-DAVIDSON
10
79
13
33
VANCE HINES
SADDLEMEN

COMPETITION

Although Harley-Davidson is not always automatically associated with the white heat of competition, it is part of the deep-seated American tradition of racing pretty much anything on wheels. The first mention of a Harley racing dates from 1904. Perry Mack (possibly the company's first employee) set a speed record on a local Milwaukee track as early as 1905. The first recorded "factory" win in actual competition came in 1908, with Walter Davidson at the controls.

Company presidents don't figure among the results any more, but Harley-Davidson has won since on tarmac, dirt, boards, ice, grass and just about any other medium possible. Much of this success has been in the spectacular field of American Flat Track racing, a 140mph (225kph) speedway where huge fields of riders compete like fury on thundering V-twins. On the Grand Prix front, Harley's Italian connection Aermacchi brought Walter Villa four world crowns in the 1970s. Since then, the factory has road raced with bikes ranging from the VR1000 of the 1990s to giant Baggers of recent seasons. Harleys have also competed successfully in events from hill-climbing to drag racing and set speed records at Daytona and on the Bonneville salt.

LEFT Harley's King of the Baggers riders put on a show for their home crowd at Elkhart Lake, Wisconsin in 2023 as Kyle Wyman leads Vance and Hines H-D's Hayden Gillim (79), from Kyle's brother Travis Wyman (10) on the second factory Road Glide.

EARLY RACING

Harley-Davidson's early years were marked by racing successes too numerous to mention. The firm's growing involvement in competition not only helped build a reputation for performance and reliability but also formed an important proving ground for technical developments.

One of the earliest successes came in 1908 when one of the first V-twins, ridden by company president Walter Davidson, claimed victory in the FAM (Federation of American Motorcyclists) seventh annual endurance event in New York's Catskill Mountains. The 365-mile (587km) course was dauntingly rugged, yet "so strong was my confidence," Davidson later said, "that I carried with me no additional parts." This was in marked contrast to several other manufacturers, whose machines were followed by car-loads of spares.

In July of the same year, the Chicago Motorcycle Club sponsored a hill climb in nearby Algonquin, Illinois. Fastest time of the day went to Harvey Bernard riding a Harley-Davidson. Oddly, contemporary photographs clearly show Bernard aboard a V-twin machine, yet the model did not officially appear until early the following year.

The succeeding years were distinguished by numerous, similar Harley-Davidson successes, yet they almost exclusively involved machines which were privately owned and run.

ABOVE The early board tracks genuinely were frighteningly steep, but photographic limitations meant images such as this were trick shots using wires.

A company advertisement from September 1911 bragged, "We don't believe in racing and we don't make a practice of it, but when Harley owners with their own stock machines win hundreds of miles from the factory, we can't help crowing about it."

This boast was nowhere more graphically demonstrated than in the San José road race of 1912, in which a 61-inch Model X8E triumphed by the small matter of 17 miles (27km). That same year, Harley-Davidson twins won at Bakersfield and the following year took first, second and third place in a 225-mile (362km) dash from Harrisburg to Pennsylvania and back, but these were private machines contesting relatively obscure races.

In 1914 – four years after Indian had won the prestigious Isle of Man TT – Milwaukee bowed to the inevitable when Bill Harley established a works race department that was to continue its winning ways for many decades of competition. Some reports refer to instant success in taking that year's Dodge City 300-mile (480km) race, when in fact only two Harleys finished, well off the pace, in a race dominated by Indian. Clearly, the battle-hardened Springfield eight-valve twin was a formidable foe, but under the direction of the Bills Harley and Ottaway, Harley's progress was rapid. By 1915, Milwaukee twins were the bikes to beat.

LEFT Harley had major success in racing from the outset.

RIGHT The Wrecking Crew at Dodge City in 1920. From left: race boss Bill Ottaway, Maldwyn Jones, Ralph Hepburn, Fred Ludlow, Otto Walker, Ray Weishaar, Jim Davis and mechanic Hank Syvertsen.

The step from factory racers to racer production was a short and logical one. By 1916, $250 would buy any aspiring racer a special stripped-down competition version of the Harley twin, producing 11 horsepower and capable of around 75mph (120kph).

As well as speed, Harley iron chased many endurance records during the same period. In 1917, a Harley-Davidson ridden by Alan Bedell covered 1,000 miles (1,610km) non-stop at Ascot Park, taking almost 21 hours and averaging a remarkable 48.3mph (77.7kph).

In the same year, another Harley set a similar mark fitted with a sidecar.

THE WRECKING CREW

During the buoyant 1920s, Harley-Davidson's competitive exploits were even more remarkable than the salvos of new models roaring out of Milwaukee. In 1920, a Harley became the first powered vehicle to top California's 10,000ft (3,050m) "Old Baldy" hill-climb. In February 1921, at Fresno, a Harley became the first bike to win a race at an average of more than 100mph (161kph).

Many of the factory's innumerable successes came courtesy of the legendary Harley-Davidson "Wrecking Crew". The Crew was almost unbeatable on the dirt and boards of America from the days before the First World War until the factory briefly pulled out of racing following the 1920 slump. Board racing, on banked ovals of raw wood, was uniquely – and spectacularly – American.

The Crew included barnstorming individuals: Eddie Brinck, Otto Walker, Jim Davis, Leslie "Red" Parkhurst and many more. Walker marked the factory's withdrawal by

BELOW Ralph Hepburn with the Harley factory eight-valve racer at the Dodge City track in 1921.

LEFT An unnamed Harley rider reaches the summit in spectacular style at a hill-climb event in 1940.

taking a 61cu in, eight-valve machine to victory in a 50-mile (80km) race at San Joaquin, California, at the sensational average speed of 101.43mph (163.23kph). The crew began 1920 by taking the first four places in the Ascot 100-mile (161km) race on America's fastest track. In February, Harleys set 23 records, including four by Parkhurst at the kilometre, mile – both at more than 103mph (165kph) – two-mile and five-mile marks.

These men, riding in little more than cloth caps, sweatshirts and jodhpurs, were tough little heroes in the same mould that was later to produce stars such as Cal Rayborn, Jay Springsteen and Scott Parker. The racing life was hard and cruel. Eddie Brinck himself was killed when a tyre blew out in a race at Springfield, Massachusetts.

As America's road system developed, it was natural that riders would create some form of contest on it. As early as 1920, Hap Sherer took a Sport Twin (584cc boxer) from Denver to Chicago in 48 hours – no easy feat even today. In the same year, Walter Hadfield retook the "Three Flags Run" record from Vancouver (Canada) to Tijuana (Mexico), a route on a 61ci Harley, riding over 1,650 miles (2,655km) down America's west coast in 49 hours. Perhaps most impressive of all was the remarkable Earl Hadfield, who covered more than 3,000-plus miles (4,800km) between New York and Los Angeles in less than 78 hours.

BELOW Ray Weishaar celebrates a 1920 win with Harley's pig mascot, which led to Harleys being called Hogs.

THE HOLE IN THE WALL GANG

In the Depression years of the 1930s, people would try almost anything to turn a buck. If Evel Knievel enlivened the 1970s, the 1930s shone for an assorted bunch of desperadoes who might be called the "Hole in the Wall Gang". These weren't Butch and Sundance but a fellowship of maniacs who believed that if you hurtled a bike fast enough at a solid timber wall, you could punch clean through it.

The first recorded case of a Harley-Davidson attempting the stunt came in Texas in 1932 when Daisy May Hendrich thudded repeatedly through inch-thick boards. (Daisy May, incidentally, was a man.) J.R. Bruce of Wooster, Ohio, went one better by setting the wall ablaze before the stunt. Wall stunts, burning or not, were a common feature of American county fairs in the 1930s before the public's interest eventually faded.

ABOVE A quartet of early hill-climbers, with chained rear tyres for extra grip, on display at the Harley Museum.

At around the same time, the immortal Windy Lindstrom was king of America's booming hill-climb scene, on specially-modified Milwaukee iron.

Harley victories were by no means confined to the United States. Harley-Davidson found willing, winning pilots as far apart as Scandinavia and Australia, notching up successes in fields as diverse as ice speedway and grass track. At the legendary banked Brooklands track in Surrey, England, Douglas H. Davidson (no relation) took a factory 1,000cc ioe twin to a record-breaking average of 100.76mph (162.15kph) over a flying kilometre. Within a few months, a similar machine ridden by Claude Temple had taken records in the hour, five mile, flying mile and kilometre.

Yet even these efforts paled when compared to those of the mercurial Englishman, Freddy Dixon, riding a special twin with four pipes and eight overhead valves. Dixon was nearly unbeatable in all forms of competition from hill-climbs to long-distance events around the daunting Brooklands circuit. On 9 September 1923 at Arpajon, near Paris, Dixon set a new world speed mark of 106.8mph/171.8kph (a record Harley-Davidson would not hold again until 1970). Ten months later he was at it again, flying through the half-mile at the Clipstone Speed Trials at 103.44mph (166.47kph). In 1925 he averaged 100.1mph (161kph) winning the Brooklands 1,000cc championship – possibly the noisiest victory ever, for the machine had no exhaust pipes.

BELOW Factory ace Joe Petrali with a hill-climber, just one of the many bikes on which he was successful.

FLAT TRACK

Flat track racing – or dirt track, as it is also known – spans the decades and is the essence of American motorcycle sport. The battle for the prized "Number One" plate of the AMA champion is the craziest and meanest of two-wheeled contests.

Although superficially similar to speedway, flat track is held on oval circuits a mile or half-mile long where 750cc machines reach speeds in excess of 140mph (225kph).

At the highest level, flat track is oddly balletic, almost poetry on wheels. But it can go wrong with sickening suddenness, ending in a maelstrom of muck, blood and machinery. In the famed movie *On Any Sunday*, riders are thrown through four-inch fence posts, clamber to their feet, dust off the dirt and the straw and climb right back on their bikes. Riders who can't walk drift both wheels at three-figure speeds. Dick Mann saws off a plaster cast – "I'm a fast healer" – just to chase that Number One plate.

Flat track grew up on the county fairgrounds of middle America, a sort of rodeo on two wheels, and an alternative to the steep board tracks. In 1946, the AMA founded the national championship, which was initially awarded to the winner of a single race, the Springfield Mile, held at the Illinois State Fairgrounds track. After Norton's Chet Dykraaft won the first, Harley won four times in a row, with three victories for Jimmy Chann, one of the greatest dirt-track racers of all time.

From 1954 the format was changed to a series comprising quarter-, half- and mile flat track racing, plus TT Steeplechase (a cross between flat track and motocross) and road-racing.

ABOVE Harley aces Jay Springsteen, Ted Boody, Korky Keener and Mike Kidd lead the flat track pack in 1977.

LEFT Kenny Coolbeth, who won a hat-trick of AMA titles for Harley from 2006 to 2008, throws his XR750 into a turn at the head of the field in the Springfield Mile.

RIGHT The start of the "Dash for Cash" race at Daytona. Winner takes all.

Harley-Davidsons dominated, winning 12 of the next 13 championships with riders including triple champions Joe Leonard and Bart Markel, and Carroll Resweber, who won four in a row from 1958.

The AMA's production-based Class C regulations allowed side-valve engines of 750cc, while limiting overhead-valve bikes to 500cc. Harley's side-valve KR750 racer was sufficiently fast to keep the factory team competitive through the 1960s, with wins for Roger Reiman, Markel and Mert Lawwill. Harley's famed "Number One" logo was designed to celebrate Lawwill's 1969 AMA Grand National title win.

In 1969, flat track rules changed to allow 750cc engines with no limitation on valve type. Harley responded by introducing the XR750, with an overhead-valve engine based on the Sportster unit. Although initially uncompetitive and unreliable, the XR was soon much improved. Harley's Mark Brelsford took the No.1 plate in 1972 – beginning a hugely successful period for Milwaukee and one of its greatest ever models.

ABOVE Reigning AMA champion Kenny Coolbeth's XR750 wears the coveted No. 1 plate as he battles on a Springfield Mile straight in 2008.

LEFT Scott Parker rockets the XR750 around the Del Mar track.

ABOVE LEFT Harley's Rich King leads a train of riders onto the straight, his throttle wound open and his left hand held low to minimize drag.

ABOVE Jared Mees searches for traction as the AMA champion powers his factory XR750 out of a turn at the DuQuoin Mile in 2015.

FROM XR750 TO XG750G

Harley-Davidson was the most successful manufacturer in flat track racing in the 1970s and 1980s but the Milwaukee factory team did not have things all its own way. The XR750 won the majority of titles during both decades, following the introduction of an improved version of the V-twin, with cylinder heads made from aluminium instead of iron, that Mark Brelsford rode to victory in 1972.

But Triumph's Gene Romero and BSA's Dick Mann had won the decade's first two championships, and Yamaha's Kenny Roberts won in 1973 and 1974, all of them riding parallel twins in the flat track events. And although Harley finished the decade strongly, two of the next five titles went to XR-riding privateers, Gary Scott and Steve Eklund.

Harley's struggles in the early 1970s followed the takeover by AMF, which had left few resources for racebike development. The initial iron-head XR had frequently overheated but the cooler-running alloy engine was soon successful. Jay Springsteen and the XR750 formed a formidable partnership, taking a hat-trick of championships from 1976.

The XR began the 1980s with three titles before the emergence of a new rival. Honda's RS750 followed the XR format of aircooled, 45-degree V-twin engine but used twin overhead cams and four-valves-per-cylinder horsepower to win four consecutive championships before Honda quit the scene. Then came a remarkable period from 1988 to 2005 during which Harley factory aces Scott Parker and Chris Carr won 16 titles, Parker taking a record nine of them.

Flat track's format changed several times over the next few years but the

BELOW Brad Baker throws up the dirt as he slides his XR750 through a turn on the way to victory at the Lima Half-Mile in Ohio in 2016.

ABOVE Decades of Harley racing history are on show as the venerable XR750 (left) is pictured with its XG750R successor in 2020.

BELOW A flat track racer's most vital piece of kit is the steel shoe, strapped to the left boot for broadsiding through the left-hand turns.

ABOVE Jesse Janisch powers through a turn on the Vance & Hines Racing XG750R on which he won the AMA's Pro Twins class in 2022.

XR750 continued to dominate, Kenny Coolbeth and Jared Mees each winning three titles. The V-twin had evolved over the decades; Parker estimated that its output had increased from 70 to 105bhp. Its rider-friendly power delivery and ability to find traction in the dirt, both vital to its success, had very much remained intact.

In 2017 the Grand National series was revamped and renamed American Flat Track. In the same year, Harley announced that it would no longer be racing the XR750, ending a story that had lasted almost 50 years, and produced 37 Grand National championships and more than 500 main event victories.

That left the XR's replacement, the XG750R, with huge boots to fill – a task made more difficult because the liquid-cooled, eight-valve XG's arrival coincided with the return of Indian, who developed a powerful V-twin racebike, hired triple champ Mees and won a string of titles.

The XG750R struggled to match its old rival in the premier Super Twins class, but had more success in the supporting Pro Twins category where James Rispoli won the championship in 2020 and Jesse Janisch followed two years later. By this time Harley-Davidson had disbanded its factory race team, in favour of offering support via dealers. Milwaukee's decades of domination had ended. But as long as flat track racing exists, riders will be competing in the familiar orange and black.

GREAT RIDERS

Over more than a century, many dozens of fine riders have won races and championships, set records and entertained crowds aboard Harley-Davidson motorcycles, on dirt, boards, sand, asphalt, salt and more. These are just a handful of the giants who have left a lasting impression.

JOE PETRALI

More than perhaps any other man, Petrali single-handedly made Harley-Davidson an unbeatable force during the late 1920s and throughout the 1930s. Born in Sacramento, California in 1904, he owned his first bike at 13 years of age and was racing – and winning – on boards by the time he was 16. Petrali first hit the big time when he showed up bike-less at Altoona, Pennsylvania, in 1925. Luckily for him, former Wrecking Crew man Ralph Hepburn had broken a hand.

Petrali took over the factory Harley-Davidson instead. He was practically unknown at the time. Less than an hour later, Petrali was a legend. He left the entire field of hardened pros in a cloud of dust, averaging 100.32mph (161.45kph) in the 100-mile (160.93km) race over Altoona's lightning-fast boards. From then on, there was no stopping Petrali. In 1935, he won every single event of the National season, including five wins in a single day at Syracuse, New York. Petrali was versatile, too. He won five straight national hill-climb championships from 1932 to 1936, and the following year rode a Harley streamliner to a record of 136.183mph (219.159kph) at Daytona Beach.

ABOVE The legendary Cal Rayborn on the XR750, Brands Hatch, 1972.

BELOW Joe Petrali with a four-stroke dirt-track single in the mid 1920s, towards the start of his Harley career.

CAL RAYBORN

Cal Rayborn never won the coveted Number One plate but he was the consummate road racer. The Californian won Daytona twice and took nine other major AMA road-race wins. Yet his career almost never began at all – in 1958, at only 18 years of age, he broke his back at California's Riverside circuit.

Never truly at home on dirt, Rayborn compensated with absolute mastery on tarmac. In 1968, he became the first rider to average 100mph (161kph) in winning the Daytona 200-miler (326km), lapping the field

ABOVE Carroll Resweber won a fourth AMA title in the early 1960s and returned to Milwaukee 20 years later.

on his XR750. He won again in 1969, in what would prove to be the last Daytona triumph for Milwaukee. British fans saw him trounce the field in the Easter Match Races in 1972, also on a factory XR750. Harley's big V-twin had almost been dismissed in favour of factory Triumphs, Nortons and Japanese machines, but Rayborn made the doubters eat their words.

Rayborn also followed in Joe Petrali's wheel-tracks by setting speed records, recording a best of 265.49mph (427.25kph) at Bonneville. Tragically he was killed in 1973 while riding in Australia, ironically on a two-stroke that seized and threw him into a trackside barrier.

BELOW Evel Knievel astride the XR750 on which he performed countless spectacular and bone-crunching stunts.

CARROLL RESWEBER

Texan-born Carroll Resweber won four consecutive Grand National titles on Harley-Davidsons from 1958 to 1961, with a style and determination that left an indelible impression on rivals and spectators alike. He might well have won several more, had not his career been ended during morning warmups by a crash in Lincoln, Illinois, when he was leading the 1962 title race.

Resweber had moved to Wisconsin and worked for Harley alongside his mentor and tuner Ralph Berndt. After the crash he didn't walk for two years but he returned to work in the Milwaukee race shop, and crafted the chassis of the famed Lucifer's Hammer road-racer in the 1980s.

EVEL KNIEVEL

If Harley-Davidson's earlier successes had been in racing, Evel Knievel had a better idea: he'd make them fly. A pure showman, Knievel chased women and long-jump records in roughly equal measure. Beginning in 1970, his crazy schemes ran on Harley power, mainly with a succession of XR750s.

Knievel's bikes had to be tough – if not quite as tough as the man himself. He jumped cars (21 at Ontario Speedway in 1971), trucks, buses and even the fountain at Caesar's Palace in Las Vegas. In the process, he broke most of his important bones and a lot of smaller ones. The Las Vegas leap resulted in one of his more spectacular crashes when he bounced off cars, cartwheeling through the Caesar's Palace parking lot.

In 1978, Knievel announced he would leap the Grand Canyon instead. The local Native American tribe vetoed the plan so Knievel turned his sights to the Snake River Canyon, abandoning his beloved Harley-Davidson for a rocket-powered projectile. However, the rocket only fizzed, and the attempt was a failure. In 1999, Knievel's son Robbie put the record straight when he successfully leapt the Grand Canyon.

THE MICHIGAN MEN

Flint, Michigan, must be a remarkable place. Jay Springsteen is from Flint, where they build Chevrolets out of the same hard stuff. So is Scott Parker. So, too, is "Black" Bart Markel.

During a dirt-track career that began in 1957 and spanned 23 years,

BELOW Knievel was a true showman and valued his close links to Milwaukee. The tank says "Harley-Davidson", but the engine is a Triumph twin.

Markel was the original Michigan hard man. He won three national titles (in 1962, 1965 and 1966) but it was his style that caught the eye. Old boys still whistle in awe at the memory of Markel bouncing off guard rails, bales and other bikes – whatever it would take him to get to the finish line first.

Like the rest, he had to race on tarmac as well as dirt to take those titles. He crashed a lot, for the simple reason that "he refused to slow down for the turns," according to Harley-Davidson race boss Dick O'Brien. Instead, he just threw the bike sideways and slid round the turn – or slid off.

Jay Springsteen was a similarly hard-charging Flint ace who was a leading rider through four decades, mostly with Harley, and won many fans. "Springer" won 43 national races in a 25-year span and was champion from 1976 to 1978.

For a ten-year period starting in 1988, Parker was "The Man" on the ovals, picking up titles most years and smashing every record. Born in 1962, Parker started riding at the age of six and racing at 13. He picked up his first Number One plate in 1988, posting four consecutive titles before Harley-Davidson team-mate Chris Carr took the crown in 1992. Ricky Graham won the following season, but Parker struck back with five consecutive victories, in 1998 winning a record ninth Grand National crown.

ABOVE Scott Parker (left) and Jay Springsteen (right), both chips off the same Flint block.

CHRIS CARR

A career total of seven Grand National championships for Harley confirms Chris Carr as one of the great flat track racers but goes nowhere near covering his accomplishments. The Californian also won seven 600cc flat track titles, rode Harley's VR1000 road racer and twice became the world's fastest motorcyclist with records at Bonneville.

LEFT Scott Parker powers his XR750 out of a turn, showing the grace and pace that won him nine AMA Grand National titles.

LEFT Brad "the Bullet" Baker won the AMA Twins title on a factory XR750 in 2013 but suffered a career-ending crash five years later.

ABOVE Chris Carr won flat track titles and set world speed records on Harleys but even he couldn't win on the VR1000.

ABOVE Jared Mees shows the flat track style that won him four AMA championships on an XR750.

RIGHT The 2015 season brought Mees his last No. 1 plate with Harley, but he had much more success to come.

Carr's first Grand National championship came aboard the factory XR750 in 1992. By 1995 he had broadened his approach, finishing third in the Grand National series and also riding the VR1000 sufficiently well to be named the AMA's road race Rookie of the Year. Carr managed a pole position and top-ten finishes on the VR but, like its other riders, not a race victory.

Carr returned to flat track with Harley, and proceeded to win another six Grand National titles between 1999 and 2005. And Carr was not finished with fast bikes. In 2006 he rode a V4-engined streamliner to become the first motorcyclist to break the 350mph (563kph) barrier, then returned to the Utah salt flats to regain the record at 367.382mph (591.244kph).

JARED MEES

When Jared Mees won the 2023 AMA Flat Track championship to take his ninth Grand National title, he drew level with another Harley-Davidson legend, Scott Parker, at the top of the all-time champions list. But unlike Parker, whose titles were all won on XR750s, Mees had taken his last five for arch rivals Indian.

That did not detract from Mees' impact, nor from the value of the four championships that the Pennsylvanian ace had won on an XR750 between 2009 and 2015 (he also rode a Honda in the single-cylinder events). When the new-look American Flat Track series began in 2017, the combination of Mees and Indian's FTR750 proved too strong for Harley's XG750R. Few riders have brought more glory to Harley-Davidson than Mees – or inflicted more pain.

ROAD RACING

Competition on asphalt has never been Harley-Davidson's strongest suit. But the Milwaukee marque has enjoyed plenty of road-racing success over the years, with a wonderfully diverse range of bikes from lightweight, Italian-built two-strokes to hotted-up, heavyweight Baggers.

GRANDS PRIX

Whatever disappointments the arrangement brought in terms of sales, Harley's ties to Aermacchi produced success on the world stage during the mid-1970s. Factory RR250 and RR350 twins ridden by Italy's Walter Villa won three consecutive 250cc world championships and one 350cc title between 1974 and 1976. Producing 58bhp at 12,000rpm and 70bhp at 11,400rpm respectively, these were unlike traditional Harley-Davidson twins. The engines were two-stroke, initially aircooled but later with full liquid cooling. The RRs were also raced with some success in the States by riders including Cal Rayborn and Gary Scott.

LEFT Walter Villa contesting the 250cc Belgian grand prix at Spa-Francorchamps in 1977 on an RR250. Despite carrying the number 10, he was world champion at the time.

LUCIFER'S HAMMER

The legendary big twin Lucifer's Hammer began its racing life with a win at Daytona in 1983, ridden by the great Jay Springsteen. The same V-twin went on to dominate American Battle of the Twins racing (under Harley Owners' Group sponsorship) during much of the 1980s, taking Gene Church to three consecutive American titles. Powered by a highly-tuned XR1000 engine generating 104bhp, the Hammer was timed at 158mph (254kph) at Daytona. Its XR750 road-race frame, albeit heavily reworked, had debuted at Daytona fully ten years before Springsteen's epic win, showing that at Milwaukee, they build 'em to last.

SPORTSTER RACING

Two different series for hotted-up Sportsters generated thrilling racing for different generations. The 883 Sport Twins was launched in the States in 1989 as a competition for modified 883cc Harley twins, and spread to

ABOVE Based on the XR1000 roadster engine, Lucifer's Hammer surprised many onlookers by its speed in Battle of the Twins competition during the 1980s.

LEFT Former 500cc Grand Prix star Jeremy McWilliams leads the charge in a typically hard-fought round of the XR1200 championship in 2010.

ABOVE A Harley superbike – the factory VR1000.

many other countries in the early 1990s. Harley reintroduced the "one-make" format in 2010, this time with the XR1200, which made about 95bhp with a race exhaust although most engine parts had to remain standard – strict rules helped produce close racing. The XR series too was popular in America and Europe, with former grand prix star Jeremy McWilliams winning races on both sides of the Atlantic.

VR1000

This was one very different Harley: a purpose-built racebike, powered by a 996cc, liquid-cooled V-twin with cylinders set at 60 degrees. The VR1000 was produced in small numbers from 1994 to give Milwaukee a presence in Superbike competition. It was rapid – producing over 150bhp, and timed at over 170mph (273kph) – and handled sweetly thanks to a rigid aluminium-framed chassis. But although Harley hired top riders including Miguel Duhamel and Scott Russell, it never managed an AMA Superbike win. Harley abandoned the VR project in 2001, although its engine technology lived on in the V-Rod that was unveiled in the same year.

KING OF THE BAGGERS

If there has ever been a road race class suited to Harley-Davidson it is surely King of the Baggers, which introduced the spectacle of gigantic touring V-twins bashing fairings and panniers in a crazy two-wheeled equivalent of NASCAR competition.

Harleys dominated the grid at the inaugural Baggers race, at Laguna Seca in 2020, but Indian took the victory to begin a new era of America's age-old rivalry. In subsequent seasons the two firms took turns to win. Vance & Hines Harley's Hayden Gillim was champion in 2023, ahead of his team-mate James Rispoli and Kyle Wyman on the factory Road Glide.

RIGHT Kyle Wyman, son of a New York Harley dealer, won the King of the Baggers title in 2021 and raced a factory Road Glide alongside his brother Travis in the following season.

DRAG RACING

If Harley-Davidsons typically thunder, no others do so with quite such a clap as fire-breathing drag machines – highly tuned bikes built for short, often explosive duels from a standing start. Like so much else in motorcycle sport, drag racing lies deep in the soul of America.

Drag racing began in 1950 at a disused runway at Santa Ana in California, where the fastest bike was a modified 1947 Harley EL, nicknamed the "Beast", that recorded 101mph (162kph) – beating the fastest car.

By the end of the decade, drag racing had spread across America and Harleys remained at the forefront, notably the Sportster XLCH. Bikes with tuned V-twin engines and nicknames including "Turnip Eater" and "Super Sportster" set record times over the standing quarter mile (400m). In 1971, Joe Smith's Shovelhead-powered "King Rat" became the first dragster to run under nine seconds.

The 1970s saw racers including Marion Owens and Danny Johnson bolt two Harley engines into a single chassis. With capacities of over 100cu in (1,600cc) each, running nitro methane fuel, these monsters set new records, established the Top Fuel class and forged a glorious era for drag racing. Another star was Ray Price, who won three national titles and set more than 50 records, exclusively riding Harleys.

More recently Harley's drag racing efforts were led by the Screamin' Eagle/Vance & Hines Pro Stock team, headed by legendary duo Terry Vance and Byron Hines. Hines' sons Matt and Andrew, plus team-mates Eddie Krawiec and Angelle Sampey, won numerous championships and more than 100 races to maintain Milwaukee's status as a major force in the sport.

ABOVE Drag racing's fans appreciate a sport that can seem like a challenge to expend as much money and effort in the shortest time possible.

LEFT Triple world champion Angelle Sampey joined the Vance & Hines Harley team in 2019 and won her 43rd Pro Stock race the following year.

BELOW Andrew Hines leaves the line on his Pro Stock Harley, aiming to hit 200mph (322kph) in a quarter of a mile in around seven seconds.

RECORD BREAKING

Motorcyclists have been aiming to go faster than anyone else for almost as long as bikes have existed. Harley riders are no exception, and Milwaukee machines have set speed records on surfaces including the sand of Daytona Beach, Florida and the Bonneville salt flats of Utah.

Fred Ludlow posted a world kilometre best of 102.87mph (165.55kph) at Daytona in February 1920, before Leslie "Red" Parkhurst took an eight-valve racer to 111.98mph (180.21kph) two days later. They then teamed up, with Parkhurst riding, to set several sidecar records.

In 1937 another famed racer, Joe Petrali, rode a 61cu in (1,000cc) Knucklehead streamliner at 136.183mph (219.159kph) to set an enduring national record on the Daytona sand. Cal Rayborn also swapped racing for record-breaking, in his case at Bonneville in 1970. Lying almost horizontally in a streamliner built by engineer Dennis Manning and powered by an 89cu in (1,458cc), nitro-fuelled Sportster engine, Rayborn crashed at 100mph (161kph) before recording a record 265.49mph (427.25kph).

The longest-lasting Harley world record was the last one: at Bonneville in July 1990, Dave Campos rode the Easy Rider streamliner to 322.15mph (518.45kph), a speed that would stand for 16 years. The 23ft (7m) long streamliner, powered by two 92cu in (1,500cc) Shovelhead engines, was owned by *Easyriders* magazine publisher Joe Teresi. More than 10,000 readers helped fund the attempt by paying $25 to have their names on the fairing. Some were at Bonneville to spectate, and helped repair the bike after a high-speed practice crash.

ABOVE Fred Ludlow and rider "Red" Parkhurst at Daytona after being timed at over 82mph (132kph) in 1920.

ABOVE Joe Petrali with the streamlined Knucklehead that he rode to a record speed of over 136mph (218kph) in 1937.

LEFT George Roeder set a 250cc record of over 177mph (284kph) on Harley's Sprint Streamliner at Bonneville in 1965.

BELOW Rider Dave Campos (left) and the *Easyriders* team with their famous Bonneville streamliner in 1990.

HARLEY-DAVIDSON
HARLEY-DAVIDSON

THE MODELS

The section that follows is a guide to the major models produced by Harley-Davidson, from the first primitive single of 1903 to the style kings and lavishly-equipped tourers of today. It is not an attempt to cover every Harley model, but all the most important and significant examples are included.
Harley-Davidson is the most enduring of all the world's motorcycle marques, and is still enjoying much success. Over the decades the firm has remained dedicated to its original convictions of sound design and solid simplicity.
It has kept faith with its dependable, thoroughbred V-twins, adding modern technology where required – and even leading motorcycling's move towards an electric future – while maintaining a unique magic that links the machines shaped in Milwaukee.
What Harley-Davidson has managed to retain in abundance through all that time is the indefinable quality of "character" – an attribute no specification panel can reveal. Harley-Davidsons are visceral. They have guts and charisma. Only by riding one can you really begin to understand.

LEFT A line of Electra Glide Ultra Classic tourers show plenty of traditional style in 2014, when the model was updated under Harley's Project Rushmore program.

EARLY SINGLES

Harley-Davidson's future was forged not out of the rumble of V-twins, but with the thump of simple, single-cylinder engines. The very first examples differed little from the 1903 prototype, and the engines conformed to the same basic "F-head" design housed in a primitive chassis only slightly removed from bicycle practice.

It was inevitably plain and basic, but this humble single showed a ruggedness that was to become a Milwaukee hallmark. Only ten years after the debut of the first Harley-Davidson model, the company was advertising that one of its machines had travelled 100,000 miles (160,930km) on its original bearings. In those days of dirt roads, bikes had to be tough.

These attributes of durability, simplicity and economy ensured that singles figured somewhere in the Harley-Davidson range well into the 1930s. It was during the era of the singles that Harley's credo was first expressed: "Experience has shown that it is preferable to use a comparatively large motor running at moderate speed in preference to a small motor running at high speed." Those words appeared in a publicity brochure printed in 1905 but could almost have been written today.

LEFT Walter Davidson, one of Harley-Davidson's founders, boosted the firm's reputation by winning prestigious endurance and economy contests on a single in 1908.

FIRST MODELS

Harley-Davidson's first motorcycle, though nominally a single-cylinder model, evolved with the company over a production span of eight years. During that time, annual production figures soared from fewer than a handful to over 4,000 as demand – and know-how – grew in leaps and bounds.

One thing that changed relatively little was the price: $200 in 1904, yet only $25 more by the time production ceased in 1911.

The heart of the engine was a bolted-up crankshaft running car-type, plain, big-end bearings in cast aluminium crankcases. Above this sat a one-piece iron cylinder head and cylinder barrel housing an iron piston. To allow for differential expansion – its top generated far more heat than its bottom – each piston was tapered, a considerable machining achievement for the time. Valve layout was inlet-over-exhaust, the "automatic" or "vacuum" inlet valve controlled – crudely – via pressure created by the rise and fall of the piston. Removable housing permitted the extrication of both valves for servicing: no method of valve-lash adjustment was available until 1908.

ABOVE AND BELOW One of the first De Dion-Bouton-inspired singles. Pedal assistance was essential on hills. The belt final drive with its crude de-clutching mechanism is clearly seen in the lower photograph. The 1910 "Silent Gray Fellow" is altogether more sophisticated but retains pedals and belt final drive.

SPECIFICATIONS: 1909

Engine	aircooled ioe single with automatic inlet valve
Capacity	30cu in (495cc)
Transmission	single speed, leather belt drive
Power	around 3.5bhp
Weight	185lb (84kg)
Wheelbase	51in
Top speed	around 45mph (72kph)

The initial cylinder dimensions of 3 x 3½in (76.2 x 88.9mm) gave a displacement of 25cu in (405cc). In 1905, the bore increased to 3⅛in (79.4mm), giving 27cu in (440cc). At the same time, the single loop frame was redesigned, as all previous examples showed a tendency to crack at

RIGHT William Harley, Frank Ollerman and Walter Davidson scored impressive results on Harley's single in endurance events, notably in 1910.

BELOW Harley's emphasized its early singles' reliability, as here with the advertising phrase: "Always a trusty friend".

the headstock. Capacity was further increased to 30.16cu in (495cc) in 1909 by a 1/16in (1.6mm) increase in bore, by which time the exhaust port had also migrated from the side towards the front of the cylinder. Until 1910, all the motors had used horizontal "beehive" finning for both barrel and head; in 1911 this changed to distinctive vertical cylinder head finning.

Lubrication, like almost all engines of the time, was "total-loss" – a gravity feed dripping oil into the engine from a half-gallon (1.9 litre) tank, good for around 750 miles (1,200km). Transmission was of the simplest possible type with a 1¼in-wide (32mm), two-ply leather belt driving the rear wheel directly. There was no gearbox or clutch, although belt tension could be adjusted on the move by 1911.

The starting technique was straightforward, if energetic – run alongside then jump on board and pedal like mad until the motor fired.

A hand-crank starter became available in 1906 for an additional cost, and was standardized the following year, although neither method of starting was notably elegant.

Like modern motorcycles, power was governed by a twist-grip on the right-hand handlebar and a simple "coaster" brake in the rear hub slowed things down. Lighting of any kind was only made available with the introduction of acetylene lights in the final year of production. Initially, suspension consisted entirely of springs under the leather saddle – and whatever the rider could suffer – but, in 1907, a crude but remarkably effective Sager front fork was added to ease the pain.

As well as standard, conservative "piano" black, by 1906 the single was also available – at an extra cost – in "Renault" pale grey with red pin-striping. This model thus became known from then on as "The Silent Gray Fellow", partly in tribute to its unusually effective silencing. Unpainted metal parts were nickel-plated and the aluminium engine covers were brightly polished to a high shine.

HIDDEN TREASURE

The very first production Harley-Davidson may currently be among the star exhibits on display at the firm's Milwaukee Museum, but it hasn't always been quite so treasured.

The bike was originally retained by the company and sent to the Pan American Exposition in California in 1915 (since which time Harley has kept at least one example from each year of production). Upon its return, however, the company somehow "forgot" this bike was Number One. During the 1970s, it was damaged in transit to the Rodney C. Gott Museum in York, but its true identity remained unrealized, even while it was being repaired.

It was only when it underwent a recent comprehensive restoration at the hands of Harley Archives craftsman, Ray Schlee, that the machine's true pedigree was disclosed – by internal parts bearing the legend "Number 1." It is believed to have been raced in 1904 but is now housed in a 1905 frame, as all the earlier examples broke at the headstock.

This priceless machine has been valued by insurers at $15 million.

MODEL 5-35 SINGLES, 1913

Harley introduced numerous improvements but proceeded cautiously as it completed its first decade of production. The second-generation single-cylinder machine, produced from 1913 to 1918, housed a refinement of the earlier engine rather than an all-new design.

Although the bore remained unchanged at 3$\frac{5}{16}$in (84.1mm), the stroke increased from 3$\frac{1}{2}$ to 4in (88.9 to 101.6mm), giving a capacity of 35cu in (565cc). The new engine was known generically as the 5-35, signifying 5 horsepower and 35 cu in.

Many lessons learned during the troubled development of the first twin were incorporated in the new single's design. Valve layout was still inlet-over-exhaust, although now the inlet valve followed the revised V-twin practice of mechanical operation via a long push rod on the motor's right-hand side. The camshafts – one exhaust, one inlet – were driven by a chain of gears, ending with the Bosch magneto (replaced by a Remy instrument from 1915) which provided the sparks.

The iron cylinder head and barrel were one-piece, accommodating a steel three-ring piston. The crankcases were of aluminium, in which a high-grade steel crankshaft ran on phosphor-bronze main bearings, with the whole crank assembly balanced. Lubrication was still total-loss, engine oil being metered by hand from its own compartment in the tank slung beneath the frame's top rail. A sight-glass below the tank gave the rider some idea how frequently to deliver drops of oil.

SPECIFICATIONS

Engine	aircooled ioe single
Capacity	35cu in (565cc)
Transmission	1-, 2- and 3-speed
Wheelbase	55in (1,400mm)
Top speed	around 54mph (87kph) (side-valve) or 65mph (105kph) (OHV)

As well as manipulating this, the rider was required to adjust the degree of ignition advance (in other words, the precise point at which the spark plug ignited the mixture), by means of yet another control lever. In those days, getting the best out of an engine was not simple. It demanded considerable awareness from the operator.

Perhaps the most obvious difference between these early singles was the

ABOVE AND LEFT By the time this Model 9-B was built in 1913, chain drive was a factory option on single-cylinder machines and twins. Both the chain-drive and belt-drive singles cost the same: $290, $60 less than the twin.

ABOVE This and the two images below show a two-speed Model 10-C from 1914. The single-speed Model 10-B proved far more popular.

replacement of belt with chain as the drive medium, eliminating the wet-weather slip that plagued all leather belt drives. On early examples, the drive was taken direct, via roller chain, from a sprocket on the left-hand end of the crankshaft to another on the rear hub. The same hub also contained a type of rudimentary clutch operated by a long lever on the left side of the machine. Starting involved placing the machine on its stand, which lifted the rear wheel off the ground, then vigorously rotating the bicycle-type pedals. These same pedals, when rotated backwards, engaged the "coaster-type" rear brake via a chain on the right-hand side. Lever-operated brakes did not appear until 1918.

A "step-starter" and Harley's first two-speed rear hub arrived in 1914 (also in the V-twin), offering increased flexibility with maximum speeds of around 54 and 65mph (87 and 105kph) in the two ratios. Within a year, this deceptively intricate device had given way to three-speed transmission with a true sliding-pinion gearbox on better-specified models. Nonetheless, single-speed and even belt-drive models continued to be built for some years.

Chassis refinements included a more robust front suspension offering around 2in (50mm) of travel. The rear, of course, would remain rigid for many years. However, a degree of consolation was provided by Harley's patented "Full Floteing" seat.

As well as the paired springs common on other motorcycles, this seat featured a hinge at the front and a coil spring inside the seat post to cushion the rider from the worst of the bumps.

BELOW Harley's astonishingly complex two-speed rear hub is clearly visible in this view. The hub employed a ring of interlocking bevel gears to vary the final drive ratio.

BELOW Although it retained pedals, the two-speeder offered footboards for the first time. Note the ignition magneto which is below the carburettor.

MODELS A, B & C SINGLES, 1926

Although single-cylinder machines were as much a hallmark of Harley-Davidson's formative years as the firm's big V-twins, Juneau Avenue produced very few singles from 1919 until 1926, the sole exception being the Model CD.

This 37.1cu in (608cc) machine was created simply by removing one pot from the 74-inch twin. The Model CD was built in small numbers from 1921 to 1922, intended for commercial use only.

When singles did reappear, they were much smaller, displacing just 21.1cu in (346cc) compared to the earlier 30-inchers. There were two versions: Model A and Model B. The former denoted a magneto ignition; the latter that the machine had a generator and coil. This was further refined into Models AA and BA Sporting Single. The basic model, named with a simple A or B, had a side-valve engine; the second letter designated an overhead-valve design.

The overhead-valve model was an altogether more potent piece of machinery that would achieve great competition success as the Peashooter racer. Even in roadster trim it was good for almost 65mph (105kph) while its side-valve sibling struggled to exceed 50mph (80kph). Both engines were rated at 3.31hp but these power figures were simply a function of piston displacement and no reflection of performance.

By the time of the single's debut in 1926, electrical equipment had leaped forward in specification and reliability. Although full electrical equipment was optional, it was also comprehensive. Generator models featured a coil and distributor (to power and time the ignition), battery, horn, two-bulb headlight and tail-light, all controlled from a switch on the steering head.

Cycle parts were more basic, although the single wore the new type of teardrop fuel tank, which wrapped over the top frame tube rather than hung from it. Harley's familiar sprung forks gave some comfort and control, but the rear end was rigid and would remain so for another 20 years. The only brake was a small rear drum.

In 1929, the singles got a bigger brother with the introduction of the Model C. Its 30.1cu in (493cc) engine essentially comprised half of the old 61-inch Model F/J twin, mated to the 21-inch single's bottom end. This was a more elegant solution than the old racers' trick – they had simply removed one of the Model J twin's top ends and connecting rods, blanked off the hole and let rip on the track.

As a roadster the Model C was available only with a side-valve engine; its extra capacity meant this was

LEFT Dual "bullet" headlights first appeared on this 1929 500cc single, derived from the Models A and B. Note the front brake – another novelty introduced the previous year.

BELOW The OHV "Peashooter" engine. The push-rods, rocker arms and exposed valves are clearly visible.

SPECIFICATIONS: MODELS A/B

Engine	aircooled side-valve or overhead valve single
Capacity	21cu in (346cc)
Transmission	3-speed
Power	8bhp (side-valve) or 12bhp (ohv)
Wheelbase	55in (1,400mm)
Top speed	around 50mph (80kph) (side-valve) or 60mph (96kph) (OHV)

RIGHT Although only $40 cheaper, flatheads such as this Model 26-B solo comfortably outsold the more exotic OHV singles.

BELOW Note the gear lever (left) and fillers for oil and fuel. The switch console is a later addition.

sufficient for most riders' needs. An overhead-valve competition derivative, the Model CA (later CAC), was produced in small numbers. The bigger side-valve engine was slower revving than the "21", and its performance increase modest, but the Model C was good for about 60mph (96kph).

By 1929, Harley had introduced a front brake: a simple drum, like the rear, activated by a lever on the right handlebar in modern style. Early Model Cs shared the same frame and running gear as the smaller-capacity singles, but during the second year of production the larger engine was installed in a chassis borrowed from the twin, turning the robust little single into a "full-size" motorcycle.

Worthy as the Model C was, most American motorcycle buyers chose twin-cylinder power even during the Depression. In 1929, sales of the singles combined were little more than half of those of the Series D twin – 3,789 units compared to 6,856. But the light and sturdy singles, especially the larger-capacity model, were popular overseas as Harley continued to develop its international markets, where the weight and size of the big twins were a drawback. More than 5,000 units of the Series C were produced over its six-year life span.

RIGHT A 1929 500cc single. At the time, the vibrant paint job was optional only on twins.

LIGHTWEIGHTS

When the Second World War ended, Harley-Davidson was a purveyor of large-capacity, four-stroke V-twins, precisely the type of machines on which their recent success has been built. Yet it somehow became corporate policy to diversify, entering any other niche market they might find. During the next 30 years, Milwaukee's catalogues would reverberate with the sounds of two-stroke commuters, scooters, middleweight four-strokes, trail bikes, minibikes and whatever else an increasingly desperate company believed might sell – even snowmobiles.

Although some of these lightweight models were half-baked and ill-conceived, others were fine machines – but they never could be "proper" Harley-Davidsons. It took Harley many years to realise that it was not a volume manufacturer. The process involved the ultimately abortive purchase of Italian subsidiary Aermacchi, a takeover by AMF and a slow decline into crippling financial difficulties. Worst of all, the core big twin models were neglected to a degree that almost proved fatal.

LEFT The Topper scooter of the 1960s featured a 165cc two-stroke engine with a single horizontal cylinder, automatic transmission and storage under the seat.

STATESIDE STROKERS

From the late 1940s to the mid 1960s, Harley produced a variety of models powered by small-capacity, single-cylinder two-stroke engines. They ranged from roadsters with names such as Hummer and Ranger, via the dual-purpose Scat and off-road ranger to a scooter, the Topper.

MODEL S-125, 1948 MODEL ST-165, 1953 MODEL B HUMMER, 1955

Harley-Davidson's first venture into the world of two-strokes owed much to the end of the Second World War. On the one hand, it was assumed that thousands of demobbed GIs would crave almost any motorcycle they could lay their hands on, and the 125cc single was considered the ideal low-cost candidate. Second, the design was basically that of the pre-war DKW RT125.

When partition placed the factory in the new East Germany, the design passed to the Allies as war reparations. British BSA's hugely successful Bantam was also a DKW copy, as was the very first Yamaha, the YA1 "Red Dragonfly".

Producing just three horsepower from its simple piston-ported, air-cooled engine, the S-125 must have been a profound disappointment to any American biker raised on big four-stroke power.

LEFT AND BELOW Two variants of the Milwaukee two-stroke derived from the German DKW. Note rigid rear end, "Tele-Glide" front forks and the fuel tank shape which would become the inspiration for the Sportsters.

Juneau Avenue was evidently hopeful about selling these machines in huge numbers, producing more than 10,000 in the model's first year, but sales proved poor, settling to around 4,000 per annum even after the introduction of a "Tele-Glide" version with telescopic forks in 1951.

A bore increase in 1953, from 52 to 60mm, resulted in the slightly zippier 165cc Model ST. A restricted version, the STU, was also available. It produced less than 5bhp so could be ridden on the street with no licence.

Two years later, the Model B Hummer – using essentially the same 125cc engine and transmission as the first Model S – appeared in the Harley-Davidson catalogue.

From 1960 to 1961, an updated 165cc range continued as the 6bhp BT and BTU (restricted to 5bhp) Super Ten. Harley-Davidson's slogan for this model went: "keen wheeling for teen wheeling".

BELOW The first two-stroke was this Model S of 1948. Note the girder front forks.

SPECIFICATIONS: S-125

Engine	aircooled 2-stroke single-cylinder
Capacity	125cc
Transmission	3-speed
Power	3bhp
Wheelbase	50in (1,270mm)
Top speed	around 40mph (64kph)

RANGER, PACER, SCAT, BOBCAT, 1962

This quartet was another attempt to broaden the Harley range and allow Milwaukee to compete as a mass-market player. In hindsight, the strategy was clearly misguided, but Milwaukee believed there was a niche market of buyers not quite ready for the new 250cc Sprint (nor for the big twins). The Ranger and its siblings were the result.

All four machines, designated Model BT, shared a two-stroke engine derived from the Super 10, but with increased stroke from 60 to 61mm for a capacity of 175cc on all but the 1962 Pacer and Ranger. As with the Topper, "full power" and 5bhp versions were built.

Models that year were the street-only BT Pacer, the dual-purpose BTH Scat and the BTF Ranger, a stripped-down, off-road variant without lights. The first examples had rigid rear ends, but models that had swinging-fork suspension appeared for 1963.

The Ranger was dropped for 1963 while the Pacer and Scat gave way to the BTH Bobcat in 1966.

BELOW The Pacer was the pure street version of the Model BT range of 165 and 175cc two-strokes.

SPECIFICATIONS: BOBCAT

Engine	aircooled 2-stroke single-cylinder
Capacity	175cc
Transmission	3-speed
Power	8bhp
Wheelbase	52in (1,320mm)
Top speed	around 60mph (96kph)

RIGHT This Topper is fitted with a windscreen, and also appears to be bolted to a sidecar – not a typical accessory for a 165cc scooter.

Available in road and optional off-guises, this lasted for one year, proving to be the last of the American-built Harley lightweights.

TOPPER SCOOTER, 1960

The Model A Topper – which was Milwaukee's obvious attempt to cash in on the scooter boom which swept the Western world during the late 1950s – employed a 165cc two-stroke with identical bore and stroke to the old ST but with the cylinder laid down horizontally to reduce engine height.

Power was claimed to be 9bhp from the 1961-on high-compression engine (Model AH), with a "restricted" five-horsepower version (Model AU) sold in those American states which permitted the use of low output two-wheelers without a driver's licence.

Unlike earlier three-speed Harley strokers, this time the "Scootaway" transmission was automatic, using belt drive and variable flanged wheels to change ratios.

The system was unusual but by no means new – the Rudge Multi and American-built NeraCar had featured similar drives decades before – yet it did anticipate today's fully automatic commuter machines.

Other Topper novelties included a rubber-mounted engine with reed-valve induction, a parking brake, under-seat stowage space and lawnmower-style hand-starting.

By all accounts, the boxy Topper was a quirky but competent device which might have fared better had it not arrived just as the scooter market went into decline. Sales of the $430 machine went from almost 4,000 to just 500 during its six years on the books.

ABOVE A Topper in conventional livery. Although quite advanced, the $450 machine failed to cash in on the scooter boom.

Ironically – given that Harley-Davidson by then had an Italian factory – being "Made in Milwaukee" was no substitute for the true Latin style of other more genuinely Italian scooters, such as those that were made by Vespa or Lambretta.

SPECIFICATIONS: TOPPER

Engine	aircooled 2-stroke single-cylinder
Capacity	165cc
Transmission	variable belt
Power	5bhp or 9bhp
Wheelbase	51.5in (1,310mm)
Top speed	around 50mph (80kph)

FORZA HARLEY

In the early 1960s Harley-Davidson attempted to broaden its range of smaller capacity models quickly by investing in Aermacchi, the firm from Varese in northern Italy that was best known for its roadgoing and racing four-strokes with a single horizontal cylinder.

SPRINT, 1961

Harley's Sprint family of four-stroke singles, unveiled in September 1960, was the first tangible result of the firm's purchase of Aermacchi. Compared to much contemporary Milwaukee hardware, this was a technically advanced machine derived from the existing 250cc Ala Verde model, with an in-unit overhead-valve engine and superb handling from its spine frame, telescopic forks and swinging-fork rear end. With its unmistakable horizontal cylinder, variants of the same engine went on to innumerable race wins, including the famous Isle of Man TT, and remain hugely popular (and competitive) in classic racing today.

American buyers – despite the invitation to "thrill to the dynamic, virile note of its Hi-Flo tuned exhaust" – never quite warmed to the Sprint's lack of cubes and relatively revvy nature, yet the bike was as capable a standard production machine as its siblings were racers. The stock street version, the Model C, claimed a potent (if slightly ambitious) 18bhp at 7,500rpm from its eager, free-breathing engine. This was joined by the Model H, an off-road variant, one year later, with high-compression pistons and an additional 1.5bhp. The "H" quickly became the more popular model and was used in a wide range of American competitions, from flat track to motocross as well as for purely recreational use.

The Sprint Model H later became known as the Scrambler, producing as much as 25bhp at a relatively giddy 8,700rpm.

In 1967, the original long-stroke configuration changed to short stroke – "The Sprint holds two land speed world records, so we improved it", went the ad. Two years later, the first 350 Sprints appeared, the ERS dirt racer and road-going 350cc SS. The SS was joined by the dual-purpose SX-350 in 1971 and given an electric starter two

LEFT Stripped-down Sprints proved surprisingly adept at dirt-track racing.

BELOW Note the carburettor's steep downdraught angle, which is a hallmark of Aermacchi design.

BELOW This early Sprint enjoys pride of place in the Harley Museum.

SPECIFICATIONS:
SPRINT C (SS-350)

Engine	aircooled OHV horizontal single
Capacity	246cc (344cc)
Transmission	4-speed (5-speed)
Power	18bhp @ 7,500rpm (27bhp @ 7,000rpm)
Weight	unknown (355lb/161kg)
Wheelbase	52in/1,320mm (56in/1,420mm)
Top speed	around 75mph (120kph) (85mph/136kph)

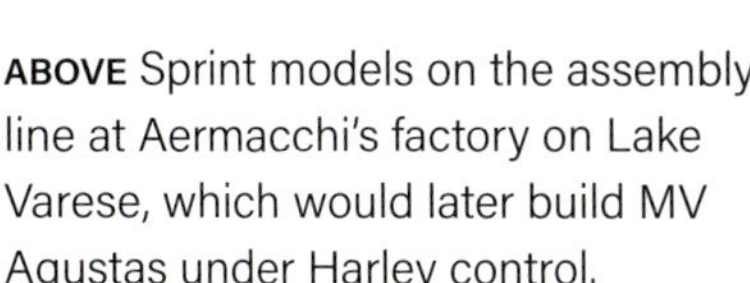

ABOVE Sprint models on the assembly line at Aermacchi's factory on Lake Varese, which would later build MV Agustas under Harley control.

RIGHT Trying hard to look like a "real" bike, with 1967 M-50 sports saddlebags and screen, despite a top speed of only around 40mph (64kph).

years later as the "Sprint" title was dropped from the range.

Pure road racing examples of the same 344cc single produced as much as 38bhp, good for 130mph (210kph) with racing streamlining. Road riders, which achieved maybe 25bhp, had to be content with top speeds in the low nineties. Although a simple spine frame was always good enough for the racers, the final SS-350 inexplicably included a heavy and wholly unnecessary twin-downtube chassis.

With a career spanning 14 years, the Sprint can rightly be regarded as one of Harley's more successful forays away from its core big twin-activities.

The Sprint's arrival coincided with the appearance of advanced, lightweight machines from Japan and, to some extent, it profited from their success.

For the first time since the 1920s, motorcycling in the United States was developing a broad appeal, and the market was soaring.

In 1971 it would peak at 2.1 million new machines sold – a 40-fold increase in less than 20 years.

The Sprint's weakness was not the way it went (when the typically feeble Italian electrical system was not playing up), but in the way its price kept rising when Japanese machines seemed, year after year, to be offering much more for much less.

SPECIFICATIONS: M-50

Engine	aircooled 2-stroke single-cylinder
Capacity	50cc
Transmission	3-speed
Wheelbase	44in (1,120mm)
Top speed	around 40mph (64kph)

M-50, M-65, 1965–71

In the mid 1960s Harley-Davidson's quest for wider markets led it into the 50cc domain, a move which was ultimately no more successful than its other oddballs of the time. Ironically those other V-twin warlords, the British Vincent company, had dabbled unsuccessfully with lightweights a decade earlier.

The range began with the M-50 in 1965 and a racier-looking Sport version 12 months later. Both were built in huge numbers – more than 25,000 in the first two years – causing massive oversupply and a sharp fall in price. 1967 brought an increase in capacity for the M-65 and Sport, and more realistic production figures.

For 1967, the original 50cc version developed much-needed extra power with the 65cc M-65, by which time some 4,000 unsold M-50s were flooding the market at knock-down prices.

Both models were available in standard and "Sport" guise, the latter with a racy fuel tank and seat.

A 65cc Leggero (which in Italian means "light") version was also built for the years 1970–1.

BELOW The M-50, one of Milwaukee's strange two-stroke mini-bike range. By 1966 it looked rather more like a motorcycle. Such lightweights never truly caught on in the USA.

STRIVING FOR SALES

Harley's attempts to diversify took many forms in the 1960s and 1970s. The Milwaukee firm put its name to a succession of trail bikes, off-road machines, minibikes and even snowmobiles, resulting in some interesting models and notable achievements, if not major commercial success.

RAPIDO, TX, SX, STX, 1968

The Rapido family of machines was yet another attempt to find a profitable niche at the lightweight end of the market, this time with mainly off-road machines (although the first batch to be built were street bikes). Powered by a simple 123cc two-stroke single with four-speed transmission, the Rapido ultimately gave way to the five-speed, oil-injected TX, SS and SX models. Although often overlooked – not least by traditional big-twin dealers – the range established its pedigree in 1969 when three Rapidos completed an epic, 2,000-mile (3,200km) ride across the Sahara. A smaller version of the TX, the 90cc Z-90, was produced.

SPECIFICATIONS: RAPIDO

Engine	aircooled 2-stroke single-cylinder
Capacity	123cc
Transmission	4-speed
Wheelbase	48.9in (1,240mm)
Top speed	around 60mph (96kph)

LEFT An SX-250, one of the Italian two-stroke singles developed in an attempt to make money from the trail-bike boom.

SS AND SX SERIES, 1974

By the start of the 1970s, off-road machines were huge business in the American motorcycle scene. Inevitably, this market was hugely competitive, with prices pared to the bone – so much so that even the super-efficient Japanese factories would soon find themselves with massive amounts of unsold stock. At the same time, environmental concerns were targeting the high hydrocarbon emissions of the two-stroke engine. It was into this unpromising scene that the off-road SX range was launched for 1974. The SX was joined by the street-only SS-250 in 1975 plus its larger dirt sibling, the SX-250, with the road-going SS-175 introduced for 1976. It was the off-roaders, however, that dominated production and sales. More than 25,000 machines were built in 1975, of which all but 3,000 were SX models. In the face of declining demand and over-supply, production slumped to 12,000 for 1976, then 1,400 in 1977 before disappearing almost completely as Harley-Davidson disentangled itself from its Italian partner in 1978.

These were actually quite competent motorcycles despite being very much copies of Yamaha's DT-series engines. The SX-250 in particular achieved quite striking competition success.

BELOW Models such as this 1970 Rapido attempted to cash in on the Stateside boom in lightweight off-road machines.

SPECIFICATIONS: SX-175 (SX-250)

Engine	aircooled 2-stroke single-cylinder
Capacity	174cc (243cc)
Transmission	5-speed
Wheelbase	56in (1,420mm)
Top speed	around 70mph (112kph) (80mph/128kph)

ABOVE Outlandishly racy, maybe, but such dual-purpose lightweights were too far from Harley's heritage to succeed.

RIGHT The X-90. Dismissed as "a menace" at the time, the minibike range is now considered cute and even collectable.

More successful still was the MX250, derived from what was substantially the same engine. Both failed to survive the closure of Harley-Davidson's Italian operation in 1978.

BAJA, SR-100, 1970

Named after the notorious desert race down Mexico's Baja peninsula, this 98cc off-roader used a high-performance engine derived from the Rapido's (with the bore reduced from 56 to 50mm) but now with five-speed transmission. The little machine was surprisingly potent and almost 7,500 were built during its five year span. It was ultimately unable to overcome both environmental concerns and the increasingly sophisticated Japanese competition, despite the introduction of an improved, oil-injected SR-100 version for 1973.

SPECIFICATIONS: BAJA SR-100

Engine	aircooled 2-stroke single-cylinder
Capacity	98cc
Transmission	5-speed
Wheelbase	52in (1,320mm)
Top speed	around 60mph (96kph)

MINIBIKES: SHORTSTER, X-90, Z-90, 1972

Anything further removed from big-inch cruisers would be hard to imagine, but that's exactly what Harley unveiled with the MC-65 Shortster of 1972. An obvious word play on "Sportster", the minibike used the M-65 engine and tiny 10in (254mm) wheels. Only 800 Shortsters were made before it grew to 90cc and became the X-90, which was built from 1973 to 1975. The Z-90 used the same engine, but in a quasi off-road chassis with larger wheels. "The Great American Freedom Machine" was how Harley billed the Italian-built two-strokes, intended mainly for hitching on the back of a camper van rather than as serious commuter machines. Almost 17,000 of these minibikes were made, plus a similar number of Z-90s.

SPECIFICATIONS: X-90

Engine	aircooled 2-stroke single-cylinder
Capacity	90cc
Transmission	4-speed
Wheelbase	40.75in (1,035mm)
Top speed	around 55mph (88kph)

SNOWMOBILE, 1970

Like the Topper Scooter, Harley's Snowmobile was a tardy response to a passing craze. The fad initiated by the Canadian Bombardier company in the mid-1960s produced many similar machines, most with the same mechanical layout. Milwaukee's version, released in 1970, was steered by paired skis linked to motorcycle-type handle-bars at the front and driven by a broad belt at the rear. It was powered by a twin-cylinder two-stroke engine and the all-chain drive featured automatic transmission. There were two capacities (398 or 433cc) and electric or manual start. The Snowmobile was dropped from 1975, the victim of three consecutive mild winters.

BELOW Harley's snowmobile sold poorly. Maybe if they'd called it a SnowGlide...

ELL BROS. CYCL
CYCLERY
MOTORCYCLES
HARLEY-DAVIDSON
MOTORCYCLES

THE FIRST TWINS

These days the expressions "Harley-Davidson" and "V-twin" are inextricably linked, but it was not always so. Expanding the Harley range from singles to twins was a logical progression as Harley attempted to broaden its share in the rapidly expanding market. The first American V-twin was the 695cc Curtiss of 1903 and Harley's first prototype was built three years later, making its first public appearance at the Chicago motorcycle show in 1907.

Two years later the Model 5-D twin was offered for sale, with the 45-degree configuration that became a Harley hallmark. In almost every other respect, however, the engine was entirely different. As with the contemporary singles on which it was based, the F-head valve layout was inlet-over-exhaust, with the inlets of the "automatic" type, in which the valve was simply sucked open by the falling piston rather than being moved mechanically by a cam.

As the 1920s drew to a close, side-valve engines became the Harley norm, heralding an era dominated by flatheads such as the enduring "45" and the mammoth 80-inch VL – machines that put the muscle into Milwaukee.

LEFT A pair of early V-twins lined up outside a prominent Harley-Davidson dealership, Powell Bros Cyclery, in San Jose in California in 1912.

EARLY TWINS, 1909

With the single having amply demonstrated its ruggedness, the twin that evolved from it ought to have been the same – only more so. But the fast-evolving Harley-Davidson firm hit an early setback when its debut model with a second cylinder generated unexpected problems.

Like the singles, the twin was single-speed with belt final drive, one-piece heads and barrels with horizontal "beehive" finning. Capacity was 54cu in (880cc), although several development engines of varying capacity had been built and even raced during the previous two years.

Yet the Model D proved remarkably troublesome, with a mere 29 built in 1909 and just one in 1910. Harley-Davidson appears to have blamed its shortcomings on its automatic inlet valves, although other sources suggest slippage of the belt drive was at fault. Either way, when the re-engineered twin returned in 1911, it had both mechanical inlet valves and a simple but sturdy belt-tensioning device which could be operated on the move by the rider's left hand.

Although still designated the Model D, other changes included a slightly reduced capacity of 50cu in (811cc). Beehive finning had also given way to vertical cylinder-head finning. By all accounts, the revised twin proved far more dependable. Although little faster on the flat than the 30-inch single, it climbed hills far better – not least because the belt tensioner allowed the rider to maintain drive. Even so, 1912 brought a new frame and a free-wheel clutch assembly in the rear wheel that freed the rider from the need to kill the engine to halt the machine.

The same year saw the introduction of the first "one-litre" Harley, the 61-inch X8E, which also featured chain final drive. The Model G "Forecar", a 61-inch twin with front-mounted luggage box, arrived in 1913. A year later the Model 10F and Forecar debuted a two-speed rear hub. This intricate device comprised no fewer than five bevel gears, yet was replaced by a true three-speed gearbox after only one year.

By 1915 the Harley range comprised just two single-cylinder roadsters but

LEFT A 1913 61-inch single speed twin. Although this example has no lights, an acetylene kit was supplied as an optional extra.

SPECIFICATIONS: 1911 MODEL D	
Engine	aircooled F-head V-twin
Capacity	50cu in (811cc)
Transmission	single speed, leather belt drive with freewheel "clutch"
Power	around 7bhp
Wheelbase	56½in (1,435mm)
Top speed	around 60mph (96kph)

BELOW LEFT AND RIGHT Two views of another 1913 twin. Note the long push-rods to the inlet valves, far more dependable than the earlier "automatic" mechanism. The colour is "Renault Gray".

ABOVE By the time this twin was built in 1917, three-speed transmission was available for an extra $25.

six twins, including the three-speed Model K "Stripped Stock" – a race replica for its time. Among six "Speciality" twins were the even hotter "Fast Motor" K12 and pure racers such as the KRH. So comprehensive was the 61-inch F-head's evolution that, by the time it was discontinued in 1929, almost no part from the original twin would fit.

The Model W "Sport Twin", developed during the war years and released in 1919, was a very different Harley: a 35.6cu in (584cc) "boxer" with cylinders set at 180 degrees, arranged in line with the bike, as favoured by British firm Douglas.

This layout could have made the Sport Twin long, but its wheelbase was actually three inches shorter than that of the existing V-twin. It was also low, and weighed 100lbs (45kg) less than its V-twin siblings. The horizontally-opposed cylinders bestowed perfect primary balance, making it smooth. As well as the standard equipment of magneto ignition and gas lights (fed by acetylene gas produced "on the move" by dissolving calcium carbide in water), optional equipment included coil ignition and true electric lighting.

ABOVE The cam drive is clear in this sectioned F-head twin.

All in all, the Model W was neat, light, economical and innovative. Unfortunately it was way down on power compared to the 61-inch Harley V-twin and similar offerings from Indian, with a top speed of little more than 50mph (80kph). American riders demanded more performance and, although its agility was useful on Europe's more tortuous roads (almost one third of exports to Britain in 1919 were Sport Twins), the Model W was never a success at home and was produced for just four years.

ABOVE An exquisite 1916 board-racing twin. Note the Bosch magneto and single carburettor.

RIGHT The very Model W machine that set the Three Flag record, riding from Canada to Mexico in less than 75 hours.

MODEL JD & FD BIG TWINS, 1921

Milwaukee's first 74-inch (1,216cc) model, the so-called "Superpowered Twin", hit America's streets for the 1921 model year. Producing 18 horsepower, the big engine was intended to compete with Indian's big twins, and with fours from Henderson and others.

The "74" followed the "61" by employing inlet-over-exhaust valves (the F-head layout) driven by a single camshaft on the engine's right.

Many major components – crankcases, cylinders and heads – were new, and both bore and stroke were increased. The transmission was three-speed. An "automatic" oil pump lubricated the bearings but, as with almost every other motorcycle of the time, used oil was burned or dripped on to the ground.

Although often referred to generically as the JD, up to 1925 the 74-inch twin might more helpfully be called the Model D, with the addition of familiar prefixes. "JD" indicated a complete electrically equipped version; the magneto model was designated "FD". Where fitted, electrical equipment comprised a six-volt generator, battery, contact breaker points and coil, headlight, tail light and oil warning indicator light. An additional "S" indicated a sidecar model, with lower compression ratio and gearing. Other suffixes covered piston material – A for aluminium, B for iron.

The single-loop steel frame held a "Full-Floteing" Mesinger saddle. Front suspension comprised similar double sprung girder forks to the smaller twin. Carrying echoes into the styling of today's Harleys, 1926 found the big twin equipped with broad "balloon" tyres and a curvaceous "teardrop" fuel tank. Only a rear brake was fitted until 1928 when a front drum brake also became standard. Over its eight-year career, the "74" proved itself a brisk performer which enhanced Milwaukee's reputation for building dependable motorcycles.

ABOVE An immaculately restored 1928 Model JD, one of the first to feature a front brake.

SPECIFICATIONS: 74-INCH SUPERPOWERED TWIN

Engine	aircooled F-head V-twin
Capacity	74cu in (1,216cc)
Transmission	3-speed
Power	18bhp
Wheelbase	59½in (1,510mm)
Top speed	around 75mph (120kph)

BELOW This 1925 61-inch twin retains the original olive green colours with maroon and gold pinstriping.

BELOW Sidecars, such as this mated to a Model J, were huge business.

JH, JDH TWO-CAM, 1928

Twin-cam and even eight-valve machines had formed the cutting edge of Harley-Davidson's official racing efforts since the First World War, yet the ordinary road-going motorcyclist could only dream of such performance for most of the first decade after the conflict's end.

ABOVE The 1928 JDH Two-Cam was only available for two years.

All that changed in 1928 when Harley offered a two-cam motorcycle to the general public at an affordable price. These special J-series machines were available for two years only, as the 61-inch JH and the awesome 74-inch JDH, which were priced at $360 and $370 respectively.

"The magic words 'two-cam' mean exceptional speed and power," extolled contemporary advertisements, with some justification. Not for the last time, Milwaukee was treading the fine line between effective salesmanship and encouraging public disquiet over bad boys on antisocial machines.

Both twin-cam engines featured inlet-over-exhaust valve operation driven by paired, gear-driven cams in a timing case on the right side of the engine. Instead of operating via Harley-Davidson's customary roller arms, the cam lobes acted directly on tappets, offering more accurate valve control, higher revs and improved combustion. The height of each cylinder's inlet valve necessitated flamboyant clearance cutaways in the narrow fuel tank, which gave the "JH" its characteristically racy appearance.

The two engines differed in both bore and stroke, as well as in the use of Dow metal pistons, but were built on essentially the same crankcases. These were connected by roller primary chain to a multi-plate dry clutch and three-speed gearbox, which in turn drove the rear wheel by chain.

As well as the choice of capacities, two specifications of the Two-Cam were offered, although numerous racing specials would be created in private hands. As well as the competitive potential of stripped-down Model Js, Juneau Avenue anticipated a demand for an exclusive road version – or "superbike" as it might be known today. Thus the Two-Cam was available with full electrical equipment, carburettor air cleaner, fully valanced mudguards and front and rear brakes.

BELOW The difference between the Two Cam's timing cover and that of the standard twin is clear.

Echoes of the machine's racing pedigree were retained, however, in the slimline "sport" chassis, single seat and racer-style two-gallon (7.5 litre) fuel tank.

Even as a roadster, the Two-Cam was billed as "the fastest model ever offered by Harley-Davidson" with the JDH specially recommended "for greatest speed and maximum performance."

With an 80-inch version available on special order in 1929, this olive green projectile was no less than the American equivalent of Brough Superior's sensational SS100 in Europe.

Yet even this degree of exclusivity was priced too high for an American market more interested in cars, and the Two-Cams passed into legend after spending two short years in the Harley-Davidson range. Hopes for these models effectively ended on "Black Tuesday" in October 1929, when the Wall Street stock market crashed to begin the Great Depression.

SPECIFICATIONS

Engine	aircooled 2-cam, F-head V-twin
Capacity	60cu in (988cc) or 74cu in (1,216cc)
Transmission	3-speed
Wheelbase	60in (1,525mm)
Top speed	around 85mph (137kph)

45-INCH TWIN, 1929

One of the most enduring motorcycles in Harley-Davidson's history was announced in October 1927, hitting the road just over 12 months later. This relatively simple and inexpensive twin would go on to serve with distinction for more than two decades.

The Model D, as it was first styled, was the first of a new generation of side-valve "flathead" V-twins – far cheaper to create than the relatively complex F-head engines. Not much more than a pair of 21-inch "Ricardo" singles on a common bottom-end, it featured three-speed transmission and a spindly frame almost identical to the little single's.

If the beginnings were lacklustre, improvements came fast. Within a year, the "45" benefited from a sturdy new frame with lower saddle but increased ground clearance. It was now available in four guises: D (low compression solo), DS (sidecar), DL (high compression Sport Solo) and DLD Special Sport Solo. Two years later, it emerged from a comprehensive redesign as the Model R. This included aluminium pistons in place of Dow metal (with magnesium offered as a special option from 1933), new crankcases with improved oiling and a sturdier frame.

In 1933, of course, the Depression was at its deepest. A sign of these cash-strapped times was that this much-improved machine now cost just $280 – $10 less than the Model D had at its introduction. After a further steady regime of continuous improvement, the "45" was transformed once again to become the

LEFT An early Model D "45". The unfinned timing cover is one obvious difference from the later Model W.

SPECIFICATIONS: 1929 MODEL DL

Engine	aircooled side-valve V-twin
Capacity	45cu in (742cc)
Transmission	3-speed
Power	around 22bhp
Weight	395lbs (179kg)
Wheelbase	56½in (1,435mm)
Top speed	around 65mph (105kph)

BELOW LEFT AND BELOW RIGHT Art-deco influences are evident in the styling of these two striking WL45s. The inspiration for modern Springers is clear in the girder forks, especially on the chrome-plated example on the right.

LEFT AND RIGHT The inspiration for the "flathead" nickname is obvious (left). Note the streamlined instrument console, which remains a Milwaukee hallmark.

Model W in 1937. Although the most obvious difference was the adoption of styling from the Knucklehead released the previous year, there were numerous engine improvements as well, with its troublesome crankcase oiling and breathing system getting the lion's share of attention.

The range now comprised not only standard (W), sidecar (WS), Sport (WL) and Special Sport (WLD) models, but also the WLDR Competition Sport Special, a mean-looking stripped-down racer – though by 1941, the WLDR machine was a "Special Sport" roadster, the racer being known by a simple "WR". Four-speed transmission, adopted from the bigger twins, appeared in 1938, and by 1940 the WLA Army version was on the books. By now, the WLD and WLDR versions carried light alloy cylinder heads with more fin area and a larger carburettor, improvements that would not reach the base models for another five years.

Indeed, the engine would receive almost no more significant changes during the WL's final decade – a far cry from the 1930s when anything from 15 to 30 modifications were made each year. Instead, Harley-Davidson directed its efforts into its overhead-valve models, confining the "45" mainly to cosmetic revisions, partly inspired by the Hydra-Glide. Civilian production of "45"s ceased after 1951, although some military versions were produced later, and the same side-valve engine would continue to power the Servi-Car into the 1970s. The WL is – and was for most of its life – a crude, heavy machine better suited to the American Prairies or war-torn battlefields than any road with bends. By the time it went out of production, it was a motorcycling dinosaur. Though it was slow, outdated and cumbersome, it was also strong as an ox and almost indestructible: this model had proved itself to be a tough old Hog that for more than two decades had dependably delivered the bacon for Harley-Davidson.

BELOW A 1942 WL45, one of the last pre-war civilian models. The "Boat-tail" rear fender appeared in 1939.

74-INCH SIDE-VALVE TWIN, 1930 80-INCH SIDE-VALVE TWIN, 1935

Far from being the dependable machine the market required, the model which propelled Harley's big-inch fortunes into the troubled 1930s was even more bothersome than that very first V-twin of 20 years earlier. It also arrived at a particularly difficult moment in US history.

Launched just in time to see the New York stock exchange collapse in 1929, the Model V "Big Twin" began life as a fiasco.

With the original twin, valve gear was the problem. With this new 74-inch model it was almost the entire machine. As William H. Davidson recalled: "bad engine... bad clutch... flywheels too small... frames broke... mufflers became so clogged the engine lost power."

It's a mystery now – and probably was for Harley at the time – why the first of this line were so very poor. The cylinder heads, though now of side-valve layout, retained the proven "Ricardo" pattern of the earlier single.

At 87.3 x 101.6mm, the bore and stroke dimensions were unchanged from the Model D. As before, a single dependable Schebler carburettor metered fuel via a forked manifold. Testing showed that power was up 15 per cent on the old "74".

There were novelties, of course, but nothing suggesting the trouble to come. Primary drive was now based on duplex chain, far stronger than the single chain used previously. Revisions to the oil-circulation system promised the rider a less oil-soaked time, as did full enclosure of the valve gear, which was impracticable on the old ioe twin. Other improvements that ought to have been welcomed by serious users included interchangeable quick-release wheels (at a time when punctures were a daily hazard) and an improved electrical system with better weather protection. The frame, too, was new: lower, heavier and reputedly sturdier than before.

SPECIFICATIONS: 74-INCH (80-INCH) TWIN

Engine	aircooled side-valve V-twin
Capacity	74cu in/1,216cc (79cu in/1,293cc)
Transmission	3-speed (4-speed from 1937)
Wheelbase	60in (1,525mm)
Top speed	up to 90mph (145kph)

ABOVE The mighty VL, the top of the Milwaukee range before the arrival of the Knucklehead.

LEFT A 1936 VLH 80-inch twin. The spring shield on the girder forks was new for that particular year.

For a company trading on unsurpassable reliability, the "74"s problems were serious indeed. No matter how handsome the new machine was, dressed in olive green with red pinstriping, no-one would buy it if it didn't work. To its credit, Milwaukee dropped everything to fix all the faults and the Model V proved dependable for the rest of its days.

ABOVE A drab army 74-inch twin. Note the metric engine capacity in the "1200" on the tank.

ABOVE Hand gear-change would remain a Milwaukee norm until the 1950s. The foot pedal operates this VL's "suicide" clutch.

Having benefited from the fixes applied to the 74-inch model, the 80-inch model released for 1935 proved almost completely problem-free. The bigger engine was substantially similar to the contemporary "74", the extra capacity resulting from an increase in stroke from 101.6 to 108mm.

For 1937, the V-series gave way to the U-series big twins, with four-speed transmission, improved engine oiling and both the running gear and styling from Knucklehead twins. Both were capable of up to 90mph (145kph), had vestigial brakes and no rear suspension. Production of the "80" effectively ceased after 1941.

NAME GAMES

Not for the first time, Harley-Davidson's model nomenclature looks confusing viewed from decades distant. Sometimes called the "VL", the 74-incher was available from the outset as a straight Model V, with "VL" representing the high compression version, "VS" the sidecar puller and "VC" signifying the use of nickel iron rather than light alloy pistons. This continued until 1934, when options included the VLD ("Special Sport solo" with TNT motor), VD (low compression, solo), VDS (low compression, sidecar gears) and VFDS (heavy duty commercial, TNT motor). In 1935, the 80-inch model appeared and was dubbed VLDD (Sport solo) or VDDS (sidecar), alongside existing 74-inch models. This all changed for the 1937 model year, with "U" replacing "V" (alphabetically backwards). From then on, all the big side-valve twins' model designations began "U-" (80-inch models were indicated by a subsequent "H"). Thus a simple "U" indicated the basic 74-inch model and the plain "UH" was the equivalent 80-inch model.

RIGHT AND BELOW With the change to four-speed transmissions in 1937, the Model V became the Model U, one year before this handsome 80-incher was built. Note the revised timing cover.

SERVI-CAR, 1932

Although we think of them now as kings of style even when carrying the Highway Patrol along California's freeways, in their earlier years Harley-Davidsons were no strangers to humble workaday vehicles. This was especially true of one notably enduring three-wheeler.

As early as 1913, the range included a "Forecar" delivery van, the Model 9-G, essentially a 61-inch F-head twin with front-mounted luggage box. Sidecars and sidecar accessories had been an integral part of the Milwaukee range since 1916, with a huge sidecar production facility in operation at Juneau Avenue since 1926.

With the Wall Street Crash and its aftermath placing a particular premium on cheap, dependable commercial transport, it was perhaps no surprise that 1932 marked the debut of one of the strangest – and most enduring – Harleys ever produced. The Model G Servi-Car was a more-or-less conventional V-twin from the saddle forward, but the rear looked for all the world like an ice-cream van. Although it resembled a car rear axle crudely grafted on to a conventional bike (and topped off with a metal and fibreglass boot (trunk)), the Servi-Car was a practical and cheap working vehicle which found a steady market in Depression-torn America.

Some suggested that it was inspired by Far East rickshaw-style machines; however, the Servi-Car was initially intended for the recovery of broken-down cars – hence the tow-bar and huge 60 amp/hour battery fitted as standard. Perhaps surprisingly, given the fraught circumstances of the time, it combined both sound design and solid engineering – so tough and enduring in fact that it remained in production from 1932 until 1974. From the outset, it employed a purpose-built frame with chain drive from the gearbox turning a car-type rear axle complete with differential. It enjoyed conventional drum brakes in each wheel, plus a parking brake mounted inside the rear axle housing. Power

ABOVE The Servi-Car's large trunk helped make the three-wheeler popular for store deliveries in the 1930s.

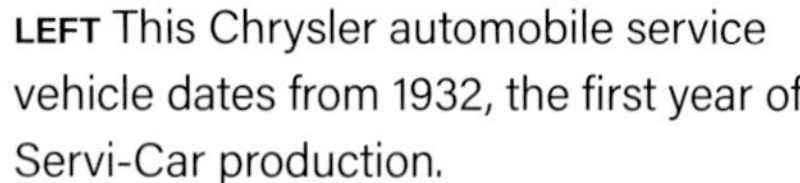

LEFT This Chrysler automobile service vehicle dates from 1932, the first year of Servi-Car production.

SPECIFICATIONS

Engine	aircooled side-valve V-twin
Capacity	45cu in (742cc)
Transmission	three forward speeds, one reverse
Power	around 22hp
Wheelbase	61in (1,550mm)
Width	48in (1,220mm)
Top speed	around 60mph (96kph)

came from the same 45cu in (742cc) flathead V-twin fitted to the Model R. It may have been sluggish but it was undeniably dependable.

The first examples had the same three-speed gearbox as the roadster solo but within two years a reverse gear (not to mention contemporary art-deco

ABOVE A Servi-Car kitted out for police duty, as so many examples were. Note the additional lights and large siren on the front mudguard.

styling motifs) had been added. By this time, the three-wheeler range was popular with police, garages, motoring organizations and small businesses alike and comprised no fewer than five models. In fact it was almost everything such enterprises needed: practical, reliable and cheap.

Above all, it was easy to drive, so there was usually need for only a minimum of operator training. One clever and user-friendly touch was the adoption of the same 42in (1,067mm) wheel track as the typical car – inexperienced Servi-Car drivers would not need to forge their own ruts in mud and snow. At its introduction, it was priced at just $450; by 1969 this had risen to $2,065.

With such a lengthy life-span, inevitably there were other changes too numerous to list. A radical styling change was introduced in 1937, echoing the new 61-inch Knucklehead (indeed the factory briefly dabbled with a prototype shaft-driven Knucklehead Servi-Car). This included a white-faced speedometer calibrated to 100mph (161kph), which would have been terrifying were it not at least 35mph (56kph) over the machine's capabilities.

At the same time, the revised flathead twin from the Model W provided the power – and would continue to do so for the rest of the Servi-Car's days.

Electric start was finally added in 1964 and rear disc brakes toward the end of 1973, at which time annual sales still exceeded 400. Volume production of Servi-Cars ceased after 1973, although some were made to order the following year.

The Model G's most obvious drawback – the absence of heater and roof – had finally brought about its demise, although it could still be seen in service with United States' police forces well into the 1990s.

ABOVE Proving that any Harley can be customized, although tassels were never a Servi-Car factory option.

RIGHT This is a more original example, and here it is painted in colours of the fire department.

WLA & XA, 1940

By far Harley-Davidson's greatest contribution to the Second World War effort came with the hardy "45" that was successfully used in huge numbers, but Milwaukee also produced larger-capacity V-twins, plus a boxer twin that was specially designed for the conflict.

WLA, 1940

If the Willys Jeep was the archetypal American military four-wheeler during the Second World War then Harley-Davidson's rugged old 45-inch flathead twin was its two-wheeled equivalent. By the time the United States entered the war in December 1941, the "45" had proved itself during a dozen years of civilian development and was the obvious choice for an army workhorse. The first example, dubbed WLA (the A stood for "army") appeared in 1940 and was initially scarcely more than a drab green WL. By 1941, it had acquired blacked-out auxiliary lights, an oil-bath air-cleaner (intended for North African conditions) and a quieter fishtail exhaust. Depending on the precise military requirements, luggage racks were added, front and rear, plus a gun scabbard and under-sump bash plate.

That pivotal year also brought the first of around 18,000 WLC models built for the Canadian military, which differed principally in having a foot-

LEFT The redoubtable WLA. Note the large auxiliary air-cleaner to prevent the motor choking in dusty conditions.

SPECIFICATIONS: WLA

Engine	aircooled side-valve V-twin
Capacity	45cu in (742cc)
Transmission	4-speed
Power	around 22bhp
Weight	varied with specification
Wheelbase	59½in (1,510mm)
Top speed	limited to 65mph (105kph)

BELOW Although American-liveried models are best known, over half of military WL production went to other countries' armies.

ABOVE AND BELOW The key to the WLA's success was its low-tuned, dependable engine, which had already enjoyed over a dozen years of development since the original Model D of 1929. Later examples had slotted "black-out" lights.

LEFT Most observers would fail to recognize this as Milwaukee iron: the horizontally-opposed XA twin.

BELOW Note the shaft drive coupling and large air-cleaner on this flathead XA.

operated gear change on the right, rather than hand-change on the left. Anti-hertz suppressors and more comprehensive blackout gear were added later, and by late 1943 – the year in which WLA/WLC production peaked, at over 27,000 – even the crankcases were painted olive drab. Each machine bore a plate warning the rider not to exceed 65mph (105kph), not that the WLA was capable of very much more. Of around 88,000 WLs produced for war-time service, many went to Russia, of which later examples were specified WSR models. It is reputed that some 30,000 Red Army Harley-Davidsons entered Berlin as the war in Europe drew to a close. Milwaukee's contribution to the war effort was marked by no fewer than three Army/Navy "E" awards for excellence in military production – although this was to backfire commercially on the company when thousands of WLAs were sold as war surplus after 1945, damping-down the post-war recovery.

XA, 1942

Although Milwaukee built some military versions of the 74-inch side-valve twin (UA) and even fewer ELC Knuckleheads for the Canadian forces, the factory's second-string army model was the curious XA. Powered by a horizontally-opposed 45cu in (739cc) twin with shaft final drive and plunger rear suspension, the XA was expressly designed for use in the North African desert. The transmission was four-speed, with foot change and twin carburettors feeding the two side-valve cylinder heads. This may seem reminiscent of contemporary BMWs: this was a direct copy of the German machine. Juneau Avenue did not copy the opposition's reliability, for it reputedly suffered serious bearing failures due to the Sahara's heat and sand. As a result, only around 1,000 XAs were built, all during the years 1942–3, though this may have been because the North African campaign was drawing to a close. There was also a rare XS variant with sidecar. A civilian prototype derivative of the XA was tested during 1946 but failed to reach production.

SPECIFICATIONS: XA

Engine	aircooled side-valve horizontally-opposed twin
Capacity	45cu in (739cc)
Transmission	4-speed
Power	around 25bhp
Wheelbase	59½in (1,510mm)
Top speed	around 65 mph (105kph)

BELOW Note the instruction plate: the military ensured that as little as possible was left to chance.

BELOW Although most XAs were intended for North African use, this example is painted in non-desert livery.

MODEL K, 1952

If a single model demonstrated Milwaukee's problems during the post-war years, it was surely the Model K, unveiled in November 1951. The side-valve V-twin was stylish but simply lacked the pace to compete with more technically advanced rivals from across the Atlantic.

Virtually a technological throwback, the "K" was born into an age when competition from Europe was intensifying almost monthly. Opposition machines offered high-performance overhead-valve engines with 100mph- (161kph-) plus performance and the finest chassis ever built. In response, Harley-Davidson offered as its premier model an antiquated, long-stroke, side-valve twin as its premier sports model, which struggled to reach 80mph (129kph).

Advertised as "America's Most Sensational Motorcycle", the "K" was "designed to outperform, outride, outlook, outvalue ... any motorcycle in its class." Of course, this was only true if a class existed for absurdly slow and out-dated machines – which it might if Milwaukee's plea for a 40 per cent tariff on imported motorcycles had succeeded in May 1951. Harley literature claimed 30 horsepower for the Model K, only a little less than the contemporary 650cc Triumph Thunderbird. Whether true or not, the V-twin was no match for the 103mph (166kph) Britisher. Yet remarkably, Joe Leonard became first American national champion in 1954, on a machine substantially derived from the K. Its other saving grace was that it was the only large-capacity motorcycle Hollywood stars could be insured to ride – in other words, the K was so slow, it was considered safe.

True, the K was the first Harley-Davidson twin to feature suspension at both ends: "easy riding" double-action telescopic forks up front with a swinging-fork rear end (oddly, a sprung seat was retained.) By the standards of Triumph, BSA and Norton in particular, the handling was ponderous and mushy, although the eight-inch (200mm) brakes weren't bad for the

LEFT Harley's bold Model K advertising did not reflect the V-twin's disappointingly modest performance.

BELOW Pictured here is a handsome example of a 1956 Model K.

SPECIFICATIONS

Engine	aircooled side-valve V-twin
Capacity	45cu in (742cc)
Transmission	4-speed
Peak power	30bhp
Wheelbase	60in (1,525mm)
Top speed	around 80mph (130kph)

RIGHT The Model K might not have been the quickest or most robust sports model of the early 1950s, but it was surely one of the most attractive.

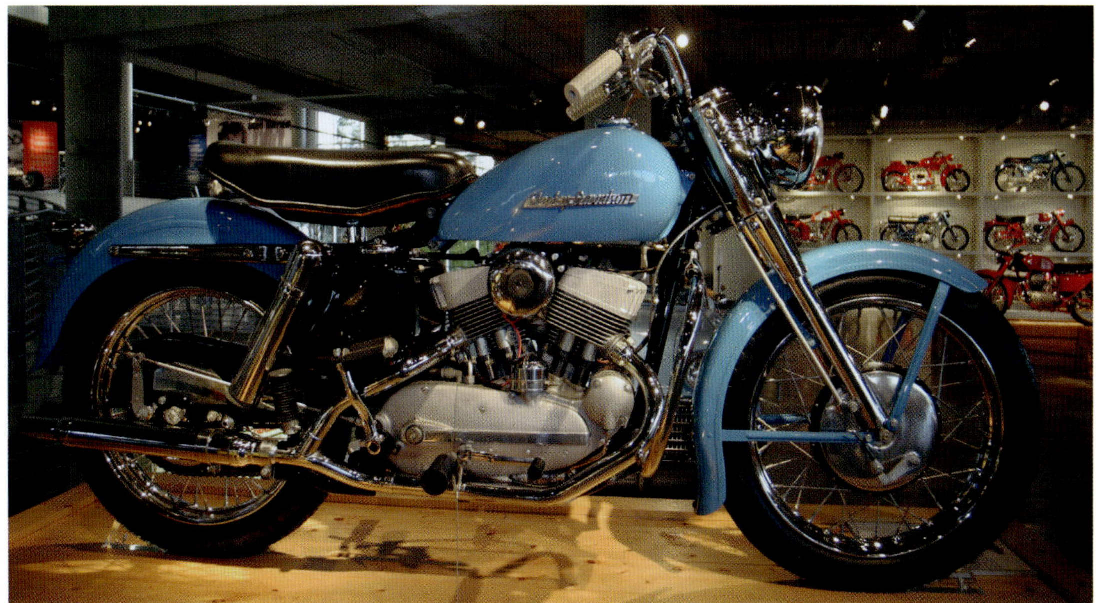

time. It offered a hand-operated clutch and in a demonstration of supreme optimism, its speedometer was graduated to 120mph (193kph).

Nor was the K dependable, at least initially, as it was beset by a variety of performance and reliability problems. Perhaps the worst was its habit of breaking its "large, rugged" transmission gears, until a switch to forged parts after 1954. In many other respects, the bike was sturdy and sensibly conceived, such as in the use of taper-roller bearings for the swing-arm pivots. Bore and stroke were identical to the WL's: 70 x 97mm. The four-cam, air-cooled engine enjoyed generous finning to its aluminium heads and iron barrels, and it featured in-unit construction of engine and gearbox, with triplex chain drive, long before this became widespread among competitors.

Some years after the age of the K, Harley revealed what many had suspected – that it was only a stop-gap model to see the company through until something better could be developed. Although history records that the Model K was superseded by the Sportster, something more radical was envisaged originally. The familiar 45-degree V layout was dropped in favour of a wider 60-degree engine to be known as the KL, with "high" cams, twin carburettors and side-by-side rather than forked connecting rods. This would have increased secondary vibration, although the wider V angle would have gone some way to reducing primary imbalance.

Evidently, the KL project ran into patent conflicts with Vincent and ran out of development time, although it is possible that the progress of European machines convinced Harley that something even more potent was required. By way of a stop-gap to the stop-gap, a drastic 19mm increase in stroke raised the Model K's capacity to 55cu in (883cc) for 1954, and power to a claimed 38bhp, in an attempt to stay at least within sight of the Brits. The cover of *The Enthusiast* showed one Elvis Aaron Presley on board just such a machine in 1956, by which time work on the model's successor was already well in hand. As well as the basic KH, a tuned Super Sport Solo KHK model with high-lift camshafts, polished ports, leaner styling and lower handlebars arrived in 1955. Though they were ostensibly intended for racing, most found their way on to America's streets where they proved far more acceptable to American sports riders – their top speed exceeded 90mph (145kph). After 1956, the old flathead expired and was replaced by the first of the overhead-valve Sportsters. As the KR and KRTT, it soldiered on for more than a decade as Milwaukee's principal racing iron.

BELOW The tuned Model KHK added welcome speed on its launch in 1955.

HARLEY-DAVIDSON

KNUCKLES, PANS AND SHOVELS

Knucklehead, Panhead, Shovelhead – these familiar names represent almost half a century of Milwaukee overhead-valve twins and many motorcyclists' idea of the quintessential Harley-Davidson.

Yet the career of each of these stalwarts was blighted. The Knucklehead project began in 1931 and may well have reached fruition in 1934 but for government restrictions aimed at reducing unemployment. When it finally arrived in 1936 the 61-inch twin was a sensation, but no sooner was a 74-inch version released than the Second World War halted civilian motorcycle production. By the time the dust had settled, the age of the Panhead had come, making the Knuckle "74" one of the rarest and most prized Milwaukee twins of all.

The Pan offered more power and refinement, plus the distinction of propelling one of the most celebrated Hogs – the first Electra Glide – and yet, during this period, Harley's sales slid to their lowest since 1921. Next, the Shovelhead which was better still, but coincided unhappily with a revolution in motorcycling with which it was ill-equipped to compete. Both the Pan and Shovelhead have their fans, but they almost rang the death-knell for Harley-Davidson.

LEFT The timeless beauty of a Panhead-powered Electra Glide from the late 1960s makes it easy to understand why modern Glides bear such a strong resemblance.

MODEL E, 1936

It's difficult to appreciate the impact Harley-Davidson's first overhead-valve roadster twin must have had on a motorcycling public that was emerging groggily from six long years of Depression. No previous Milwaukee model was ever quite so comprehensively new.

Not only was the legendary Knuckle's engine a major departure, but it sat in an equally new twin-cradle frame, with just the mudguards and generator remaining from the flathead VL. Its striking styling owed much to the art-deco innovations of the Depression years, capped by a teardrop-style tank, complete with an audacious white-faced Stewart-Warner speedometer calibrated to 120mph (193kph). Fanciful, perhaps, but factory testers had reported 100mph (161kph) during development. Little wonder that would-be owners queued in droves when the first examples were shipped to dealers in January 1936, despite the $380 Knuckle costing $40 more than a contemporary 80-inch twin.

SPECIFICATIONS

Engine	aircooled OHV V-twin
Capacity	61 or 74cu in (989 or 1,207cc)
Transmission	4-speed, hand change
Power	40 or 45bhp
Weight	565lbs (256kg)
Wheelbase	59½in (1,510mm)
Top speed	up to 90mph (145kph)

Designed by William S. Harley and Lothar A. Doerner (the latter tragically killed while testing a 1937 model), the 61cu in (989cc) twin underwent no fewer than 70,000 hours of testing, according to contemporary claims. As with previous mainstream models, the Knuckle was initially available in three guises: E (standard, discontinued after 1937, but restored during the Second World War), ES (sidecar) and EL (high-compression sport). All proved free-revving and eager, while the EL in particular – with 40 horsepower at 4,800rpm – offered a huge performance increase over the laggard side-valvers. Even the mighty 80-inch VL couldn't come close to an OHV twin.

Yet despite the time-consuming route to production – and not for the first time – there were initial problems.

ABOVE Knuckle-shaped cylinder heads confirmed the OHV advantage.

Many changes were implemented during the first year of production, including frame reinforcing and revisions to the kick-start gears. The

BELOW The first Model E's art deco inspired styling added to the excitement generated by the V-twin's improved performance and refinement.

ABOVE This 1946 FL Knucklehead looks better now than it did when new.

rocker assemblies became enclosed for 1938, by which time the patented tank-mounted instruments also included warning lights for low oil pressure and generator output.

But the 61's worst fault concerned its dry-sump lubrication. Some parts got too little oil while others – including the road underneath – got too much. A partial fix was introduced in 1937 but the glitch was not completely solved until the arrival of the centrifugally-controlled oil pump bypass of the 74-inch (Model F) Knuckle of 1941. The crankshaft main bearings had been up-rated in 1940, perhaps in anticipation of the extra loads on the bigger engine.

The arrival of the more potent "74" also brought larger 8½in (216mm) diameter flywheels, revised crankcases, an up-rated seven-plate clutch and a carburettor choke increased to 1⅛in (28.6mm). By now, the two OHV models combined were comfortably out-selling Milwaukee's established range of side-valve twins. Given

LEFT AND BELOW LEFT A finned timing cover (left) identifies this as a post-1941 Knucklehead. Compare this with the "smooth case" example below. A host of other changes also came in for 1942.

further development, the Knuckle could surely have become better still, but with the outbreak of war in December 1941, production concentrated almost exclusively on military side-valve twins and development of the OHV models all but ceased.

Milwaukee lore has it that the very best of the big Knuckles were those built in that final pre-war year, but hostilities meant that relatively few Model Fs reached the road until 1947, when the line's reign was almost over.

Not surprisingly, that first overhead-valve "74" remains one of the most prized Harley roadsters of all.

By 1948, however, a new pretender was on the scene: the age of the Panhead had arrived. At last it was goodbye, finally, to oil leaks from the rocker box, which was a problem that had never been completely solved on the Knucklehead.

HYDRA-GLIDE, 1949

For the 1948 model year, Harley-Davidson had unveiled its new Panhead engine, mating it to a revised "Wishbone" frame with characteristic "dog-leg" front downtubes. Within a year, it had been eclipsed by the first of Milwaukee's "Glide" models.

Although retaining a rigid rear end, the Hydra-Glide broke with the company's usual reliance on leading-link sprung forks. Instead, here was a Hog with a modern oil-damped telescopic front-end. As if to compensate for this fit of novelty, the Hydra persevered with a uniquely American hand-change gearbox until 1952 and even later as an option for true die-hards.

For the present, however, it was as close to modern as heavyweight Harleys would get. Billed with characteristic restraint as "the nearest thing to flying and as modern as a spaceship," the first Hydra-Glide was, in truth, only a relatively slight departure from the model that went before.

As was company tradition, a host of detail changes would follow year-on-year. Many of these would be cosmetic (the speedometer alone received an astonishing degree of attention), but most concerned the internal workings of the engine and chassis, making the final Hydra-Glide of 1957 very different from the first. It should be remembered, however, that in the American automotive industry in general, the 1950s and 1960s were characterized much more by developments in styling than in functional engineering.

In essence, the Panhead engine comprised new cylinders and heads grafted on to the Knucklehead bottom end. The heads were now aluminium with hydraulic valve lifters (tappets), and internal oilways had replaced the Knuckle's external lines.

SPECIFICATIONS

Engine	aircooled OHV V-twin
Capacity	61 or 74cu in (989 or 1,207cc)
Transmission	4-speed, hand change
Power	around 50/55bhp
Weight	560lbs (254kg)
Wheelbase	59½in (1,510mm)
Top speed	around 95mph (152kph)

ABOVE RIGHT Although the Panhead shared its bottom-end with the Knuckle, the heads, valve gear and oil feeds were all new.

ABOVE The Hydra-Glide's new front end added comfort and control to the two-up touring experience.

LEFT Add electric start and rear shock absorbers and you'd have an Electra Glide. The real thing was to take another 17 years.

RIGHT White tassels probably weren't around when the Hydra-Glide was king of the road, but whitewall tyres certainly were.

Like the Knucklehead it replaced, this new Panhead was produced in both 61- and 74-inch (989 and 1,207cc) versions, designated models E and F respectively. Six versions comprised the initial range: Model F Sport Solo, FL Special Sport Solo and FS Sidecar twin, with the designations repeated for the 61-inch motor. All featured four-speed transmission, while sidecar models had lower gearing and reduced compression ratios. At their launch, all sprung-fork Model Es cost $635, with the larger engine adding a mere $15 to the price. Within a year, the introduction of the Hydra-Glide had upped those figures by precisely $100. Just to be on the safe side, sprung-fork models – designated ELP and FLP – remained in the range for one transitional year.

Of literally hundreds of detail changes, the first major improvement came in 1950 when revised cylinder heads with larger ports added a claimed ten per cent more power. The 61-inch Model E was dropped for 1953, by which time annual sales of the smaller Panhead had slumped to below 1,000. The same year – the company's 50th anniversary – brought about Harley-Davidson's familiar "mid-series" bottom-end redesign. This included major changes to both crankcase halves as well as the relocation of the hydraulic lifters from top to bottom of the pushrods. A new "straight-leg" frame was brought in for 1954, followed by the FLH Super Sport model (the "H" stood for "hot") 12 months later, with gas-flowed heads and 8:1 compression ratios.

Even the FLH was no tyre-shredder, though, retaining the low-revving, high-torque virtues of every Milwaukee V-twin. These were very much machines in the American tradition, having ponderous steering, limited ground clearance, marginal brakes and hand gear change.

In terms of styling, the Hydra-Glide was pure 1950s – or any decade since, given that so many modern Harleys echo its visual themes. Central to this was its low-slung profile with "Air-Flow" front and rear fenders.

A chrome-plated tubular steel front "safety guard" was offered as an option from 1950, with "Hydra-Glide" emblems available one year later – both mimicking those gracing the very latest FLs.

It had some early "innovations" – like black silencers and fork sliders – that did not last, but overall the Hydra-Glide made an impact that is still very much with us today.

BELOW This 1953 Hydra-Glide could almost be a modern Glide, as most Harley updates are so well disguised.

FL DUO-GLIDE, 1958

By 1958, Harley-Davidson was already in grave difficulties as annual sales hovered around a paltry 12,000 under intense competition from European machines. This was well below half the figure of ten years earlier, representing an unsustainable rate of decline.

To make matters worse, the start of the Japanese invasion was just one year away – though no-one knew it at the time – with the arrival of Honda into the American market.

One way in which the company responded was through increased diversification of its range – first the Model K, and then the Sportsters took different directions from the heavyweight twins. But by the late 1950s, the latter – the FL models – were woefully outdated and badly in need of a major overhaul. Instead, they got little more than a facelift.

After the Hydra-Glide, the Duo-Glide was the logical next step. As well as real, oil-damped telescopic front suspension, the Duo floated on a swinging-arm rear end, hence the name. This was a major improvement on the face of it, even though the Model K had beaten it comfortably for the distinction of being the first Harley-Davidson twin with rear suspension. By the time it appeared in 1958, however, pretty much everything it offered had already been done – and done better – by every other major motorcycle manufacturer, with the exception of the Duo's hydraulic rear brake. Unfortunately this was little more than a gimmicky novelty, since both hubs contain tiny, ineffective single-leading shoe drums.

SPECIFICATIONS

Engine	aircooled OHV V-twin
Capacity	74cu in (1,207cc)
Transmission	4-speed
Power	55bhp
Weight	575lb (261kg)
Wheelbase	60in (1,525mm)
Top speed	around 95mph (152kph)

With major engine revisions having been implemented in 1953 and in 1956, the Duo-Glide's engine might as well have been called the "Panhead Mark II". It also benefited from more generous finning than previous Pans for 1958, as well as an up-rated generator. With the 61-inch Pan long departed, all Duo-Glides enjoyed 74-inch (1,207cc) power. The range offered a choice of hand or foot gear-change and Sport or Super S port ("H") tune, making four models in all. In 1958, the hotter specification added $65 to the standard $1,255 purchase price.

Central to the machine's layout was a new "Step-down" frame with larger diameter backbone and attachment points for the twin rear shock absorbers. These incorporated oil-damping (typical of the time, for rebound only) and their springs were enclosed in gleaming chrome-plated

ABOVE The distinctive speedometer is original; the handbag is not.

BELOW The chrome crash bars, fender rails and panniers were available as part of 16 Harley-Davidson option groups.

ABOVE It was still a Panhead, but with the arrival of the Duo-Glide the FL had springing at both ends.

RIGHT Few would dispute that a Duo-Glide is a striking machine, especially a neatly restored and mildly customized example such as this.

shrouds. The new frame necessitated many other modifications – to the oil tank, toolbox and fork yokes – although the first Duos looked rather like soft-tailed Hydra-Glides.

If the Duo's looks weren't enough for aspiring owners, 1958 also introduced a huge expansion in the number of factory "option packs" including no fewer than nine for the new Duo-Glide. These comprised accessories groups for "Chrome Finish", "Road Cruiser" and "King of the Highway", with a bewildering array of lights, luggage items and other paraphernalia. The "King of the Highway" package included front and rear nudge bars, twin rear lights and a dual exhaust system.

Unfortunately it didn't sell very well, being particularly unsuited to most export markets, although it accounted for around 40 per cent of Milwaukee's sales at home. The Duo didn't much like corners, and was woefully under-braked. Even the "H"-designated Super Sports models, with optional high-lift camshaft and higher compression pistons, weren't rapid. Vibration was intense at high engine speeds, leaving much of their potential power unused most of the time, except by the most determined riders – who would probably seek the high-rev thrills of a Triumph Thunderbird anyway.

Then, as now, the Duo-Glide was about a different sort of motorcycling, with its big, slow-revving engine and charismatic looks. It was undeniably a Harley, with all the attributes and vices of the breed. And it was also indisputably beautiful.

BELOW An original 1961 example shows how Harley intended it to look.

HARLEY-DAVIDSON

SPORTSTERS

The Sportster was launched in 1957 to begin one of Harley-Davidson's most enduring model families. The original 883cc XL Sportster featured overhead valves, a unit-construction engine and gearbox, and a chassis with swing-arm rear suspension. It was an instant hit, accounting for a fifth of Harley's production in its first year.

As well as meeting performance expectations, the Sportster looked the business; its lean, purposeful lines, capped with a minimalist fuel tank and "shorty" exhausts, would remain unmistakable for decades. Not that Harley stood still. The first electric-start model arrived in 1967, more power in 1968 and more again with the 1,000cc version of 1972. The Evolution-engined models of 1986 gave a choice of either 883cc or 1,100cc engines, the latter growing to 1,200cc.

The Sportster lost its performance edge over the years but improvements continued, notably in 2004 with rubber-mounted engines. Subsequent models including the Forty Eight and Iron 883 maintained the trademark blend of raw style and character until emissions regulations finally ended the aircooled line after 65 years of production. The introduction of the all-new, liquid-cooled Sportster S in 2021 began a new era for the famous old name, but that's a story for a later chapter...

LEFT The Sportster XL1200R Roadster of 2004 combined familiar family style with technical improvements including the first rubber-mounted engine.

XL SPORTSTER, 1957

After the debacle of the side-valve Model K, the Sportster series roared across America like a refreshing gale, finally giving Harley a model that could compete with rival parallel twins. At its heart was an overhead-valve engine displacing the same 883cc as the XLs of much more recent times.

That first Sportster featured cylinder barrels and heads made from heavy cast iron, the latter with a hemispherical combustion chamber.

Each valve had its own gear-driven camshaft, operating the valve via "High Speed Racing" roller tappets and solid push-rods. A single Linkert carburettor fed mixture into the cylinder, where shallow-domed pistons offered a compression ratio of 7.5:1. In 1957, peak power was around 40bhp but this rose considerably with the ported, high-compression "H" and "CH" versions, reputedly reaching 58bhp at 6,800rpm by the mid-1960s. By then, a good one could exceed 110mph (177kph).

SPECIFICATIONS: XL SPORTSTER 1957

Engine	aircooled OHV V-twin
Capacity	883cc
Transmission	4-speed
Power	40bhp
Weight	438lbs (199kg)
Wheelbase	58.5in (1,485mm)
Top speed	95mph (152kph)

Cosmetically, even fully-equipped versions of the XL were as lean as motorcycles can be. Not so much as a pillion seat was permitted to mar their purposeful lines. The chassis was adequate if altogether less persuasive. A combination tubular steel and cast iron frame married "easy riding" telescopic forks and twin rear shock absorbers, with the swing arm pivoting on taper roller bearings. Each 18in (457mm) wheel held an underwhelming eight-inch (200mm) drum with shoes one inch (25mm) wide.

In truth, the handling wasn't great, although (for a Harley) the Sportster was light and low enough for a good rider to manhandle it into shape. An improved front fork helped matters from 1968 but the XL only really began to behave with the appearance of a lighter and stiffer frame, universally praised in press road tests, in 1982. By this time, the old one was very much feeling its age. Those first Sportsters were comparable with almost anything on the road and, at $1,103 apiece, sold like "Competition Hot-cakes". By the late 1960s, this was comfortably Harley's best-selling range.

ABOVE The 883cc OHV engine was a big improvement on the Model K unit.

SPORTSTER EVOLUTION

Following its introduction in 1957, the XL Sportster became the bread and butter of the Harley-Davidson range. Within a year, the stock Sporty had been joined by the high-compression XLH Sportster Sport, the legendary XLCH "Competition Hot" (as it is

BELOW LEFT Owners of the Sportster enjoyed new-found admiration but rued its lack of a pillion seat.

BELOW In 1957 the first of the Sportsters proved to be a giant leap forward from the primitive side-valve Model K.

ABOVE With its clean lines, tiny peanut tank and open pipes, the XLCH was a gloriously purposeful machine.

BELOW Early Sportsters had the name in capitals on the left engine case.

commonly called, although it actually meant "Competition High-compression") and the stripped-down XLC Sportster Racing. Perhaps surprisingly, the latter, intended for off-road use, lasted for only one year.

Originally marked for a life on dirt, the XLCH featured the 1.8 gallon (8.2 litre) "peanut" tank (standard was 3.5 gallon /16 litres), big valves, magneto ignition – and neither lights, speedometer nor battery. It was superseded by a fully road-equipped XLCH one year later. Detail changes included a switch to 12-volt electronics in 1965, two years before the first Sportster electric start – or "Push the button... ZAP... and away you go" as Milwaukee promoted it.

For 1971, the previous dry clutch gave way to a wet one. The first 1,000cc examples were the XLH/XLCH Super H and Super CH of 1972, the extra displacement coming from a 4.5mm increase in bore size to offer around 60bhp. (The captivating XLCR and XR1000 are dealt with in detail later.) Another spin-off from the Sportster line was a series of hybrid models, hoping to hit any untapped market niche. The XLT Touring came out in 1977, equipped with saddlebags, high bars and a thicker seat. More than 1,000 were built in the first year, a mere six in the second, giving way two years later to the XLS Roadster, with extended forks, highway pegs and a 16in (406mm) rear wheel. That year might be remembered as the last year of the legendary XLCH. A lasting hybrid was the optional Hugger package of 1980, offering shorter shocks and a thinner seat. The equally far-reaching XLX61 came out in 1983: a stripped-down, budget-priced version of the XLH1000 aimed at cash-strapped riders. It became Milwaukee policy to produce a cut-price "entry-level" model. When the 883 and 1,100cc Evolution models arrived for 1986, it was to be the beginning of a new chapter in the Sportster story.

BELOW The Sportster's profile changed remarkably little through the aircooled V-twin family's six decades.

XLCR CAFÉ RACER, 1977

The lean, all-black Café Racer was another of Willie G. Davidson's variations on an old theme, in this case re-working the basic 1,000cc Sportster, which had first appeared in 1972, to create a lean black V-twin that looked more like a European superbike than a traditional Harley.

When the XLCR arrived for the 1977 model year, it was revolutionary – the most unashamedly different Harley-Davidson yet.

At its heart was the then biggest XL engine grafted into a redesigned frame, with extended rear frame rails allowing more vertical shock absorbers than before. Most striking of all was the "Black-on-Black" paint job. This included gloss black bodywork, crinkle-black engine finish and a black Siamesed exhaust which snaked together below the air-filter housing – which, naturally, was black.

The 3.8 gallon (14.5 litre) fuel tank – black, of course – was unique to the XLCR, as were a fibreglass "bikini" fairing and single seat. The latter ended with a racing-style "bum stop" – although a dual seat option was available for 1978, the model's second and final year of manufacture. Cast aluminium Morris wheels, as well as rear-set "race replica" footrests and controls, were also provided as standard.

The move to more vertical shock absorbers was a not particularly successful attempt to improve the Sportster's habitually sloppy handling.

SPECIFICATIONS

Engine	aircooled OHV V-twin
Capacity	992cc
Transmission	4-speed
Power	around 60bhp
Weight	540lbs (245kg)
Wheelbase	58.5in (1,485mm)
Top speed	110mph (177kph)

At the same time, twin hydraulic front discs were fitted in much-needed pursuit of improved braking. They proved moderately powerful, if rather lacking in feel.

Visually, this "top Sportster" was superb. True, it wasn't to everyone's taste, but most bikers would cast admiring glances at this stylish symphony in black. For all its eye-grabbing credentials, however, the XLCR was far from a runaway success.

On the one hand, most Harley die-hards found it visually too radical. On the other hand, more neutral buyers found sport-bike image and performance far more effectively packaged in Japanese and Italian machines. For all that, the

ABOVE The stylish XLCR, with its "race replica" footrests, did not produce the kind of sales that Harley had hoped for.

RIGHT In truth the XLCR looked better than it went.

RIGHT In 1977, riders were required to enjoy the machine alone. A dual seat became an optional extra for 1978.

XLCR is a desirable classic now, though at the time it was neither a vintage Harley-Davidson model nor a competent sports machine.

With an output of 60bhp and top speed of around 110mph (177kph), the XLCR was certainly no slug, but the bald truth was that it went at least 25mph (40kph) slower than rival sports machines, with equally inferior handling and braking. Worse still, the XLCR bore all the worst hallmarks of the AMF years. Contemporary road tests might praise the marque's "indefinable magic" but they would equally slate the Café Racer (and its siblings) for being "appallingly built and hideously unreliable", to which was usually added "prohibitively expensive".

By the end of the model's brief reign, Harley-Davidson's share of the American motorcycle market had slumped to a paltry four per cent, yet it would be several years before the reborn company would seriously set about tackling its manufacturing shortcomings. This wasn't specifically the fault of the XLCR, of which just 3,124 examples were built, but this model did illustrate Harley-Davidson's problem – that beauty had to be much more than skin-deep.

RIGHT The problem wasn't so much the name on the tank as the AMF logo on the side panel. Just nine were made for the 1978–9 model year.

XR1000 SPORTSTER, 1983

Unveiled at Daytona in March 1983, the XR1000 was the closest Harley-Davidson fans would ever get to a road-going XR racer. Even this far on, it's still many people's idea of the ultimate Harley Sportster – tuned, minimalist, loud and unashamedly aggressive.

This should have come as no surprise because the big XR roadster was designed (and the prototype built) in the official factory race shop under the direction of Dick O'Brien. The 1000 could scarcely have enjoyed a better pedigree – O'Brien had managed Harley-Davidson's racing efforts since 1957 and overseen every moment of the XR750's career. Fittingly, O'Brien retired in the same year as the XR1000 roadster was released, making it an appropriately snarling swansong.

The $6,995 1000 wasn't quite a big-bore factory racer with lights but it was pretty special all the same. The engine employed a normal Sportster bottom end capped by special cylinder barrels, heads, fuel and exhaust systems. The aluminium heads were based on those of the racing XR, each reputedly shipped to Los Angeles to be ported and polished by legendary tuner, Jerry Branch (although it's likely that Branch simply oversaw the work, since a total of 1,777 XR1000s were built).

SPECIFICATIONS

Engine	aircooled HV V-twin
Capacity	998cc
Transmission	4-speed
Power	70bhp
Weight	487lbs (221kg)
Wheelbase	59.3in (1,505mm)
Top speed	115mph (185kph)

Induction was in the capable hands of twin 1½in (36mm) Dell'Orto carburettors with accelerator pumps, each breathing through huge, free-flowing K&N air filters stacked, flat-track style, on the engine's right side. Although stock Sportster camshafts were employed, valve-lash was adjusted by racer-style eccentric rocker shafts. The push-rods, too, were special lightweight alloy components. Lumpy pistons gave a 9:1 compression ratio. Paired high-level black megaphone exhausts growled back along the machine's left side.

ABOVE Not quite a racing XR750 for the road, but visually the XR1000 came close.

This bespoke engine was red-lined at 6,200rpm but there was no earthly need to spin it that high, since the spread of power was immense.

Peak power – a claimed 70bhp – arrived at 5,600rpm but the engine pulled strongly from as few as

RIGHT Possibly the most prized of all AMF-era models, the XR1000 was race boss Dick O'Brien's major contribution to Harley roadsters.

ABOVE Harley did not need dry ice smoke to make the XR seem smokin' hot.

2,000rpm. Maximum torque was 48lb/ft (65Nm) at just 4,400rpm. The speedometer was calibrated only to 110mph (177kph), a figure a good XR could reach comfortably.

With optional performance kits offering more than 90bhp, the sky was almost the limit.

In truth, the XR's chassis was far less impressive than its engine. The frame and running gear were based on the XLX61, which was also new for 1983, with a nine-spoke, cast 19in front wheel and 16in rear. Rear suspension was in the hands of twin shock absorbers of no great quality, adjustable only for spring pre-load. Travel was quite short and the action harsh, making the XR nervous when ridden hard on bumpy surfaces. The brakes, however – twin 11½in (292mm) front discs – were surely the best Harley-Davidson had put on any roadster model up to that time and improved even further for 1984.

During the model's second year, it was offered with optional black and orange "factory" racing paintwork as well as the original steel grey. This seemed to be a suitably fitting livery for such a great machine.

The XR1000's reign as the ultimate sporting Harley-Davidson ever to have been produced by Milwaukee came to an end when production of this model ceased in 1984.

ABOVE Strangely, Milwaukee didn't offer the XR in their classic orange and black racing livery until 1984. In comparison this relatively standard machine looks mundane.

RIGHT That's better: the same colours flown by Jay Springsteen, Scott Parker and the rest of the champion racers.

EVOLUTION SPORTSTERS, 1986

The Sportster got a boost in 1986, when Harley fitted a new Evolution motor with traditional 883cc capacity and aluminium top-end, shortly followed by a larger, 1,100cc version. Both Evo models combined reliable performance with subtly uprated chassis, and both proved hugely popular.

Competitive pricing contributed to the success, especially with the smaller model. Back in 1983, Harley had introduced the 883cc XLX61 with a price tag of just under $4,000, making it precisely the type of entry-level machine so conspicuously absent from the range in the past. In 1987, would-be owners got an even more irresistible package with Milwaukee's innovative buy-back scheme: "Trade in your XLH against an FX or FL within two years and we'll guarantee $3,995 on your old machine." How could anyone lose?

By the start of the 1990s the larger Sportster's engine had been bored out to create the XLH1200, and both models had received major updates. The most important were the addition of a fifth ratio to the gearbox, and the substitution of the drive chain by a belt – a narrower version of the Kevlar item used on Harley's 1,340cc models, and as fitted by many Sportster owners in the past.

The 1200's changes were part of a redesign that left only its carburettor, pistons, conrods and cylinders untouched, and boosted peak output slightly to around 57bhp at 5000rpm. The 883's extra gear transformed the 52bhp smaller Sportster from a relatively buzzy, busy machine into a far more laid-back device, with the bonus of a better gearshift. The tooth-belt drive was also smoother than a chain, with the added benefits of low maintenance and cleanliness.

As well as gaining a ratio, the gearbox was uprated with new shafts,

LEFT The 883's performance was nothing special, but it was seriously cool.

BELOW The XLH1200 engine featured significant updates including a fifth gearbox ratio and final drive by belt instead of chain.

BELOW With no frills, no tassels or baubles, the 883 was the most honest-to-goodness model in the Milwaukee range.

SPECIFICATIONS: XLH883

Engine	aircooled OHV V-twin
Capacity	883cc
Transmission	5-speed
Power	52bhp
Weight	489lb (222kg)
Wheelbase	60.2in (1,530mm)
Top Speed	95mph (153kph)

ABOVE The XLH1200 Sportster was surely one of 1990's most stylish streetbikes, if not one of its quickest.

ABOVE A blend of looks, adequate performance and competitive price kept the XLH883 Sportster hugely popular well into the 1990s, helped by Harley's promotional deals.

gears and bearings. The alternator moved from the clutch to the end of the crankshaft, allowing the clutch to borrow some components from the big-twin unit. Detail modifications included new one-piece pushrods to reduce oil leaks, a more sophisticated engine-breather system, and reworked oil-pump and tappet assemblies.

The updates made the Sportsters even better at what they had long been good at – being a lean, spare and handsome means of filling practically all the space between headstock and rear spindle. They had no tassels, no gratuitously shiny but ultimately useless bits – just plain, single-seated function.

Of course, like all Harleys, the function in question had relatively little to do with sheer speed, handling or stopping. A Sportster looked cool while allowing its rider to appreciate, with as little intervening sanitation as possible, the most intimate doings of the internal-combustion engine.

Even the larger model's acceleration was brisk rather than vivid, although the ample torque meant there was always power on hand. The 883 was notably easy to handle. Many female riders, in particular, appreciated its Hugger variant, whose shorter suspension and thinner seat gave an ultra-low seat.

In the mid-1990s the Sportster was the best-selling motorcycle on the US market. In 1995, the 883 version alone outsold every other bike in the States, and the 1200 was fourth best-seller, behind only Honda's Gold Wing and Harley's own Electra Glide. Pretty good for a model that was almost 40 years old.

BELOW A 1996 Hugger 883, even lower to the ground than the stock Sportster.

XL1200S SPORTSTER SPORT, 1996

The Sportster Sport proved that Harley had been listening to the feedback from customers, particularly in export markets including Europe, who for years had been complaining about the Sportster's mediocre handling and stopping ability.

There would soon be a boost to straight-line performance, too, but on the Sport's launch in 1996 its key features were suspension, brakes and tyres.

New cartridge front forks and rear shocks, both from Showa of Japan, were fully adjustable for preload, compression and rebound damping – a major first for Harley. The front brake featured not one but two drilled, floating discs, and was bolted to a 19-inch cast wheel which, like its 16-inch rear counterpart, wore a respectably soft and sticky Dunlop tyre.

LEFT Once sorted, the Sportster Sport represented a quantum leap in Harley-Davidson engine power, handling and stopping prowess.

Compared to the Sportster's previous chassis parts, this was serious stuff. Front brake performance was notably improved – the big twin discs allowing two-finger braking instead of the vice-like grip previously required at the lever – and the grippier rubber made the most of it. Most important, though, was the Harley's uprated suspension, which was comfortable on its standard settings and could be fine-tuned to give more control for hard riding.

Sportster fans had to wait another two years before the Sport model truly reached its peak, but the updated 1998 version was worth the delay. In broad terms, the engine was little changed from previous Sportsters, with its hydraulic tappets, dry sump and triple-row primary chain driving a wet multi-plate clutch and toothed-belt final drive.

However, a comprehensive engine revamp raised torque figures by an average of 15 per cent throughout the twin's 2,000–5,500rpm operating range. The model now had both the chassis and the engine to justify its "Sport" aspirations at last.

Essential to these improvements was an all-new ignition pack igniting not one, but two spark plugs in each cylinder, promoting quicker, more efficient burning of the incoming fuel/air charge. Although a conventional carburettor was retained – a 1½in (40mm) constant velocity Keihin instrument equipped with an "accelerator" pump – combustion control was further improved by an electronic management system even more sophisticated than the V Fire III set-up fitted to its sister models. The system, incidentally, also afforded

LEFT The Sportster Sport was extremely popular, and the 1998 model pictured was long-awaited by its devotees.

SPECIFICATIONS

Engine	aircooled OHV V-twin
Capacity	1,203cc
Transmission	5-speed
Power	61bhp
Weight	518lbs (235kg)
Wheelbase	60.2in (1,530mm)
Top speed	105mph (169kph)

TOP One of the first examples of the 1200S. Later versions were better.

ABOVE The Sportster is really a joy to ride.

ABOVE Clean lines are common, but note improved calipers between this early example and the 2000 Sportster that is pictured below.

high-tech electronic diagnostic capabilities. These measures allowed Harley-Davidson's engineers to bump up compression from 9:1 to 10:1, offering a substantial increase in mid-range power.

As well as lumpier pistons, the revised powerplant benefited from a larger, less restrictive exhaust system and new camshaft design. The camshafts offered both higher lift and longer duration, again with the emphasis on enhancing mid-range torque. Harley could claim a peak torque figure of 78lb.ft (106Nm) at 4,000rpm, over 50 per cent higher than the 883. With not only much improved power characteristics but better throttle response as well, the Sport felt even stronger than the figures showed. The 1200S looked every inch as mean and muscular as a Sportster should, with its clean lines and understated black engine highlights. Nor was this a deception, for the twin-plug Sport package delivered genuine punch.

Better still, it stopped and handled in an almost un-Milwaukee-like manner – a mantle several more recent models subsequently adopted, to welcome effect.

In short, this not only proved to be the best XL for years, but perhaps was also the model with which Harley rediscovered the Sportster's roots, and made a great addition to the range.

LEFT Getting back to its roots: the XL1200S.

XL1200R ROADSTER, 2004

Continuous development had long been a Sportster trait when the XL1200R Roadster and more laid-back XL1200C Custom were launched in 2004, but few steps had been as big as this: their V-twin engines were rubber-mounted in the frame for the first time.

Their new chassis was also adopted by the two models' XL883 contemporaries, instantly raising their level of comfort.

Harley's development team had investigated using engine counter-balancers before opting to rubber-mount the engines in a new frame. In developing both chassis and powerplant they worked closely with engineers from Buell, whose bikes had long used tuned and rubber-mounted, Sportster-based motors.

The Sportsters' new twin-cradle frame used two large rubber mounts, located low down at the front and rear. Each mount incorporated two rubber pucks. Three Buell-style metal tie-rods limited the engine's vibration to a rotational movement along the line of

ABOVE Along with its retro paintwork and new frame, the XL1200R featured cast wheels and twin front discs.

RIGHT Harley fitted the rubber-mount frame to the XL883 (front), XL1200C Custom and XL1200R Roadster.

SPECIFICATIONS

Engine	aircooled OHV V-twin
Capacity	1,202cc
Transmission	5-speed
Power	70bhp
Weight	552lbs (251kg)
Wheelbase	59.8in (1,520mm)
Top speed	115mph (185kph)

the bike. Because the engine was no longer a stressed member of the chassis the frame was made stiffer, with a thicker main spine. Other changes included a wider rear tyre and new twin-piston Nissin brake calipers.

Changes to the 1,200cc engine started with improved cooling due to increased fin area on cylinder heads and barrels. The pistons were cooled by oil jets in Buell fashion, and used new rings also borrowed from Buell, who also provided the valves and high-flow cylinder heads. Lighter pistons and conrods allowed the rev limit to be increased from 5,500 to 6,000rpm; peak output was up 15 per cent to 70bhp.

The previous, solid-mounted engine had felt like a bag of nails at high revs, but the Roadster's rubber-mounted V-twin picked up speed with much less vibration. There was slightly more midrange urge, and the still carburetted Harley remained crisp below 2,000rpm. The new model felt much faster, though, because more of its rev range could be used.

Much of the Sportster riding experience was familiar, though the way the aircooled motor jiggled about in the frame at idle was not. At very low revs the rubber mounting removed some of the old V-twin's engagingly mechanical feel. But on the open road with its throttle wound open, this Sportster happily rumbled towards its top speed of slightly more than 100mph (161kph), feeling sufficiently smooth to make the experience enjoyable.

Stability and handling were respectable, although Harley had saved money by abandoning the multi-adjustable suspension of the Sportster Sport. The basic forks and shocks gave a fairly comfortable ride most of the time, but struggled when the bike was ridden harder. At least the twin-disc front brake gave plenty of stopping power.

The Roadster was a significant improvement on previous Sportsters, mainly because its motor was so much more useable. Previous XL1200s had looked great but shook too much to be fun when ridden hard. All of a sudden, the Sportster had become a reasonably quick and practical bike, without losing any of its style or its competitive price.

ABOVE The XL1200C Custom differed from the Roadster with its wire-spoked wheels, single front disc, more pulled-back bars and a larger fuel tank.

RIGHT Base model of the new Sportster family was the XL883, featuring a peanut tank and single seat with the new rubber-mount frame design.

XR1200, 2008

In many ways the XR1200 could hardly have been more American, inspired as it was by the XR750 flat-tracker which, on the roadster's launch in 2008, had already won 28 Grand National championships to become indisputably its nation's greatest ever competition machine.

So it was ironic that, having been conceived by Harley-Davidson Europe and developed for the European market, the XR1200 became the first Milwaukee model that was initially not sold in the land of its birth.

The motive for the XR1200's creation was European Harley enthusiasts' desire for sportier bikes, in sharp contrast with the preference of customers back home. Although flat track racing did not have much of a following across the Atlantic, Harley's XR750-styled XL883R model had sold sufficiently well to suggest that a more authentic dirt-track replica would be popular.

The XR1200 did a good job of replicating the lean XR750 racer, thanks largely to its distinctively shaped gas tank and tailpiece, especially in its orange paint option. Its handlebar was wide, but by Harley

SPECIFICATIONS

Engine	aircooled OHV V-twin
Capacity	1,202cc
Transmission	5-speed
Power	90bhp
Weight	550lbs (250kg)
Wheelbase	59.6in (1,515mm)
Top speed	125mph (201kph)

ABOVE Harley tuned the 1,202cc Sportster engine with downdraft induction, hot cams and lighter internals, increasing output to 90bhp.

BELOW Its factory style orange and black paint option gave the XR1200 some of the XR750's look, helped by its small tank and racy tailpiece.

ABOVE The XR1200's chassis was revamped with a new rear subframe, lighter swing-arm and stiffer shocks.

standards quite low. A white-faced rev-counter dominated the view of the new instrument panel.

Power came from an uprated 1,202cc Sportster powerplant, breathing through a new downdraft intake system and tuned with higher compression ratio, racier cams, and a lighter Buell-sourced flywheel that allowed quicker revving. Revised lubrication, stronger connecting rods and bigger crankpins provided enhanced strength.

The XR accelerated notably harder than a standard Sportster, pulling enthusiastically through the midrange and revving rapidly to the higher, 7,000rpm limit. It sounded good, too, thanks to an induction roar that Harley's engineers had provided by meeting noise regs with help from an electronically operated flap in the airbox. Shorter overall gearing for the five-speed box added to the punchy midrange, but limited top speed to about 125mph (201kph), at which point the bike was redlining in top. That gave a slightly busier feel at speed, but the motor was smooth enough to cope.

Handling was where the XR had its biggest advantage over a standard Sportster. The steel frame was essentially unchanged, but a new rear subframe gave steeper steering geometry. The new aluminium swing-arm was lighter and more rigid. Suspension was stiffer than standard, its rates set after development testing by nine times AMA champ Scott Parker.

That all made the XR fun on a twisty road, despite its weight and unfashionable (for sporty bikes) 18-inch diameter front wheel. It steered precisely, stayed stable, and could be cornered hard thanks to grippy tyres and adequate ground clearance. Twin Nissin front brake calipers gave powerful stopping too.

ABOVE The XR's lighter steering and firmer suspension helped make it more fun than a standard Sportster when ridden hard on a twisty road.

The XR1200's Sportster-like character, flat track inspired looks and uprated performance made an attractive combination. Initial response in Europe was enthusiastic, and Harley belatedly made the bike available on the American market in 2009. But ultimately the XR1200 did not sell in sufficient numbers, and production ended in 2012 with the roadster having failed to approach the impact of the XR750 that had inspired it.

RIGHT Nine times Grand National champion Scott Parker (right) had helped develop the XR1200 and joined journalists on its launch in Spain.

FORTY-EIGHT, 2010

If the Forty-Eight proved anything, with its unmistakable appearance thanks to a combination of peanut fuel tank, low-slung single saddle and fat-tyred 16in wheels, it was that some Harley-Davidsons can get away with any number of drawbacks – provided they have sufficient style.

ABOVE Fat tyres, peanut tank and minimalist rear end gave the Forty-Eight a uniquely squat, muscular look.

The Harley range contained numerous models that were more powerful and practical than this Sportster variant, and some that cost less. But the Forty-Eight's simple, squat look gave it a unique appeal and kept it popular for a decade.

Its name and look were inspired by its fuel tank. In 1948, Harley had launched the 125 S, later known as the Hummer. The little two-stroke single's tiny, distinctive "peanut" tank would become iconic. It was later used by racers, and by the factory for the XLCH Sportster that was Milwaukee's hot-rod roadster in the late 1950s and early 1960s.

That peanut tank was key to the Forty-Eight's lean, stripped-down image. It held just 8 litres; barely a couple of gallons. However you measured it, that was barely a spit. The rest of the bike was minimalist too, enhanced by a single saddle. It had a fat-tyred, 16-inch diameter front wheel with wire spokes, which gave a

SPECIFICATIONS

Engine	aircooled OHV V-twin
Capacity	1,202cc
Transmission	5-speed
Power	70bhp
Weight	552lbs (251kg)
Wheelbase	59.8in (1,520mm)
Top speed	115mph (185kph)

BELOW The characterful 70bhp engine came from the Nightster, the base-model 1200 of the Sportster family.

ABOVE Handling was respectably good despite short-travel suspension.

RIGHT For 2016 the Forty-Eight's look was revised with 1970s-inspired tank graphics, and its chassis with a fork brace and uprated suspension.

chunkier look than the Sportster 1200's typical 19-inch wheel.

Other changes included repositioning the mirrors, which sat underneath instead of above the handlebars. The footrests were positioned forward, giving a relaxed riding position. Shorter shocks lowered the seat, which was already low enough.

Its engine was borrowed from the Nightster, the base-model Sportster 1200, and produced about 70bhp. The Forty-Eight was no bike for high-speed thrills, but it happily surged clear of traffic. And thanks to the engine's rubber mounting system, it cruised respectably smoothly.

That low-slung look involved compromises, notably that the short-travel suspension tended to jar, sometimes painfully, over bumps. The Forty-Eight also scraped its footrests at modest lean angles. At least the efficient front and rear disc brakes helped it stop on a dime.

Comfort was not a major issue for the Forty-Eight, because it couldn't be ridden for long before needing a top-up. Riders would typically be looking for a gas station after just 60 miles (96km), and sweating after half as many again. By 100 miles (161km) they'd be pushing.

For most Harley enthusiasts there were models that made far more sense, but plenty of riders were happy to let heart rule head. The Forty-Eight became one of the firm's most popular models, and was boosted in 2016 when updated with new suspension, wheels and brakes.

The fuel tank gained some stripes on its side, too, inspired by Sportsters from the 1970s. One thing the Forty-Eight didn't get was additional fuel capacity. Practicality from a motorbike is good, but sometimes style is simply better.

THE SEVENTY-TWO

Two years after bringing back the peanut tank with the Forty-Eight, Harley put it centre-stage again with a different take on the 1200cc Sportster. The Seventy-Two, inspired by the choppers of the 1970s, sparkled with ape-hanger bars, metal-flake paintwork, longer suspension and a skinny, wire-spoked 21-inch front wheel. It captured the period look cleverly, and rode respectably well, but didn't match the impact of the Forty-Eight.

RIGHT Ape-hanger bars, metal-flake paint, long forks and a narrow, laced 21in front wheel gave the Seventy-Two a classical chopper style.

ROADSTER, 2017

After six decades, the aircooled Sportster line was increasingly threatened by tightening emissions regulations as the 2017 model year approached. Harley supplied a final flourish with the Roadster, which blended traditional Sportster style with best-yet engine and chassis performance.

The Roadster's design was shaped by Harley-Davidson's very different fortunes with two fairly recent attempts to diversify the famous old Sportster family.

Back in 2008, the XR1200, inspired by the mighty XR750 flat-track racer, had offered speed and sporty handling but failed to sell. By contrast the squat, bobber-themed Forty-Eight of two years later had been a hit, suggesting that in the Sportster world, edgy style trumped performance every time.

The Roadster shared the Forty-Eight's 1,202cc engine and steel frame, and echoed its minimalist style with a peanut tank, this time with roughly 50 per cent extra capacity. By Milwaukee standards it had a sporty feel thanks to a flat handlebar, relatively rearset footrests and low-slung headlamp.

The familiar V-twin powerplant meant the Roadster was respectably quick. It pulled sweetly from low revs, shook just enough to have some character, sounded good through its

SPECIFICATIONS

Engine	aircooled OHV V-twin
Capacity	1,202cc
Transmission	5-speed
Power	70bhp
Weight	570lbs (259kg)
Wheelbase	59.2in (1,505mm)
Top speed	115mph (185kph)

RIGHT New forks and rear shocks with dual-rate springs gave the Roadster good ride quality by Sportster standards.

BELOW The Roadster captured much of the Forty-Eight's compact style despite its bigger tank and longer suspension.

ABOVE The Iron 883 combined a similarly aggressive look with Harley's smaller V-twin powerplant.

side-by-side silencers, and stayed reasonably smooth as it rumbled towards a top speed of just over 110mph (177kph).

Handling was respectably good too. The chassis featured the Milwaukee rarity of upside-down front forks, which were matched to rear shock units with dual-rate springs. Braking was via twin front discs, rather than a single disc like the other Sportster models.

The Roadster required a deliberate nudge of the bars to get it to change direction quickly, but steered with an admirably neutral feel. Its fairly firm suspension had generous travel by Sportster standards, contributing to a respectably comfortable ride.

Like most Sportsters this bike wasn't designed to be practical, but its peanut tank had sufficient capacity for a range of about 100 miles (161km). The seat was not exactly comfortable for a pillion but contributed to the bike's versatility without spoiling its look.

The Roadster succeeded in recapturing some of the magic of a hotted-up Harley from the early 1960s by blending traditional V-twin appeal with plenty of attitude, sound chassis performance and enough get-up-and-go for a lively ride. In many ways it was the best, most complete Sportster yet. With time running out for the aircooled V-twin, it would prove a fitting way to end the famous line.

BELOW The Iron's straight-line performance was modest but it had plenty of aircooled V-twin character.

IRON 883

By the time the Iron 883 was launched in 2016, Harley had released the new-generation Street 750 in an attempt to attract younger riders. But riding that liquid-cooled V-twin back-to-back with the Iron confirmed that the traditional aircooled, 883cc Sportster format still had plenty to offer as an entry-level model.

By modern standards the Iron wasn't fast or sophisticated, but its rubber-mounted motor ran smoothly enough. And its chassis – which featured cartridge forks, progressively wound shocks and lightened alloy wheels – was a capable accompaniment.

More to the point, the Iron looked good, in paint options including Hard Candy Custom Gold Flake. And the 883cc V-twin had an old-school character that the liquid-cooled Street couldn't match. It was cast-iron proof of how well the Sportster concept had aged in almost 60 years.

NA DEL SOL

CRUISERS

The Cruisers of Harley-Davidson's range are essentially the laid-back Big Twins. That's pretty much how it's been for decades, although back in the day – until a major Milwaukee rejig in 2018, to be more precise – there were separate model families for Softails and Dynas, the latter distinguishable by their visible, rather than hidden, rear shocks.

Cruisers generally don't have fairings or luggage, although rules on such things can be flexible. The breed definitely included the original Super Glide of 1971, and the similarly influential Low Rider that followed six years later. The Softail of 1984 made a double impact with its Evo engine and hardtail-look chassis. In 1991 the Sturgis began the Dyna line of rubber-mounted V-twins that would endure for more than 25 years.

These days the Cruiser roster is packed with star names, from Softail to Heritage Classic, via Low Rider, Fat Boy and Sport Glide. Simplicity remains the theme, though you might find detachable windscreens and panniers here. The bikes are more powerful and more refined than ever, but the essence of their appeal hasn't changed in well over half a century.

LEFT This elegantly styled cruiser is a Heritage Softail Nostalgia from the 1990s, but with its stout forks and hardtail-look rear end it resembles a 1950s Hydra-Glide.

FX SUPER GLIDE, 1971–84

In the late 1960s, customizing was king. In California in particular, Harley-Davidson owners were tearing their machines to pieces, discarding one piece and adding another to produce unique examples of what were to become known as "blend" bikes.

Nowhere was this more publicly demonstrated than in the film *Easy Rider*, with Peter Fonda cruising to New Orleans on the outrageous "Captain America" alongside Dennis Hopper's hardtailed Duo-Glide.

Milwaukee's response was as startling as it was controversial. When the Super Glide was unveiled for the 1971 model year, it was the first example of a genre quickly dubbed "factory custom". The influential *Cycle* magazine's misgivings were typical. "Is the American motorcyclist ready to ride around on someone else's expression of personal, radical tastes?" it asked, before testing the newcomer and answering its own question enthusiastically in the affirmative. Such was the Super Glide's impact that almost every major motorcycle manufacturer has since produced its own interpretation of the "factory" custom – invariably to less effect than Harley's original. From a modern perspective, taking into account models such as the Springer Softail, the FX wasn't actually all that radical. Styled and conceived by Willie G. Davidson, it was essentially a combination of heavyweight FLH frame, 74-inch Shovelhead engine (which still carried "FLH" on the timing cover) and running gear, with the front end from the existing XLH Sportster. The rear end's styling was dominated by a fibreglass boat-tail stepped seat and integral rear mudguard which had debuted as an option on the Sportsters the previous year. Although widely viewed as a defining element of the model, this lasted for only one year and was quickly replaced by a more conventional rear mudguard.

Compared to the FLH, the Super Glide also had pegs in place of footboards, with foot controls revised to suit. Both exhausts were low-level feeding paired silencers on the right hand side. Wheels were 19in front, 16in rear, both equipped with fairly feeble drum brakes. The 3½ gallon (13 litre) fuel tank included a built-in speedometer. Functionally, it was a far from perfect machine, although it went and handled far better than the FLH

ABOVE Harley's advertising backed up the Super Glide's patriotic red, white and blue paint scheme.

SPECIFICATIONS: 1971–80

Engine	aircooled OHV V-twin
Capacity	74cu.in (1,207cc)
Transmission	4-speed
Power	around 60bhp @ 5400rpm
Weight	590lbs (267kg)
Wheelbase	61in (1,550mm)
Top speed	105mph (169kph)

BELOW Part Sportster, part FL, the Super Glide was an instant hit, with 4,700 built in the first year.

RIGHT Although the Super Glide's most eye-catching feature, the "boat-tail" rear end was an option rather than standard equipment.

from which it was derived, not least because it was more than 66lbs (30kg) lighter. The hybrid instantly struck a chord and sold well – 4,700 units in its first year, almost as many as the established FLH Electra Glide. After two years, it acquired hydraulic disc brakes at both ends and improved suspension with stiffer springs. A year later, an electric start option, the FXE, was added. Japanese Showa forks were added in 1977, electronic ignition in 1978 and twin front discs in 1979, before it developed 80-inch Shovelhead power for 1981.

For the final year of production in 1984, five-speed transmission was added; the FXR and FXRS Super Glide II models were also on the Milwaukee stocks, comfortably out-selling the old stager. Although almost two decades would pass from the Super Glide's launch to the turnaround in the company's economic fortunes, it's impossible to overstate the effect the model has had on Harley-Davidson's affairs. The FX invented the concept of the factory custom and led to landmark models such as the FXEF Fat Bob in 1979 and Sturgis 12 months later.

BELOW In 1974 the Super Glide gave rise to the FXE, featuring an electric starter. Twin discs first appeared for 1979.

BOTTOM A later, disc-braked FX. Note the "AMF" logo on its tank.

BELOW For 2006 the Dyna Super Glide came in white, blue and red "Sparkling America" paintwork to mark the original model's 35th anniversary.

FXS LOW RIDER, 1977

Willie G. Davidson and his design team created another classic with the Low Rider by reworking the Super Glide. They kicked out the front forks, shifted the footpegs forward and lowered the bars and seat. The result was one of Harley's most enduring styles and model names.

As The Man himself said, "We took the custom bubble and pushed it further." This lean piece of two-wheeled art would spawn a Milwaukee dynasty.

Described as "one mean machine" in Harley-Davidson's own publicity, the FXS was a new type of custom cruising model, intended to be as content cruising wide-open prairies as downtown avenues. It was finished in menacing gunmetal grey with flat, drag-style handlebars on pulled-back risers, resonating echoes of the choppers that countless enthusiasts had created in the past. The laid-back name came from a seat height of just 27in (686mm), a characteristic which would appear again in the Huggers of the future.

SPECIFICATIONS

Engine	aircooled OHV V-twin
Capacity	74cu in (1,207cc)
Transmission	4-speed
Power	60bhp
Weight	550lb (249kg)
Wheelbase	63in (1,600mm)
Top speed	98mph (158kph)

Although the 80-inch Shovelhead first appeared on the FLH Electra Glide in the Low Rider's debut year, the FXS was initially powered by the established 74-inch Shovel. The engine came finished in crinkle black paint with highly polished outer covers. Both exhaust pipes curved back along the right side below a new "1200" air-cleaner cover, before thumping the atmosphere through a single chromed muffler. The revised frame was heavily raked and fitted with highway pegs, allowing the rider to stretch out, like the latter-day *Easy Rider* the styling sought to emulate.

Chassis components included Japanese Showa telescopic forks, chromed twin rear shock absorbers and dual front disc brakes. Sadly, the stoppers were still disconcertingly feeble in their effect, although the rear was relatively fierce with massive leverage available at the pedal. The puny forks, too, were prone to flex while the short-travel rear suspension units were at the same time both harsh and under-damped. It would be a while before any heavyweight Harley aspired to even the sketchiest handling prowess.

ABOVE The Low Rider was built by Milwaukee, but born in the biker heaven of the United States.

BELOW The FXS-1200 Low Rider was described as "one mean machine" when it first came on to the scene.

Quicksilver handling, though, wasn't what the FXS was all about. The model was an instant success, hitting the public's wish-list almost as soon as it was unveiled. It was comfortably out-selling the Super Glide by its second year, with almost 10,000 examples built. Clearly, the Low Rider concept was here to stay and the breed benefited from a steady stream of improvements in succeeding years. Along the way, they spawned eye-catching sister models, such as the 80-inch FXB Sturgis of 1980 – the year after the FXS itself was first offered with the larger Shovelhead mill.

The biggest novelty came in 1983 with the much revised FXSB Low Rider. The "B" represented the adoption of the Aramid-fibre toothed belts first seen on the Sturgis for both primary and secondary drive.

A small number of late-1984 examples may have received the new 80-inch Evolution motor, but it wasn't until the FXRS "Custom Sport" Low Rider of 1985 that this much-improved engine became widespread. When a five-speed transmission was grafted on to the same model 12 months later, a new Low Rider era had arrived.

BELOW This 1985 FXRS Custom picks up the tradition of V-Twin power that was started by the Knucklehead, Panhead and Shovelhead.

LEFT AND RIGHT The FXS caught on almost instantly, becoming Milwaukee's best-selling model by 1978.

LEFT Although built in 1992, this Low Rider Sport displays features similar to the original FXS.

FXST SOFTAIL, 1984

The original FXST Softail was more than just a popular and significant model for Harley-Davidson. By bolting a new Evolution V-twin engine into a cleverly engineered and sumptuously styled hardtail-look chassis, the firm created a cruiser for the ages and one of its greatest ever machines.

With its classically clean look, founded on the way that its hidden suspension units gave the illusion of an old-fashioned rigid rear end, the Softail encapsulated the firm's growing design confidence and ability to combine traditional style with increasing refinement.

One reason the Softail made such an impact is that it took two great leaps forward in one model, and at a critical time for Harley. On its launch in 1984 – shortly after the management buyout, and with the company's future in the balance – it debuted the V2 Evolution engine, whose aluminium cylinder barrels and many other innovations added power, refinement and reliability over the old iron-barrelled unit.

But, as its name suggests, the Softail's defining feature was its hard-tail look chassis. The ingenious hidden suspension system was designed and patented by an independent, Missouri-based engineer named Bill Davis, as a modification to his own Super Glide. Davis discussed selling his idea to Harley and, when discussions broke down, set up a firm to market the design as the "Sub Shock", before in 1982 reaching an agreement to sell his patents, prototypes and tooling to the Milwaukee factory.

Willie G. Davidson's Softail design cleverly emphasised the apparently suspensionless rear

SPECIFICATIONS

Engine	aircooled OHV V-twin
Capacity	82cu in (1,340cc)
Transmission	4- (later 5-) speed
Power	69bhp
Weight	604lbs (274kg)
Wheelbase	66.3in (1,685mm)
Top speed	105mph (169kph)

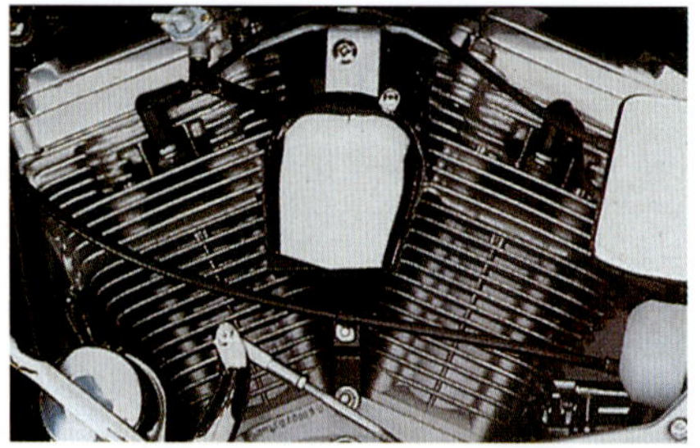

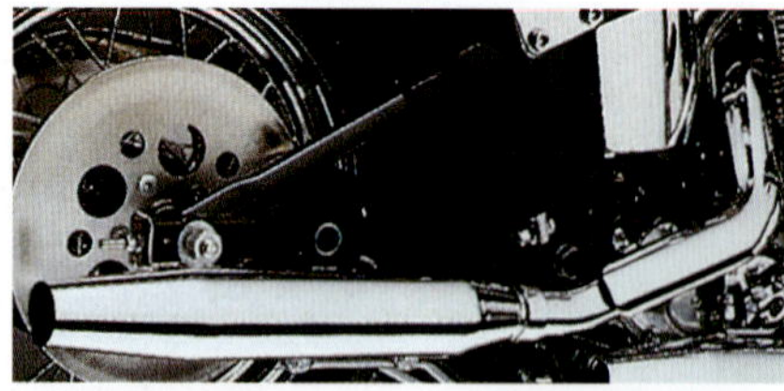

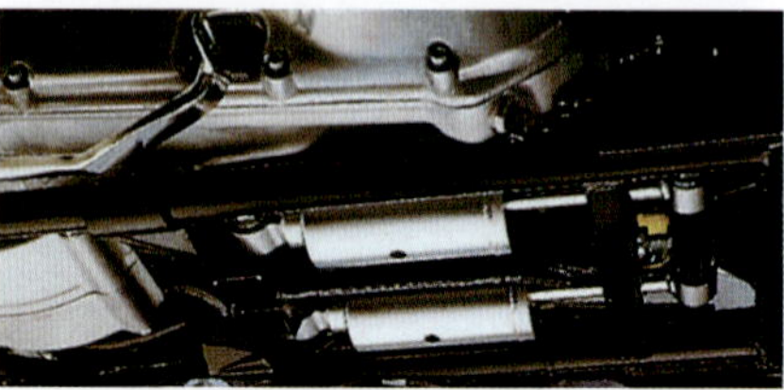

TOP, CENTRE, ABOVE AND ABOVE LEFT The earliest versions of the Softail featured Evo engines with four-speed transmissions, although contemporary FLs enjoyed five speeds. Even a kick start was originally retained.

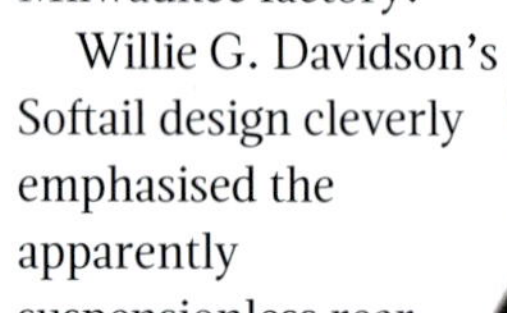

LEFT The first FXST's handsome Evo engine and hardtail-look frame was an instantly popular combination.

RIGHT Harley's promotional image adds atmosphere with dry-ice smoke but the original Softail required no assistance to make a huge mark on the cruiser market.

end, whose twin Showa shock units, working in tension rather than the usual compression, gave 4in (103mm) of travel, fairly generous by Harley standards. Such was the Softail's simple elegance that it would probably have been a hit even if powered by the old Shovelhead motor, but the adoption of the dramatically superior Evo unit confirmed that this was a mighty leap for Milwaukee.

With its new light alloy top-end the Softail produced around 70bhp at 5,000rpm and a withering 84lb.ft (114Nm) of torque at just 3,600rpm. Indeed, the spread of power was so immense that almost no-one complained that 1984 examples had to make do with four-speed gearboxes. A five-speed cluster was installed for 1985, by which time a lighter diaphragm spring clutch had also appeared. Meanwhile, the Evolution engine's redesigned combustion chambers, stronger connecting rods, new electronic ignition and uprated lubrication system had begun to earn Harley a reputation for much improved reliability

The chassis was characterized by an immense 66.3in (1,685mm) wheelbase and a seat height of 1in (25mm) lower than even a Low Rider's seat. Fuel is carried in the familiar, bulbous, two-piece Fat Bob tank, split across the mid-line, with a speedometer set in the centre. Wheels were wire-spoked, 21in (533mm) front and 16in (406mm) rear, carrying a single hydraulic disc apiece. Unlike contemporary Glides, the 80-inch engine was solidly mounted, although rubber-insulated handlebars and footrests compensated to some extent. Softails may have been stylish, but smooth they were not.

The low saddle and forward-mounted "highway" pegs imposed an appropriately laid-back riding position. As for handling: well, the Softail didn't – it just sort of rumbled from A to B and all the better if that didn't include too many fast corners. The suspension at both ends was woefully under-damped, the front forks were characteristically soft and woolly, and the rear was, frankly, harsh. Nonetheless, the expansive wheelbase and conservative steering geometry kept things more or less in line. Besides, this was a bike for cruising.

It was a measure of the overall rightness of the concept that, superficially at least, Softails would appear little changed for decades to come. This disguised the vast improvements Harley-Davidson made in build quality and detailing from the time of the FXST's launch.

Above all, there was the inescapable fact that this inspired piece of post-modern design was a huge and instant success. Although the FXST was not the most practical model that Harley-Davidson has ever built, it was one of the most eye-catching, technically brilliant and significant of all.

LEFT The Softail Custom introduced in 1987 was the first of many models inspired by the original FXST.

FXSTS SPRINGER SOFTAIL, 1988

In late 1987, the motorcycle world took one look and pinched itself – twice. The Springer Softail that Harley-Davidson unveiled for the 1988 model year not only looked distinctly different to current Milwaukee models, it looked like no new motorcycle of the previous 40 years.

Gone were the telescopic front forks to which we had become accustomed. In their place was a trellis-work of bright-chromed steel members, linkages and springs. It was called "Springer", and was as audacious as it was surreal.

As Harley said at the time, the new front-end wasn't just reborn, it was re-invented. The Springer front end was styled along the lines of the girder forks seen on almost every make of motorcycle from before the 1920s until the late 1940s, but the technology and the detail were all-new. Using computer-aided design (CAD) and the latest materials, Milwaukee had created a system which not only afforded an acceptable level of wheel travel (around 4in/100mm) and suspension control, but which freed its designers to make the styling statement of the year.

LEFT The Springer has always been exclusive. Around 1,350 were produced in its first year, compared to more than 14,000 other Softail models.

SPECIFICATIONS

Engine	aircooled OHV V-twin
Capacity	82cu in (1,340cc)
Transmission	5-speed
Power	69bhp
Weight	625lbs (284kg)
Wheelbase	64.6in (1,640mm)
Top speed	100mph (161kph)

BELOW No-one pretends Springers give state-of-the-art handling, but who needs it on a cruise in the sun?

ABOVE A modern damper unit (with Harley sticker) controls the movement of the Springer forks.

We now had retro-tech at both ends: Springer at the front to accompany Softail lines at the rear. The engine, naturally, was the doughty 80-inch Evo, styled for its new role and fitted with staggered shorty dual exhausts.

Like all "conventional" Softail models, the new Springer offered defiantly lazy steering geometry. In this case, a shallow 32-degree steering head gave a generous 5¼in (133mm) of trail. The wheelbase was a lanky 64.6in (1,640mm). Unlike standard Softails, Springers rolled on slow-steering 21in front wheels, with a 16in hoop at the rear. Inevitably, the result wasn't quite at the cutting edge of modern suspension performance. Any Softail rear end could be harsh, especially over freeway seams, and the latter-day girders lacked the control of even Fat Boy's massive telescopic forks. Such judgements missed the point, however. Of all the Milwaukee models, Springers were unashamedly machines for stately cruising – and were as far removed from a Japanese "crotch rocket" as a 1959 Cadillac.

If 1987 marked the Springer's debut, then 1997 marked what many regard as its finest hour. As well as offering practical accessories such as leather saddlebags as standard, the 1997 FLSTS

ABOVE The Springer's slender suspension arms and exposed springs give a very different look to telescopics.

ABOVE The Heritage Springer's big fenders, whitewall tyres and fishtail mufflers added to its period look.

Heritage Springer Softail went further down the classic road, combining even more vintage styling with modern retro-technology. "Loaded with chrome and leather," publicity material hailed at the time, "the Heritage Springer Softail screams nostalgia." And so it did, from its bright-chromed fishtail mufflers to its deeply-valanced mudguards and whitewall tyres. Even at first glance, the result was sublime, the level of detail extraordinary. Note the nostalgic front fender-tip light and the "retro-1940s tombstone tail-light once commonplace on Harley-Davidsons decades ago." Admire a seat with a leather fringed valance "embossed with a basket-weave pattern and accented with conchos".

The ultimate factory custom had come a long way from the original Super Glide, but that didn't stop it being discontinued in 2003.

BELOW After-market fishtail silencers and two-tone paint contrive to make this Springer look for all the world like a 1946 FL.

FXRS-CONV LOW RIDER CONVERTIBLE, 1989

Characterized by their brutal, low lines, fat rear wheels and skinny front ends, Low Riders represented one of the core "families" of Milwaukee models from 1977 until the mid-1990s.

ABOVE The Convertible became the ultimate Harley all-rounder upon its launch in 1989.

Beginning with the 74-inch Shovelhead FXS in 1977, the range grew to include seminal spin-offs such as the FXEF Fat Bob and FXB Sturgis. Along the way, Low Rider capacity grew to 80cu in (1,338cc) for 1980 and adopted toothed-belt final drive for the FXSB of 1983. The first Evolution-engine Low Rider, the FXRS Custom Sport, appeared for the 1985 model year, gaining five-speed transmission one year later. By 1987, Harley's "broadest and most versatile range" included Standard, Custom and Sport Edition models, as well as sister models such as the quintessential Super Glide and Sport Glide.

Harley-Davidson literature was always keen to stress Low Riders' unrivalled "combination of style and comfort", and it was certainly true that the range always veered towards the practical end of the style scale: cruisers that were as adept on the open road as on the city streets.

"They're in their element anywhere there's pavement" was how the brochures put it. It was no idle boast.

This was never more apparent than with the Low Rider Convertible released for the 1989 season. Although not exactly a convertible in the Cadillac

SPECIFICATIONS

Engine	aircooled OHV V-twin
Capacity	82cu in (1,340cc)
Transmission	5-speed
Power	69bhp
Weight	585lbs (265kg)
Wheelbase	64.7in (1,643mm)
Top speed	106mph (170kph)

LEFT AND ABOVE Easily detached screen and saddlebags made the FXRS equally at home in the western deserts as cruising city streets. The 1991 model (above) is en route from the Harley factory at York, Pennsylvania to San Francisco.

BELOW The FXRS-Conv's successor was the Dyna Glide Convertible, with Twin Cam 88 power.

ABOVE Hot dry air and stinging dust make the screen essential in desert conditions.

sense, this model was as close as any two-wheeler needed to be. No longer did owners need to lash luggage wherever they could – this Convertible came complete with leather saddlebags. There was a large, wind-cheating Lexan screen, too. The real beauty of both was that they were detachable, and quickly. Riders setting out for the long haul could leave them on – or, in just a few moments, whip them off for a cruise downtown.

As a touring alternative to Electra Glide overkill, the Convertible was supreme. Its plush seat, standard sissy bar and highway pegs offered reasonable comfort (although the pillion pad was always something of a style-dictated joke), while the screen kept off the worst of road grime and weather. It handled tolerably well, too. The 1½in (39mm) front forks featured air-adjustment and anti-dive. For a heavyweight Harley, ground clearance was also good. Stopping was better than the Milwaukee norm – courtesy of twin hydraulic discs at the front and one at the rear.

The Low Rider look came largely from the choice of wheels: a 19in front rim with a 100/90 tyre, compared to a 16in rear hoop with a fat, 5⅛in- (130mm-) wide tread. Power came from the Evo 82cu in (1,340cc) mill. Although the rubber-mounting wasn't quite in the same league as later Dyna models, it was pretty good. For five years until it gave way to the Dyna series at the end of 1993, the Low Rider Convertible was perhaps the most practical Harley-Davidson model. It was a neat adaptation of a well-sorted design, so there were few improvements during the time. A 1⅜in (40mm) Keihin carb and uprated clutch were introduced in 1990, and other minor details, but essentially the first one was as good as the last. In 1994, the FXRS gave way to another Convertible, the Dyna-series FXDS.

LEFT Possibly not the most handsome chunk of Milwaukee iron, but very definitely one of the most practical. This is a 1992 example.

FLSTF FAT BOY, 1990

If one model could be said to represent Harley-Davidson's relentless rise through the 1990s, it is perhaps the Fat Boy. With its curvaceous and clean lines, monotone paintwork, solid disc wheels and twin shotgun exhausts, it made a uniquely imposing style statement.

Willie G, who along with fellow Milwaukee designer Louie Netz had shaped the Fat Boy, had based it on the Heritage Softail, keeping that model's 82cu in (1,340cc) engine, shrouded front forks, fat tyres and hardtail-inspired rear while stripping back the chrome and much else for a deliberately pared-back image. Instead of the familiar classical themes, the look was 1950s industrial minimalism.

The Fat Boy was a hit and sold more than 4,400 units in its first year of production. In 1991 it was boosted when ridden by Arnold Schwarzenegger in *Terminator 2*, the year's highest grossing movie. Its impact was seemingly undamaged by controversy over its name, which some suggested referenced the Fat Man and Little Boy atomic bombs dropped on Japan during the Second World War, in a dig at rival Japanese manufacturers.

Harley vehemently denied any connection, and Willie G insisted the name had simply been inspired by the Fat Boy's size and shape, when the marketing department had been looking for something simple, memorable and irreverent to call it. Harley's design chief had put in the hard yards during the model's development in the late 1980s, twice riding prototypes to Daytona Bike Week in order to get feedback from the marque faithful.

The Fat Boy received only minor changes to its exhaust, brakes and switchgear until the 2000 model year, when the the whole Softail family got a major shake-up. Only a handful of parts were retained as the Twin Cam

LEFT Solid disc 16in wheels distinguished the Fat Boy on its launch in 1990.

BELOW Only Harley could get away with such a derogatory title – and make it sell.

BELOW The very first FLSTF in metallic grey with yellow highlights is regarded by many as the most handsome.

SPECIFICATIONS

Engine	aircooled OHV V-twin
Capacity	82cu in (1,340cc)
Transmission	5-speed
Power	67bhp
Weight	665lbs (302kg)
Wheelbase	62.5in (1,587mm)
Top speed	105mph (169kph)

TOP The Fat Boy was actually no more of a fatso than other Softails, and its lines were cleaner, as these Evo versions from the late 1990s showed.

ABOVE The Fat Boy's solid look remained in 2023 despite spoked Lakester wheels introduced a year earlier.

88 engine was adopted across the heavyweight range. This was no ordinary Twin Cam, though. Designated the 88B, the engine was developed in parallel with the "stock" 88 and used essentially the same top ends, including the same 88cu in (1,450cc) displacement.

The bottom-end, however, used Harley's first counter-rotating balance shafts to eliminate primary engine vibration. This was necessary because the Softail rear suspension pretty much demanded that the engine be mounted rigidly in the frame. As a consequence, the rubber mounting used to such good effect on other heavyweight models was not a practical option.

That update was followed by several more as Harley's development continued. In 2006 the engine was enlarged to 1,584cc, and fitted with a six-speed gearbox for the first time. In 2018, the Fat Boy was part of the revamp that merged the Softail and Dyna families. It was fitted with the new-generation 1,864cc Milwaukee-Eight 114 engine, and also got a reworked chassis and numerous detail updates.

ABOVE The all-black livery of the 30th anniversary model of 2020 suited the Fat Boy down to the ground.

In 2020, Harley celebrated the Fat Boy's 30th anniversary with a special edition, finished all in black and limited to 2,500 units. It was a fitting tribute to an iconic model that had been one of the firm's most popular for all that time, and which would surely rumble on for many more years.

LEFT For year 2000 the Fat Boy benefited from the new 88B balance-shafted Twin Cam engine.

FXDB STURGIS, 1991

The original Sturgis, the FXB of 1980, had essentially been a Super Glide that was notable for introducing the toothed rubber primary and final drive belts that Harley soon adopted widely. Its successor of 11 years later also debuted a significant technical development.

The original model's name was inspired by the annual South Dakota bike rally; the B stood for Belt.

By contrast, the "Mark II" Sturgis that was launched in 1991 seemed to add little to the Low Rider family from which it sprang. It looked like little more than a black FXRS with modest changes to its rear shocks and oil tank; indeed, the two models shared the same front end.

The major attributes of this new FXDB Sturgis were simplicity itself – just two hard-to-spot pieces of rubber – and with them, a motorcycle was transformed. The Sturgis was a limited edition model – just over 1,500 were produced – but its impact lived on in every subsequent Dyna Glide. The frame, an all-steel structure developed by advanced computer-aided design, was fabricated from a mixture of tubular and forged components with a large-diameter box-section backbone.

The engine isolation system differed from the existing Glide series and Low Rider mounts. These had used three location points with rubber-bonded bolts, rather than the two more sophisticated composite blocks of the Sturgis. The result was startling. The big twin's effective rev range had been limited by low-speed shudders at the bottom end and intrusive vibes at the top. With the Sturgis, that all changed. One could now happily ride at engine speeds where other Hogs would rattle. The FXDB Sturgis also featured a belt drive system that had been simplified and improved since the original model's launch, and was by now fitted to most models in the range.

BELOW The Sturgis was a major leap forward in Harley affairs. It was to give rise to the successful Dyna Glide series.

SPECIFICATIONS

Engine	aircooled OHV V-twin
Capacity	82cu in (1,340cc)
Power	69bhp
Transmission	5-speed
Wheelbase	65.5in (1,665mm)
Weight	597lbs (271kg)
Top speed	106mph (170kph)

ABOVE The belt final drive introduced by the original Sturgis had been widely adopted through the range, and was updated with the 1991 model.

LEFT Stars and stripes had less to do with the Sturgis legacy than did two deceptively simple rubberized blocks.

FXDWG DYNA WIDE GLIDE, 1993

By 1992, the Sturgis no longer existed, but it had spawned a growing Dyna Glide family – first the Dyna Daytona, then the Super Glide Dyna Custom. By 1993, the Dyna Low Rider was closer to the original but the Wide Glide harked back to its namesake of the 1980s.

Both, however, went one stage further than the Sturgis in the anti-vibration stakes, with revised "directionally-controlled" mounting blocks.

Harley's idea was "to combine the look of Low Riders of the late 1970s, with the handling and rubber-mounted ride of today", and it worked startlingly well. The 1993 Dyna Glides were the smoothest Hogs yet, by a margin. Milwaukee's engineers had made a good bike better, even more than they had with the Sturgis. Without so much as laying a hand on the engine, the company had broadened the big V's effective powerband by a quantum amount – a bigger bonus than adding another ten horsepower.

Much of the rest, as was Harley's way, was in the hands of the blend-men and cosmetic engineers. There were "factory ape-hangers", a "tucked-in tail light", "air-foil directionals" and a wide front fork (hence the "Wide Glide") with a 21in, wire-spoked front wheel, as well as a new, one-piece Fat Bob tank, which removed the need of having to fill up two separate fuel tanks each time you ran short on fuel.

To ride the Wide Glide was to marvel at the unprecedented smoothness of the experience – especially after you've grown accustomed to having only forward-mounted footpegs and controls.The ape-hanger handlebars towered somewhere above you, but after a couple of miles it all felt fairly natural and comfortable.

ABOVE The original Wide Glide of the 1980s was a stylish machine but a far less refined one than its namesakes of the following decade.

SPECIFICATIONS

Engine	aircooled OHV V-twin
Capacity	82cu in (1,340cc)
Transmission	5-speed
Power	69bhp
Weight	598lbs (271kg)
Wheelbase	66.1in (1,680mm)
Top speed	106mph (170kph)

ABOVE Inspiration for the Wide Glide name is clear from this shot highlighting the width between the fork legs of a 1993 model.

In that uncanny Harley-Davidson way, the steering was light with excellent low-speed balance.

Turns, however, reveal a lot about the Wide Glide. Even by Harley-Davidson standards, ground clearance was poor. The stand scraped on the left, the muffler on the right, both with sufficient force to pitch you off line. But on the straight, wide highway, it was great to ride.

LEFT For 1999 the new Twin Cam 88 engine was bestowed upon the redoubtable Wide Glide.

FLSTN HERITAGE SOFTAIL NOSTALGIA, 1993

Dubbed the "Cow Glide" on its release for the 1993 model year, the limited-edition Heritage Softail Nostalgia was the fanciest incarnation of Milwaukee's fanciest model line. It would soon prove to be one of the most popular.

The nickname came from its hairy, black-and-white natural cowhide seat and saddlebag inserts, but there were plenty more cosmetic tricks where they came from. Little wonder its creators described it as: "Without doubt, the most distinctive-looking motorcycle in Harley's 1993 line ... nostalgic-looking ... but thoroughly modern." It had already proved a winning formula.

Modern, of course, meant something else in Harley-Davidson's wondrous time-warp world – like whitewall tyres and forks straight out of the 1940s. Ever since beginning life in 1986, the Heritage Softail package had attempted to re-enact the look of the 1949 Hydra-Glide, with its "hardtail" rear and gleaming metal fork shrouds.

ABOVE "Cow Glide" nickname comes from the Nostalgia's black and white hide details.

ABOVE The engine was an 80-inch Evo like any other, but the Nostalgia package set it apart.

Fine detail isn't something you'd normally expect from a device scaling almost one third of a ton, but this was a Harley, so the tank badge was a specially fired enamel named "jewelled cloisonné." Yet at heart, it was essentially an even more customized variant on the Heritage Softail Classic, available only in Birch White and Black two-tone, with black and chrome engine trim. Power came from an identical 80-inch Evo engine booming out the same 69bhp at a mere 5,000rpm and a mammoth 70-or-so pound-feet (95Nm) of torque at an even lowlier 3,500rpm. Like the rest of the 1993 range, the Nostalgia benefited from a taller final drive (61-tooth rear pulley) for lower revs at cruising speeds. Improved brake and clutch levers, master cylinder sight glasses and a new, neater engine-breather system also arrived for the same model year.

To ride, it was inevitably much like any other Softail, particularly the Classic

LEFT The "Cow Glide" was derived from the stock Heritage Softail, here seen cruising in company with a Low Rider.

SPECIFICATIONS

Engine	aircooled OHV V-twin
Capacity	82cu in (1,340cc)
Transmission	5-speed
Power	69bhp
Weight	710lbs (322kg)
Wheelbase	64.2in (1,630mm)
Top speed	100mph (161kph)

ABOVE They say that nostalgia isn't what it used to be. No, in this case it's much better.

or Fat Boy (with which it shared wheel sizes), steering geometry (32-degrees rake, 5.8in/147mm trail), forks, footboards, handlebars and almost every other relevant dimension. The only significant differences were a fuel tank almost ¼ gallon (1 litre) larger and the addition of a hefty 93lbs (42kg) of mass compared to the basic Softail model.

With suspension springing as soft as the Cow Glide's considerable weight would allow, handling fell somewhere between sedate and ponderous. Over bumps, the steering was vague and accompanied by a slow weave whenever the road turned lumpy. As with the brakes, it was adequate if it was ridden with prudence.

Since Softail engines were not rubber-mounted, the vibrations intruded towards the top of the rev range even with its higher overall gearing – or as its makers preferred, the bike "rumbles with the echoes of Harleys past."

At a first glance, most onlookers took the Nostalgia – which was fresh from the factory floor – to be either the real 1949 McCoy or a bespoke special that had been put together at huge expense by one of Hollywood's celebrity custom farms. Harley-Davidson's retro illusion was that good, yet only 2,700 examples of the limited-edition Nostalgia were ever built.

Even at $13,000 – just $3,100 less than the most lavish Glide – demand for these highly-desirable models far exceeded supply. Second-hand "Cow Glide" Nostalgias were soon changing hands at far more than list price. Mark up another masterpiece for Willie G. Davidson and his men.

RIGHT The Heritage Softail front-end blend of fork shrouds, big fender and whitewall rubber goes all the way back to the 1949 Hydra-Glide.

FXDX DYNA SUPER GLIDE SPORT, 1999

The Dyna Super Glide Sport made a big impact on its launch, and an even bigger one when revamped just a year later. In 1999, the original Sport debuted the Twin Cam 88 engine and quickly became popular, especially in Europe.

For the 2000 model year, The Dyna Super Glide Sport's already capable chassis was uprated to create by far the sportiest cruiser ever from Milwaukee.

The Twin Cam 88 engine took its name from its twin camshafts – which still operated pushrods – and capacity of 88 cubic inches, or 1,450cc, up from the 1,340cc, 80-cube Evolution engine. Apart from its larger, oval-shaped air filter cover the new motor looked little different. But Harley had spent six years developing it, and had done a very thorough job. Besides the revised cam system and extra capacity, the Twin Cam lump was strengthened throughout with larger bearings and better lubrication, to the extent that very few Evo components remained.

ABOVE The original Super Glide Sport was among the first models powered by the Twin Cam 88 engine.

SPECIFICATIONS	
Engine	aircooled OHV V-twin
Capacity	88cu in (1,450cc)
Transmission	5-speed
Power	86bhp
Weight	614lbs (279kg)
Wheelbase	64in (1,623mm)
Top speed	115mph (185kph)

That Twin Cam unit was the original Sport's undoubted star turn, managing to retain the look, sound and feel of a traditional Harley unit while putting out enough extra power and torque to make the bike feel distinctly more lively. The Sport was stronger than any Evo-engined model both at low revs,

ABOVE The Twin Cam unit featured camshaft drive by chain and was more powerful and robust than its predecessor.

LEFT Despite its name, the Sport was happy at a gentle pace.

ABOVE The 2000-model Super Glide Sport's uprated suspension, tyres and brakes made it notably well suited to hard riding on a twisty road.

where it pulled cleanly and harder from below 2000rpm, and at higher speeds, where it accelerated with an urgency that no previous standard Harley could approach – all the way to a genuine top speed of about 110mph (177kph).

Harley said that chassis rigidity was increased by the design of the Twin Cam engine, whose gearbox was more solidly bolted on. At around 650lbs (295kg) with fuel the Sport was no lightweight, but it felt reasonably agile and handled pretty well, aided by fairly soft but competent suspension. Its twin front discs gave a reasonable amount of braking power, too, despite their low-tech caliper design, and there was a reasonable amount of ground clearance.

Chassis performance was substantially raised just a year later, though, when Harley treated the Super Glide Sport to a serious chassis overhaul. Its new Showa front forks were multi-adjustable, and were pushed further through the yokes to quicken the steering. The same Japanese firm's rear shocks gained dual-rate springs and rebound damping adjustment. The front brake was uprated with new four-piston calipers from Haynes; the rear tyre was a wider, softer version of Dunlop's Elite, giving added grip at the expense of faster wear.

The Sport's handling was a revelation, compared to most previous Harleys, and most other firms' cruisers too. Its standard suspension settings were similar to the previous model's, and were fine at a gentle pace. For harder riding both ends could be firmed-up to give a very well-controlled ride. The front brakes provided strong stopping power, too, requiring little lever effort, and the grippy tyres allowing enjoyably enthusiastic cornering.

Other updates included a tougher drive belt, uprated battery and modified sidestand. They combined with the chassis updates to make the Dyna Super Glide Sport into a more practical machine that still had all the laid-back style of a traditional Harley. But which, if someone picked a fight with it on a twisty road, was capable of taking off its jacket, rolling up its sleeves and trading blows with some much sportier looking opponents.

LEFT The FXDX had a typically clean Harley cruiser style.

FXDF DYNA FAT BOB, 2008

The Fat Bob was 100 per cent streetfighter. Twin headlamps, flat drag bars and slotted aluminium wheels enhanced its solid look. The two-into-one-into-two "Tommy Gun" exhaust system added sparkle, contrasting with matt-finish paintwork.

ABOVE The Fat Bob gleams in the sun on the bank of the Hudson River on its launch in New York in July 2007.

The image was big, bad and belligerent, and the Fat Bob felt that way from its rider's seat too, thanks to flat handlebars and forward-set footpegs.

According to Harley, this latest model in the Dyna family was named after "the iconic fuel tank shape that has defined generations of Harley-Davidson factory customs". The Fat Bob's small front fender was appropriate, given that the original "bobbers" were cut-down bikes built in the late 1940s and early 1950s, often by former American Second World War servicemen.

For all the Fat Bob's edgy style and marketing hype, the shortest of rides was sufficient to confirm that this American pit bull of a bike was as docile as a spaniel puppy. Its Twin Cam 96 engine was the same fuel-injected V-twin that powered all the Dyna and Touring models for 2008, differing from the Softail motor only in that it had no balancer shaft and was rubber mounted in the tubular steel frame. Producing a claimed 94lb.ft (127N.m) of torque at just 3,200rpm, it generated

SPECIFICATIONS

Engine	aircooled OHV V-twin
Capacity	96cu in (1,584cc)
Transmission	5-speed
Power	85bhp
Weight	671lbs (305kg)
Wheelbase	63.8in (1,620mm)
Top speed	115mph (185kph)

BELOW Twin headlights, flat bars and chunky front end gave the Fat Bob an aggressive and distinctive look.

plenty of grunt all the way from idle.

On the open road, the Fat Bob showed a deceptive ability to cover ground quickly. The efficient rubber mounting system allowed the bike to cruise effortlessly with 70mph (113kph) or more showing on its tank-mounted speedo, the big engine rustling lazily below thanks to the tall sixth gear, and with plenty of instant acceleration in hand when required.

Chassis performance was very respectable too, although the Bob's fat tyres and fairly raked-out forks (30 degrees) meant that slow-speed direction changes required firm pressure on the relatively narrow bars. The bike's length and 671lbs (305kg) of weight made themselves known at times, too. Even so its front brake blend of twin front discs gripped by four-piston calipers, plus a twin-pot caliper at the rear, slowed the bike with reassuring authority, aided by the braided hose that was introduced to all Dyna models for 2008.

Straight-line stability was predictably unshakeable, and the suspension was reasonably plush and well-damped, given that the chromed so-called "Full Metal Jacket" shocks provided a less than generous 3.1in (79mm) of travel. But the Fat Bob's wind-blown, feet-forward riding position put almost all of its rider's weight through the saddle. Although that was fairly well padded, this bike was definitely not built for touring.

For shorter trips or blasting round town, though, many found the big twin-headlamp Harley's chunky, aggressive image difficult to resist.

The Fat Bob combined tough, uncompromising style and truck-loads of V-twin character with improbably rider-friendly performance. That was enough to make it a lasting success.

ABOVE The front brake's combination of twin front discs and four-piston calipers gave reliably powerful stopping.

ABOVE The Twin Cam 96 V-twin's vibration was controlled by rubber mounts rather than balancer shafts.

ABOVE Its pair of 60W quartz halogen headlights provided the Fat Bob with plenty of candle power.

RIGHT The Fat Bob's upright, feet-forward riding position was better suited to short trips than to touring.

FXCW SOFTAIL ROCKER, 2008

In 2008, almost four decades after *Easy Rider*, a second bout of chopper mania had swept through the United States. Harley-Davidson, so central to the story of American motorcycling since the movie's launch in 1969, joined in with a spectacular creation of its own.

Milwaukee's response to the hordes of chopper manufacturers was the Softail Rocker which, with its kicked-out front forks and minimalist rear end, was the firm's most radical bike yet.

The Rocker had the air of an exotic, hand-built creation from *American Chopper* or *Biker Build-Off*, popular TV shows that had fanned the chopper craze. Above its Twin Cam 96B engine was a stretched-out gas tank, a low-slung single saddle, and a swept-back, V-shaped handlebar on curved risers. The forks' length and radical 36.5-degree rake put the slim, five-spoke front wheel way out front.

At the back, the contrastingly fat, 240mm rear Dunlop's width was emphasized by a tight-fitting hugger.

SPECIFICATIONS

Engine	aircooled OHV V-twin
Capacity	96cu in (1,584cc)
Transmission	6-speed
Power	85bhp
Weight	660lbs (300kg)
Wheelbase	69.3in (1760mm)
Top speed	115mph (185kph)

RIGHT The Rocker went round corners remarkably well for a bike with such long, kicked-out forks and a truck-like wheelbase.

Harley's "Rockertail" rear end was a variant of the familiar Softail design, giving a hardtail look while incorporating twin shocks beneath the engine. The Rocker was seriously long and low, with a gigantic, 69.3in (1,760mm) wheelbase, and a seat height of 24.5in (622mm) that was the lowest in Harley's range.

Even its finish was distinctive. Frame colour matched that of the tank and fenders, which on the standard model came in black, blue or dark red. The Rocker C added pinstripe flames on tank and front fender, and also featured the ingenious Trick Seat – a pillion pad that folded away beneath the rider's saddle when not in use.

Harley's development team had managed to make the radical Rocker ride remarkably normally. Its big Twin Cam 96B lump was torquey, smooth due to its balancer shaft, and long-legged thanks to its overdrive sixth gear. And it handled improbably well given its length and geometry, steering without too much effort and absorbing most bumps to remain reasonably comfortable.

LEFT The Rocker C differed from the base model with its flame-effect tank graphics and retractable pillion seat.

So the Rocker looked a million dollars and was great fun to ride. But unfortunately for Harley, its launch in 2008 coincided with the chopper craze collapsing along with the global economy. This most radical of Softail models was also one of the shortest lived.

RIGHT Inevitably the Rocker's rear view was dominated by twin exhaust mufflers and a hugely wide tyre.

FAR RIGHT The Twin Cam 96B engine gave the Rocker a smooth cruising feel with the help of its balancer shaft and a tall, overdrive sixth gear.

BREAKOUT

Harley returned to the long, low theme in 2013 with the Breakout, which echoed the Rocker with its kicked-out front end, this time holding a thin, 21in front wheel with distinctive cast spokes. The rear tyre was contrastingly fat, combining with the Breakout's minimalist style to give a drag-bike image. Power came from a Twin Cam 103B engine, or the bigger, 1,802cc Twin Cam 110B in the limited-edition CVO Breakout.

Both engines delivered plenty of straight-line punch, to match handling that was resolutely stable in a straight line but required plenty of effort on a twisty road. The Breakout was popular, even so, and in 2018 was uprated with the more powerful Milwaukee-Eight engine. By 2023 it was powered by the even gruntier Milwaukee-Eight 117 unit, and had become an established star of Harley's cruiser family.

ABOVE The Breakout caught the eye with its long, low profile and large-diameter cast front wheel.

BELOW Flat bars contributed to the Breakout's drag bike image.

RIGHT Handling was reassuringly stable, but the Breakout was far better suited to straight-line cruising than to twisty roads.

FXLRS LOW RIDER S, 2016

The Low Rider S was a Milwaukee mongrel. As its name suggested, the black bike was a development of the standard Low Rider, latest in a distinguished line dating back to the famed original of 1977. And there was something distinctly special about the S model.

LEFT Its flat bars, low seat and black finish gave the Low Rider S a purposeful feel, even before its hotted-up Twin Cam 110 engine was fired up.

BELOW The S-model's black finish extended to its Showa rear shocks and its exhaust system, which featured shotgun silencers on the right side.

While the standard Low Rider was a member of the Dyna family of rubber-mounted V-twins, the Low Rider S joined the Fat Boy S and Softail Slim S in an elite group of S models, powered by the 110cu in (1,802cc) engine from Harley's Custom Vehicle Operation special editions.

SPECIFICATIONS

Engine	aircooled OHV V-twin
Capacity	110cu in (1,802cc)
Transmission	6-speed
Power	80bhp
Weight	670lbs (305kg)
Wheelbase	64.2in (1,630mm)
Top speed	115mph (185kph)

Essentially the Low Rider S was a hotted-up version of the standard Low Rider, and was sufficiently aggressive to justify that S in its name. Its near-flat handlebar sat behind a bikini fairing, and combined with the ultra-low seat and mid-mounted footrests to give a slightly sportier riding position than the standard model's.

The key feature was that engine, officially the Screamin' Eagle Twin Cam 110. It was basically the standard Low Rider's Twin Cam 103 lump, bored-out from 1,690cc to 1,802cc. The S-model also gained a high-performance air filter sticking out on the right, and a new twin-pipe exhaust. That was finished in black, as was just about everything else including the fairing, gas tank and tailpiece. There

ABOVE Twin front discs gripped by radial calipers gave the Low Rider S plenty of stopping power; front suspension was from Showa of Japan.

ABOVE A high-performance air filter helped the Screamin' Eagle Twin Cam 110 V-twin engine deliver exhilarating midrange performance.

was also plenty of black on the upgraded forks and shocks, which were from Showa of Japan.

The Low Rider S was a classical hot rod, designed primarily for straight-line thrills. The big motor's peak output was only about 80bhp, but its low-down grunt made the S-bike seriously quick. When the throttle was wound open at low speed, the rider was shoved against the seat-back as huge reserves of midrange torque sent the bike charging forward like a rampaging buffalo, staying smooth thanks to the engine's rubber mounting.

The chassis backed it up, providing high-speed stability plus respectably light and neutral steering. The S-model was no lightweight, at 670lbs (350kg) with fuel, but its suspension worked well, delivering decent ride quality and control. There was powerful braking from twin front discs with radial calipers. For a cruiser there was even generous tyre grip and ground clearance.

If the S-model's storming performance and capable chassis impressed, its character very much added to the experience. At idle there was something distinctly malevolent about the bike, with that huge rubber-mounted engine jiggling about. With a blip of the throttle it magically smoothed, as the slurping from the air intake was drowned by the din from the shotgun pipes.

This big black bruiser was also respectably practical, provided its rider didn't want to carry a pillion. Its bikini fairing gave some wind protection without generating much turbulence; its big tank was good for over 150 miles (241km); its seat was reasonably comfortable.

Less positively, the Low Rider S was far from cheap, costing almost 20 per cent more than the standard model. But it was much less expensive than Harley's exotic CVO factory customs. And the S-bike delivered an adrenaline hit to compare with any previous aircooled streetbike from Milwaukee, plus a feeling of riding something special.

BELOW Well-damped suspension and generous ground clearance helped make the S-model fun on a twisty road.

FXBB STREET BOB, 2018

The 2018-model Street Bob highlighted Harley-Davidson's ability to revamp models over the years while maintaining their essential style and market positioning. The original Dyna Street Bob of 2006 had earned its name by taking the bobber concept seriously.

That original Dyna Street Bob was a stripped-down streetfighter with ape-hanger bars, solo saddle, laced wheels and plenty of attitude; the base-model bike of the twin-shock Dyna family. It hit the spot so sweetly that it became Harley's best-selling model in Europe. Two years later it was among the Dyna models updated with the new 1,584cc Twin Cam 96 engine.

For 2018 the Street Bob was comprehensively updated and no longer a Dyna, having been given a new single-shock chassis and incorporated into the expanded Softail family.

This new-generation Street Bob was powered by the Milwaukee-Eight 107 powerplant, with twin camshafts and capacity of 1,745cc. It was a much more powerful and refined bike than the original model, but it still featured ape-hangers, solo

ABOVE For 2013 the Street Bob came with optional metal-flake paintwork and was a member of the Dyna family, with twin rear shock units.

ABOVE The Milwaukee-Eight 107 engine was the smaller of Harley's eight-valve units but had plenty of punch.

LEFT The 2018-model Street Bob followed its old namesakes' bobber-inspired format of high bars, laced wheels and minimalist rear end.

SPECIFICATIONS

Engine	aircooled OHV V-twin
Capacity	107cu in (1,745cc)
Transmission	6-speed
Power	90bhp
Weight	653lbs (297kg)
Wheelbase	64.2in (1,630mm)
Top speed	115mph (185kph)

seat and laced wheels, and was the least expensive bike in an all-new Softail range.

In many ways it was one of the best, too. Unlike some siblings, the Street Bob was initially available only with the smaller, 107cu in eight-valve V-twin, rather than also with the torquier, 1,868cc Milwaukee-Eight 114 unit. But that was not a major drawback. Even the smaller Milwaukee-Eight 107 engine produced a generous 107lb.ft (145N.m) of torque at just 3,000rpm, and always seemed to generate sufficient grunt for entertaining performance.

The solidly-mounted V-twin impressed whether it was pulling crisply with barely 1,500rpm showing on the small digital display set into the handlebar clamp, or staying smooth when spinning harder. The relatively light V-twin also handled sufficiently well to be fun, steering with ease and even managing respectable lean angles before its mid-mounted footrests touched down. Its single-disc front brake was no more than adequate, but could be relied on when given a firm squeeze of the lever.

This Street Bob was a bike that at first glance resembled something straight out of a 1970s movie, but which performed, handled and looked after its rider as a modern motorbike should. As a stripped-down street-fighter with plenty of attitude, it hit the mark just as surely as its namesake had back in 2006.

ABOVE The Street Bob was relatively light and had generous ground clearance by Harley standards, which helped make it around the bends in the road.

ABOVE Small headlight and front fender were Street Bob staples but the 2018 model's gaitered forks were new.

BELOW Its Softail rear end and blacked-out exhaust mufflers gave this Street Bob a distinctly different look.

SOFTAIL STANDARD

The Street Bob had traditionally been the base model of Harley's big twins, but in 2020 – following the demise of the liquid-cooled Street and aircooled Sportster families – it provided the entry-level model for the whole marque – albeit with the new name of Softail Standard.

With unchanged Milwaukee-Eight 107 engine, paintwork in black only, and front forks with no gaiters, the Softail Standard offered unchanged performance and plenty of opportunity for customization. A year later, the Street Bob itself was upgraded with the Milwaukee-Eight 114 engine, adding punch along with a choice of four colour schemes.

BELOW For 2020 the Softail Standard came with paintwork in any colour provided it was black.

FXFBS FAT BOB, 2018

The word "bobber" had become a motorcycling cliché in 2018, with numerous manufacturers having launched models of that name, inspired by the original "bob-jobs" that had had their front fenders removed and rear ends shortened, or bobbed, after the Second World War.

Harley-Davidson, of course, had originally produced most of those bikes, and had been humming the bobber tune for years. The Fat Bob name had been introduced back in 1979, and returned to the line-up in 2008 with a fat-tanked, stripped-down Dyna model notable for its round twin headlights.

Ten years later, a rectangular LED headlight was the most visible feature of this new-generation Fat Bob, which was arguably the star of the revamped, eight-model Softail family that combined the old Softail and Dyna clans. All eight bikes were powered by the Milwaukee-Eight engine, which had been introduced in the touring range a year earlier. The Fat Bob was one of several that came in both Milwaukee-Eight 107 and 114 sizes, equating to 1,745 or 1,868cc.

SPECIFICATIONS

Engine	aircooled OHV V-twin
Capacity	114cu in (1,868cc)
Transmission	6-speed
Power	90bhp
Weight	673lbs (306kg)
Wheelbase	63.6in (1,615mm)
Top speed	120mph (193kph)

ABOVE The Fat Bob lived up to its name with its wide headlight, chunky look and cut-down fenders.

BELOW Graphics featured bar-and-shield badge, with Harley name on the top.

ABOVE Like several of the new Softails the Fat Bob came with either Milwaukee-Eight 114 or 107 engine.

Harley's product planning chief called the Fat Bob the firm's "zombie apocalypse escape vehicle", and there was a distinct touch of two-wheeled Hummer about the chunky V-twin. Its drag bars, tank-mounted instrument panel, relatively tall seat and forward-set footrests combined to give an aggressive, snub-nosed look and a wind-blown but roomy riding position.

Chassis design was all new, a lighter and stiffer steel frame and swing-arm contributing to a handy 33lbs (15kg) weight reduction. All the new Softails received uprated suspension and single, instead of twin, rear shocks. The alpha-male Fat Bob alone was awarded a higher specification, incorporating steeper steering geometry, upside-down front forks and a second front brake disc.

BELOW Instrumentation was a tank-mounted tacho with digital speedo inset.

With its larger engine option, in particular, this Fat Bob was a distinct step up from its predecessor in both engine and chassis performance. The Milwaukee-Eight 114 powerplant churned out V-twin torque almost from idle, feeling docile around town and then tuning all American pit bull when the throttle was tweaked.

Although the standard exhaust was fairly quiet, the solidly mounted motor added character by vibrating just enough to be involving but not annoying.

That stiffened chassis worked well too, though the Fat Bob's broad tyres meant it required a fair bit of muscle to initiate quick direction changes. The suspension was fairly firm yet gave supple ride quality, and the big bike cornered well enough to be fun, even offering a respectable amount of ground clearance. The second front disc helped it stop hard, without requiring a fierce squeeze of the lever.

The Fat Bob was respectably sophisticated, too, with features including keyless ignition, and a USB socket under its steering head. Almost four decades after the original Fat Bob had introduced the combination of big-inch V-twin engine, wide tank and cut-down fenders to the masses, its latest descendant had its stubby finger right on motorcycling's pulse.

BELOW Straight-line performance from the 114cu in engine was immense, with strong torque almost from idle.

FLHCSANV HERITAGE CLASSIC ANNIVERSARY, 2023

When Harley was looking for ways to celebrate its 120th anniversary, a special edition model was an obvious choice. The firm ultimately created seven breathed-on bikes for 2023, including the Heritage Classic Anniversary that gave one of its best-loved models a subtly different look.

The Heritage Classic Anniversary – or FLHCSANV, as the recipient of possibly Milwaukee's longest ever model code was surely known by very few people – was the latest in a line that stretched back to 1986 and the Heritage Softail. Variations on the Heritage trail since had featured two-tone paintwork, whitewall tyres, and even the cowhide seat and pannier inserts of the 1993-model Heritage Softail Nostalgia.

The Anniversary gained its distinct look from unique red-and-black paintwork, new badges and a numbered plaque on its handlebar clamp. Fresh details included colour-matched inserts in its air filter cover, and premium material used for the seat covers.

Everything else remained as it had been since 2018, when the Heritage Classic had been introduced as part of the merging of the Softail and Dyna families, at which point it was fitted with the Milwaukee-Eight engine in either 107 or 114cu in capacities. Styling was

ABOVE The Anniversary model was based on the standard Heritage Classic that had been a versatile and popular model since its launch in 2018.

SPECIFICATIONS

Engine	aircooled OHV V-twin
Capacity	114cu in (1,868cc)
Transmission	6-speed
Power	90bhp
Weight	726lbs (330kg)
Wheelbase	64.2in (1,630mm)
Top speed	115mph (185kph)

LEFT Harley's Anniversary finish included red-and-black paintwork, new badges and revised covers for the seat and air filter.

RIGHT When powered by the big Milwaukee-Eight 114 engine, in particular, the Anniversary offered effortless straight-line performance.

BELOW Behind the removable windscreen, the Anniversary's handlebar clamp incorporated a plaque confirming the bike's vehicle number.

revamped at the same time, as Harley attempted the difficult task of making it look more up-to-date, without losing its retro appeal.

The new Classic's LED lights, blacked-out engine and other parts give a subtly different, edgier vibe. "It's Young Elvis from the 1960s, with energy and black leather, not the 1970s Elvis with his white jump suit and more weight," explained Harley stylist Kirt Rasmussen.

Inevitably some of the previous model's vintage charm was lost along with the chrome and whitewalls, but the new look was fresh and striking. More to the point, the Heritage Classic was improved in most aspects of its engine and chassis performance, while retaining the versatility provided by its semi-rigid panniers and a screen that could be unclipped in seconds to turn tourer into cruiser.

The Milwaukee-Eight engine was strong and smooth, especially in its larger, 114cu in (1,868cc) form. The bike felt effortlessly long-legged, thanks to its low-revving, flexible engine and smooth-shifting six-speed gearbox. On the freeway it cruised effortlessly at 70mph (112kph), the non-adjustable screen doing a useful job of diverting the breeze. Stability was very good, and the suspension reasonably compliant yet well-controlled, although the rear shock's inaccessibility hindered adjustment.

If the Classic wasn't the most luxurious model in Harley's range, it was certainly well equipped. As well as the removable screen and lockable panniers, its features included a large fuel tank, USB socket and self-cancelling indicators. There were Harleys that were better for cruising, and others that were better for touring. But for riders who wanted to do both, there was arguably no better bike with which to celebrate the firm's 120 years of production.

RIGHT For 2023 the Heritage Classic was also available in standard form, in a variety of shades including yellow.

114

TOURERS

Harley-Davidson calls them Grand American Tourers these days; for decades most were simply known as the Glides. Either way, Harley's touring models have long stood at the pinnacle of the hierarchy – the best equipped and most expensive in the range. With their big engines and long, slow-steering chassis, they are the long-haul kings of America.

The line dates back to the Hydra-Glide and Duo-Glide that brought suspension to the Big Twins in the 1940s and 1950s. The Electra Glide arrived in 1965 and raised the touring bar through the 1970s. By the end of that decade, the FLHC Electra Glide Classic's standard equipment included a fairing and windshield, saddle bags, crash bars, luggage rack and running boards – previously available only as "Tour-Pak" optional extras.

The Tour Glide added comfort with its rubber-mounted engine in 1980, since when the Road King has supplied retro charm and the Street Glide has led the bagger movement, becoming a best seller in the process. Relentless development has improved the touring family, notably with a new chassis in 2009, the Project Rushmore revamp of 2014, the Milwaukee-Eight engine three years later, and the gradual adoption of liquid-cooling. Like the big tourers themselves, their evolution will just keep on going.

LEFT The Electra Glide Highway King, released in 2023 as the third of Harley's Icons series, was a thoroughly modern tourer with the style of a 1968 FLH Electra Glide.

FL ELECTRA GLIDE, 1965

Of all Harley-Davidson models, the enduring Electra Glide is perhaps the one that best epitomizes the breed. The "FL" designation actually arrived with the first 74-inch Knucklehead of 1942 and became a mainstay of the Milwaukee range.

The model that carried those initials with the greatest distinction was the thundering Electra Glide – the quintessential model following its 1965 debut.

Yet for all its lusty pedigree, that first Electra Glide was little more than a Duo-Glide with the addition of 12-volt electrics and an electric starter which – initially, at least – did not prove very dependable.

Just as there was a 12-month hiatus between the introduction of the Panhead and the Hydra-Glide, Harley-Davidson waited until 1966 before giving the Glide something new. From its second year of production, it was powered by the new Shovelhead mill with its (relatively) more efficient "Power-Pack" heads. Initial examples used the alloy-headed Panhead engine which had first appeared in 1948 and gone on to propel the first Glide (the Hydra-Glide of 1949) and the Duo-Glide of a decade later. The Hydra- had been the first big twin with telescopic forks while the Duo- added swinging arm rear suspension.

The starter motor itself lived behind the rear cylinder and engaged on the rear of the primary drive. The Duo-Glide frame had to be opened up slightly to accommodate it, yet still

SPECIFICATIONS: 1965

Engine	aircooled OHV V-twin
Capacity	74cu in (1,207cc)
Transmission	4-speed
Power	around 55bhp
Weight	595lbs (270kg)
Wheelbase	60in (1,525mm)
Top speed	95mph (152kph)

RIGHT The Electra Glide of the 1960s was a handsome, fairly simple machine.

BELOW The last of the Panheads: in 1970 the Shovelhead took its place.

ABOVE For little more than $1,500 this Milwaukee dream could be yours – at least in 1965.

ABOVE Arizona bike cop Robert Blake and his *Electra Glide in Blue* were stars of the silver screen in 1973.

BELOW It would do considerably more than 12mph (20kph), but in Harley-land style counted as much as numeracy.

there was no room for the earlier model's tool kit. Surprisingly for a unit "borrowed" from an outboard motor, the first starters were troublesome when damp and the kick start was prudently retained. Harley later adopted Homelite starters, which proved much more reliable.

Like all Harley big twins, the OHV engine ran forked con-rods to eliminate rocking couple (so the rear cylinder was precisely, rather than roughly, masked by the front). Primary drive was by chain to a four-speed box (with a sidecar option, up to 1980, of three forward and one reverse). Capacity was 74cu in (1,207cc): the bigger 82cu in (1,340cc) engine didn't arrive until 1970 with the new generation of "alternator" Shovelheads. The rest was almost unchanged from the Duo-Glide, complete with five-inch (127mm) whitewall tyres and running boards, although for the first time a five-gallon (19-litre) "Turnpike" tank was fitted. Of the four-model range, two versions retained hand gear change, which would remain an option until 1972.

In short, this was never a state-of-the-art machine. Indeed the "King of the Road" touring pack offered in 1966 required the rear shock absorbers to be relocated forwards, to the detriment of the Glide's handling, which had already proved to be rather pedestrian.

For all that, it was a strikingly handsome machine – one that looked far better than it performed. As with most Harleys, the rear brake was good but, prior to the arrival of a front disc in 1971, no prudent rider attempted to stop a Glide in a hurry.

This was a device for getting into top gear and staying there as you cruised serenely to the next horizon.

BELOW As leaps forward go, the Electra Glide was conservative: both hand-change and foot-change versions were available until 1972.

FLT TOUR GLIDE, 1980

Like most things Harley-Davidson, the Tour Glide didn't suddenly appear out of the Milwaukee ether, it evolved. One fundamental element, the 80-inch Shovelhead engine, first emerged on the 1978 FLH Electra Glide. It would take a new fairing and considerably more to create the Tour Glide.

Some of those extras arrived a year later with the FLH Classic, which featured special paint and wheels plus a set of "Tour-Pak" parts, comprising saddlebags, luggage rack, "batwing" fairing and chromed crash bars.

In 1980, Harley bundled the two together, adding a few other choice ingredients, and the FLT Tour Glide was born. The most obvious change was the replacement of the Electra Glide's handlebar-mounted fairing with a bigger, more protective frame-mounted fairing, equipped with twin headlights.

The engine and transmission were now bolted rigidly together; the transmission was five-speed for the first time on any big twin Harley roadster, permitting even more long-legged gearing. Final drive was still by chain but now fully-enclosed in its own oil bath. Toothed belt drive would arrive with the FLTC Classic in 1984, and become standard across the FL range the following year. A new frame with box-section backbone provided increased suspension travel. Crucially, for the first time the engine was installed using a clever three-point rubber-mounting system designed to isolate the rider from vibration.

This made the Tour Glide smoother and more usable than any previous big twin, and launched a generation of Milwaukee luxury tourers. Anyone with $6,013 to spare in 1980 could buy what was undoubtedly the smoothest, most comfortable and lavishly-equipped motorcycle Harley had ever produced; a machine tailor-made for demolishing large distances.

ABOVE All Tour Glides enjoyed five-speed transmission and rubber engine mounts. The Evo powerplant brought further refinement from 1984.

ABOVE Early Tour Glides are easily distinguished by their huge twin headlamp fairing, which gave excellent wind protection.

SPECIFICATIONS

Engine	aircooled OHV V-twin
Capacity	82cu in (1,338cc)
Transmission	5-speed
Power	65bhp
Weight	765lb (347kg)
Wheelbase	62½in (1,590mm)
Top speed	100mph (161kph)

RIGHT The Tour Glide's tall screen allowed high handlebars that gave an upright and relaxed riding position.

FLTCU TOUR GLIDE ULTRA, 1989

Harley refined the Tour Glide's "fully-loaded" concept through the 1980s, notably with the adoption of the smoother and more reliable Evolution V2 powerplant and belt final drive in 1984, but as the decade drew to a close an even more luxurious carriage was needed.

It arrived in 1989 with the awesome Tour Glide Ultra Classic – 82cu in (1,340cc) of imposing, luxurious brawn.

As well as new fairing lowers to protect the rider, the big Glide featured a welter of electronics, including electronic cruise control, CB radio and a sophisticated stereo hi-fi system. The pillion was provided with separate speakers; a built-in intercom allowed rider and passenger to chew the fat. A cigarette lighter was standard and even the self-cancelling indicators were micro-processor controlled. To cope with this plethora of added electrical demands, a new high-output 32-amp alternator was fitted.

Overkill? Perhaps, but profoundly practical too. The panniers and capacious "Tour-Pak" top-box swallowed two weeks' luggage. The screen kept wind and dust at bay; the plush, upholstered saddle was good for long days on the road. Perhaps the powerful hi-fi system wasn't strictly necessary, but who could resist cruising to a favourite blues tune, with the backbeat of a thundering Milwaukee twin?

Harley dropped the Tour Glide from its line-up following the fuel-injected FLTCUI model of 1996, after 16 years as the long-haul king of America's open roads. Its core feature, the frame-mounted fairing, would reappear a few years later with the even longer-lasting Road Glide.

RIGHT A 1991 Tour Glide in its element, easing across the high desert plateau of Utah, in the south-western United States.

SPECIFICATIONS

Engine	aircooled OHV V-twin
Capacity	82cu in (1,340cc)
Transmission	5-speed
Power	69bhp
Weight	765lbs (347kg)
Wheelbase	63in (1,600mm)
Top speed	105mph (169kph)

BELOW The majestic spirit of the Glides lives on in this 1992 Tour Glide.

FLHR ELECTRA GLIDE ROAD KING, 1994

As standard equipment became even more comprehensive at the top of the Electra Glide range, there came a demand for a model more like the stripped-down FLs of the 1960s – a bike with touring ability but not the bulk and weight of a full-blown tourer.

Harley-Davidson's response was the FLHS Sport of 1987 – a real lightweight at "only" 690lbs (313kg). The FLHR Road King that followed was in much the same mould.

Launched for the 1994 season, the Road King was an attempt to bridge the gap between Milwaukee's custom and touring models. Although in essence a full-on Electra Glide minus the fairing, with a "retro" chromed headlight and tank-mounted speedometer, its long, low silhouette belied its super-heavyweight roots. Here was a machine that could hit the highway with the same authority as any other Glide – once the detachable windscreen was installed. As well as the QD windshield (an idea borrowed from the Low Rider Convertible), the panniers and pillion perch were also easily removed, changing the machine's profile and character in the wink of an eye. Thus stripped, the King had all the languid grace of a custom cruiser.

To many eyes this was the best looking of all the Glides, the normally ponderous lines replaced by a machine which, if not exactly svelte, had a certain grace. Where fully-loaded FLs tended to obesity, the Road King had style. It was a Harley-Davidson for those who wanted their heavyweight cake in custom clothes. Equally, its touring roots made the King an eminently practical custom bike. Six hours in the saddle was hard work on any Softail but a Glide could comfortably knock that off – and more.

ABOVE Cleaner, lower lines distinguish this king of the road from other heavyweight FLs.

BELOW Adding a few of Milwaukee's many accessories can undermine the effect.

The rubber-mounted Evo engine kept vibration at bay but let that evocative rumble pour through. Parked anywhere it looked good; on the open road, it worked.

The first fuel-injected Road King, the FLHRI, came in 1996, although carburetted versions continued to be produced in parallel. The ESPFI (Electronic Sequential Port Fuel Injection) system was based on a similar Italian Magneti Marelli design to that of Ducati V-twins, although in this case the emphasis was on user-

SPECIFICATIONS

Engine	aircooled OHV V-twin
Capacity	82cu in (1,340cc)
Transmission	5-speed
Power	69bhp
Weight	692lbs (314kg)
Wheelbase	62.7in (1,590mm)
Top speed	105mph (169kph)

ABOVE Chrome plate and an abundance of lights are traditional features of the Road King's front end.

RIGHT With its screen in place the Road King is very much a tourer, but a naked cruiser is just seconds away.

friendliness rather than sheer power. Though some owners preferred the reassuring simplicity of a stock single carb poking out of the right hand side, the fuel-injection system was a major bonus. As well as improving emissions, it offered slightly higher torque (83lb.ft rather than 79lb.ft) and much better driveability, particularly at high altitude. The fuel system was improved across the Injection range for 1997.

High-tech was largely absent elsewhere, except of course for Harley-Davidson's trademark belt final drive. Suspension was adjustable only for air pressure in the twin rear shock absorbers. Both wheels were cast light alloy, 16in (406mm) in diameter, wearing characteristically fat Glide rubber.

Twin hydraulic disc brakes graced the front, with a single disc at the rear. All three of these brakes had a lot of work to do on a machine that scaled 692lbs (314kg), but by this time Harley-Davidson stoppers worked fairly well. Like most of the Glide family, the Road King's top speed was a shade over 100mph (161kph), although screaming the big twin that hard was a futile pursuit.

The Road King was happiest when ambling along at a disdainful 75mph (120kph); if you travelled at much above 85mph (140kph), a disconcerting weave could sometimes intrude. To rule the asphalt the Milwaukee way, you didn't need to be the fastest, just the coolest – as a much-updated Road King would still be confirming three decades later.

LEFT A 1996 Road King – or should that be FLHR-Convertible? Both the windshield and pillion seat are quickly detachable.

ULTRA CLASSIC ELECTRA GLIDE, 1995

By the mid-1990s the Electra Glide seemed to have been around for ever, becoming as much a part of American motoring legend as the Corvette or Mustang, such was the strength of its name and its status at the top of Harley-Davidson's model line-up.

Since its introduction in 1965 it had undergone countless updates, starred in a Hollywood movie (*Electra Glide in Blue*, in 1973) and fashioned a mighty reputation as a devourer of serious distances.

The Ultra Classic Electra Glide was launched in 1995, initially a US-market special edition created to mark the model's 30th anniversary. While the age-old Electra Glide look and most of the features of the previous range-topping Ultra Classic were retained, it was a notable step forward, for one important reason: fuel-injection.

Behind the familiar round cover on the right of the unchanged 82cu in (1,340cc) Evolution V-twin motor sat not the familiar Keihin carburettor but the body of an injection system built by Weber-Marelli, the Italian firm that had equipped numerous Ducatis and Milwaukee's own VR1000 racebike. Harley claimed the system gave smoother, cleaner running and improved fuel consumption by ten per cent, which turned out to be broadly true.

ABOVE With plenty of room to store luggage, this is the ultimate long-haul Hog.

Just two years later the Ultra Classic was uprated even more substantially. For 1997 it gained a new frame with lower saddle height (27in/685mm) and many other detail changes, and Harley's first new engine for 15 years. The bigger Twin Cam 88 gave the massive Electra Glide a welcome boost to more than 80bhp, the 88cu in (1,450cc) unit producing a prodigious peak torque of 86lb.ft (117Nm).

With a wider spread of torque and the driveability that only fuel

LEFT Its adoption of the Twin Cam 88 engine in 1997 gave the Ultra Classic a notable boost in both performance and refinement.

RIGHT The Evo-engined Ultra Classic of 1995 was one of the first Harleys to benefit from fuel-injection's improved smoothness and economy.

BELOW Touring riders know that one key to two-up touring harmony is a comfortable pillion – and the Ultra Classic very much delivers.

injection could bring, the big V-twin's legendary ability to gobble up countless miles was improved. Now it shrugged off gradients and altitude with even greater ease than before. Everything about the big Glide, from its fat tyres and sofa-like saddle to lazy, laid-back steering geometry, marked it out as the grandest of open-road tourers.

Scaling a hefty 776lbs (352kg) without a drop of fuel in the tank, this was the heaviest Hog of them all. Most of that weight was good, solid Milwaukee metal, but much of the rest aimed to pamper the rider like no bike known to humanity. The rubber-mounted engine ensured that vibration was enough to say "Harley" but did not intrude. The amply padded seat was huge and welcoming; the adjustable footboards gave room to move and relax.

Meanwhile the panniers, fairing pockets and copious, carpet-lined "King Tour-Pak" top-box simply swallowed up luggage. Harley described its top model as "fully loaded" and wasn't exaggerating. Depending on the market, it came with passing and running lamps, more instruments than a Boeing and even a cigarette lighter. There was a voice-activated intercom, CB radio and electronic cruise control. The 40W-per-channel cassette radio incorporated four speakers and separate passenger controls, and responded automatically to ambient noise levels. If any Harley-Davidson was as much fantasy as motorcycle, this was it.

SPECIFICATIONS

Engine	aircooled OHV V-twin
Capacity	82cu in (1,340cc)
Transmission	5-speed
Power	80bhp
Weight	763lbs (347kg)
Wheelbase	62.7in (1,592mm)
Top speed	105mph (169kph)

RIGHT An Evo-engined predecessor to the full-on Ultra Classic 88. But who'd want his electricity bill?

FLTR ROAD GLIDE, 1998

The Road Glide had a complicated start to life before becoming an enduring staple of the touring family. It was launched on the US market in 1998, powered by an 82cu in (1,340cc) Evolution engine and with either carburettors, as the FLTR, or fuel-injection, as the FLTRI.

Just a year later The Road Glide went on sale worldwide, by now fitted with the more refined, 1,450cc Twin Cam 88 engine that was Milwaukee's key release of 1999.

Through all three early variations on the Road Glide theme, one thing was soon crystal clear: Harley had a hit with its format of frame-mounted half-fairing, low windscreen and dual headlights. The new model was based on the Electra Glide's chassis, but its fixed, so-called "shark nose" fairing gave a distinctly different feel to the familiar handlebar-mounted "batwing".

The frame-mounted fairing had to be set further forward to allow clearance for the handlebars, which gave a roomier riding position that some appreciated. Wind protection was not notably reduced, and the benefits included slightly lighter low-speed steering, unencumbered by the fairing's weight. The frame-mounting also enhanced stability, allowing the Road Glide to track straight and true at

SPECIFICATIONS: 1999

Engine	aircooled OHV V-twin
Capacity	1,450cc (88cu in)
Transmission	5-speed
Power	70bhp
Weight	759lbs (345kg)
Wheelbase	62.7in (1,592mm)
Top speed	105mph (169kph)

ABOVE The Road Glide's frame-mounted "shark nose" fairing was set a fair distance ahead of the rider but still gave excellent wind protection.

LEFT The Road Glide's distinctive shape was already familiar to US riders in 1999, when it was updated and sold in export markets for the first time.

ABOVE Twin headlamps and a twin-disc front brake gave the Road Glide plenty of lighting and stopping power.

ABOVE The 1999-model Glide's Twin Cam 88 powerplant was a welcome upgrade on the old Evolution unit.

ABOVE Footboards and a heel-and-toe gearshift contributed to the Road Glide's comfort and convenience.

speeds that would have had the bar-mounted batwing provoking a weave.

This was arguably the first genuine high-speed tourer from Milwaukee, especially after it had been boosted by the Twin Cam 88 engine in time for its belated appearance in export markets. The big bike pulled hard from low revs, surged towards a top speed of just over 100mph (161kph) on the straights, and cruised with a long-legged feel, and just enough V-twin vibration to make life interesting.

Equally importantly, its chassis did a good job of keeping up. The Road Glide sometimes felt rather vague in fast curves, but generally stayed stable, with the help of compliant but fairly well-controlled suspension. Its twin front and single rear discs brought even this heavyweight to a halt without too much fuss. That big twin-headlamp fairing kept off most of the elements, although the screen was low and non-adjustable. The seat was well-padded, the footboards gave plenty of leg-room.

All contributed to making an enjoyable and practical machine well suited to both everyday riding and longer trips. The Road Glide was gradually improved, too, notably in 2007, when fitted with the torquier, 1,584cc Twin Cam 96 engine; and two years later with the new chassis that was introduced across the touring range, featuring a stiffer frame, uprated suspension and Brembo brakes.

Harley also did a good job of broadening the Road Glide's appeal. In 2010 it embraced the booming bagger movement with the stylish FLTRX Road Glide Custom, featuring larger 18in front wheel, shorter, tinted windscreen and low, stripped-down rear end. The following year's FLTRU Road Glide Ultra went the other way, providing long-distance touring ability with the more powerful, 1,690cc Twin Cam 103 engine, a taller screen, luxurious dual-seat and top-box.

BELOW The Road Glide Ultra was designed for serious long-haul comfort.

FLHRCI ROAD KING CLASSIC, 2000

The Classic version of the Road King took up where the standard model left off. Introduced at the turn of the millennium, it transported its rider and any pillion or onlookers back in time by several decades with an immaculately detailed look inspired by the Glides of old.

There was something quintessentially American about the Road King, all the more so in Classic guise with its typical combination of two-tone paintwork, white-wall tyres and leather-covered panniers.

In fact the two models were initially almost identical, or at least could be. The 2000-model Road King came as standard with a big, round chromed headlamp in a polished nacelle, inspired by the Duo-Glide of 1958. It had wide, "buffalo" handlebars, a removable windscreen and tank-mounted instruments. It was powered by the 1,450cc Twin Cam 88 engine that had been introduced a year earlier.

The Classic differed in that its engine was fuel-injected, rather than fed by a 40mm Keihin carburettor, although the standard model could be injected at extra cost. Similarly, the Classic came with wire-spoked wheels and the standard Road King had cast, but could be ordered with laced spokes for an additional charge. The Classic also had leather saddlebags with rigid inserts to keep them in

ABOVE This 2009-model Road King Classic with its Twin Cam 96 engine manages to look much like a Duo-Glide from half a century earlier.

SPECIFICATIONS

Engine	aircooled OHV V-twin
Capacity	88cu in (1,450cc)
Transmission	5-speed
Power	80bhp
Weight	710lb (322kg)
Wheelbase	63.5in (1,612mm)
Top speed	110mph (177kph)

LEFT Windscreen, whitewalls and panniers add to the period look.

ABOVE Tank badge and two-tone paint confirm Harley's passion for detail.

RIGHT The Classic's removable screen contributes to touring comfort along with the footboards and plush seat.

shape, in place of the standard model's fibreglass panniers.

Either way, you got big fenders, cruise control, generous footboards, air-adjustable rear suspension and plenty of Twin Cam performance. The result was a bike that not only epitomized Harley-Davidson's ability to blend retro style with modern technology, but which had distinct advantages of its own.

The windscreen, for example, couldn't match the protection of other touring models' big fairings, or their boredom-relieving option of a sound system on long freeway trips. But it kept off most of the wind, and gave a notably easier steering feel. For everyday riding, being able to remove the screen in seconds added a dimension of naked-bike cool.

The rider's view of the shiny chromed nacelle was spectacular, but having the instruments on the tank top meant they were out of immediate sight, and prevented the use of a tank-bag. The Classic's leather-covered panniers weren't as convenient or secure as Harley's top-opening hard cases, which the Standard model adopted, but were still mighty useful.

Both the standard Road King and the Classic were upgraded with the 1,584cc Twin Cam 96 engine in 2007, and took another step forward two years later when they gained new chassis as part of Harley's overhaul of the touring family. Stiffer frames and swing-arms, firmer suspension and a wider, 180-section rear tyre improved both straight-line stability and cornering poise.

The result was a pair of bikes that performed better than ever, yet whose appearance remained as determinedly in the 1950s as ever. Especially so in the case of the Classic, which retained its laced 16in wheels and white-wall Dunlops, while the standard Road King joined the other touring models in adopting a 17in front wheel. Some Classic features, clearly, were strictly non-negotiable.

RIGHT For 2017 the Classic was updated with the Milwaukee-Eight 107 engine and new parts including lights, suspension and saddlebags.

FLHX STREET GLIDE, 2006

One way of describing the Street Glide would be as an ideal compromise between minimalist cool and long-distance comfort. Another would be as a brilliant example of Harley-Davidson's ability to stay in tune with customers and provide them with what they wanted.

In the early years of the new millennium, Harley's big twin range was split between the stylish Softails and Dynas on the one hand, and the luxurious but less fashionable Electra Glides and other tourers on the other. Increasing numbers of riders started looking for a middle ground: stripping down the big Glides in search of reduced weight and a leaner look, while retaining wind protection and some practicality.

They removed the bulky Tour-Pak rear luggage, big seats, unwanted lights and chrome fittings, in a variation on the old chopper scene of decades earlier. They further customized them with shorter screens, lower suspension and sometimes bigger wheels. These bikes became known as baggers, and

ABOVE Key to the Street Glide's success is its ability to provide wind-cheating and luggage-carrying practicality along with plenty of Harley cool.

RIGHT The distinctively curvaceous batwing half-fairing is vital to both the Street Glide's look and its function.

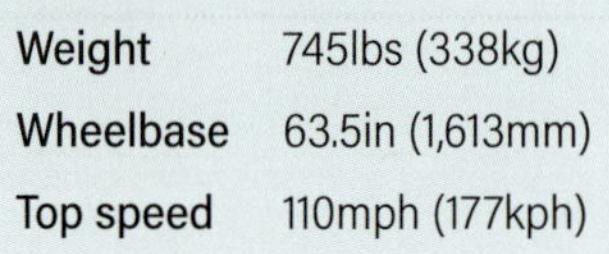

SPECIFICATIONS	
Engine	aircooled OHV V-twin
Capacity	88cu in (1,450cc)
Transmission	5-speed
Power	80bhp
Weight	745lbs (338kg)
Wheelbase	63.5in (1,613mm)
Top speed	110mph (177kph)

ABOVE Street Glide features that have inspired the bagger movement include a low, comfortable seat and a useful pair of hard panniers.

RIGHT The Street Glide's super-power was its ability to cover serious distance on the open road while also having the streetwise style of a cruiser.

they were noted with interest in Milwaukee, and especially by Willie G.

Harley had previously used the Street Glide name in the mid-1980s, for a fully-dressed, Evolution-engined tourer, but that bike had made little impact. In 2006, the firm introduced a completely new Street Glide, powered by the current Twin Cam 88 engine, featuring an Electra Glide style batwing fairing and a clean, low-slung rear end.

This time round, the Street Glide quickly became popular. Its appeal was easy to understand. The FLHX was lighter, lower and more manoeuvrable than a big tourer. Although it had a stubby windscreen and short-travel suspension it was reasonably comfortable, the ride enhanced by features including sound system, cruise control and smartphone integration.

This was a bike that you could happily use for short trips and cruising during the week, then load up for some serious distance at the weekend. It was enjoyably quick, respectably smooth, and around town benefitted from a notably light clutch action. It also looked good in standard form and was modestly priced by big twin standards, adding to its appeal for customization.

The Street Glide had hit the sweet spot, and its popularity grew in 2007 when it was revamped with the gruntier 1,584cc Twin Cam 96 engine and six-speed gearbox, along with ride-by-wire throttle and bigger gas tank. Two years later its chassis was updated as part of Harley's overhaul of the touring family, gaining a stiffer frame and swing-arm, a revised rubber-mounting system for its engine, a longer wheelbase for improved stability, and a twin-disc Brembo front brake system.

At the same time it was given shorter rear shocks with just two inches (51mm) of travel, which made it even lower and more manageable, at the expense of jarring over bigger bumps. As before with the Street Glide, most riders seemed happy with the compromise. By this time it was America's best selling motorcycle, and the leader of a bagger movement that included machines from numerous rival firms.

BELOW By 2009 the Street Glide had been updated with the Twin Cam 96 engine and a new chassis with stiffer frame and shorter rear shocks.

FLHTCUTG TRI GLIDE ULTRA CLASSIC, 2009

With its powerful engine, luxurious features and price tag to match, the three-wheeled Tri Glide Ultra Classic was very different to Harley's old Servi-Car, which had remained in production for more than 50 years based on its appeal as a practical and inexpensive working vehicle.

By contrast the Tri Glide Ultra Classic was a high-end tourer whose name reflected the fact that it was based on the Ultra Classic Electra Glide.

The Tri Glide's inspiration came from Harley's ageing customer base; often mentioned as a problem for the company but here an opportunity. As older riders had struggled with the size and weight of its tourers, some had looked to three-wheelers from

ABOVE The Electra Glide's influence is clear in this 2014-model Tri Glide Ultra's features including batwing fairing and roomy dual-seat.

BELOW The much-requested CVO Tri Glide of 2020 featured a Milwaukee-Eight 117 engine along with special paint, wheels and audio system.

SPECIFICATIONS

Engine	aircooled OHV V-twin
Capacity	103cu in (1,690cc)
Transmission	6-speed
Power	80bhp
Weight	1,157lbs (525kg)
Wheelbase	66.6in (1,692mm)
Top speed	100mph (161kph)

RIGHT Riding the Tri Glide, in this case a 2021 model, is an acquired skill and requires plenty of force through the bars for quick direction changes.

specialists including Lehman Trikes of South Dakota, self-styled "Leaders of the Three World".

John Lehman's firm already produced luxurious models including the Harley-powered Renegade, which resembled an Electra Glide with an additional rear wheel. In 2006, Harley-Davidson signed a deal with Lehman to develop a range of Harley-branded trikes. The Tri Glide Ultra Classic went on sale in 2009 and was initially assembled at Lehman's base in Spearfish, after Harley had transported Electra Glide front ends from its York factory.

That front half included the Electra Glide's batwing fairing and 1,690cc Twin Cam 103 engine, including its six-speed transmission and belt final drive, although the heavier trike was geared slightly lower via two extra teeth on its rear sprocket. And it certainly was heavier – at 1,157lbs (525kg) it weighed half as much again as the Electra Glide, making the optional electric reverse gear highly advisable.

Chassis changes included new triple clamps that kicked the forks out to 32 degrees and reduced trail, to reduce the amount of effort required through the bars. A steering damper added stability. The stiffened frame held a swing-arm that splayed out to a pair of 15in diameter rear wheels, which wore car tyres, in contrast to the 16in diameter bike tyre up front.

The Tri Glide was designed as a grand tourer with plenty of features, including the Electra Glide's 80W audio system, CB radio and passenger intercom. Below the standard Tour-Pak was a trunk that more than trebled the storage space.

Performance was very respectable, although the three-wheeler handled nothing like a motorcycle, and demanded that its rider work hard on a twisty road. Its acceleration was inevitably down on the Electra Glide's, due to the extra weight. But the Tri Glide was happy to cruise at 70mph (113kph) or more on the freeway, and was stable at speed.

By 2011 its name had been shortened to Tri Glide Ultra and Harley had moved production to York. The three-wheeler stayed in the range and was updated along with the other touring models, notably in 2017 when it was fitted with the Twin Cooled Milwaukee-Eight 107 engine, and in 2019 with the Milwaukee-Eight 114.

In 2020 Harley unveiled the "most requested model in the history of Custom Vehicle Operations": a CVO Tri Glide, powered by a 1,923cc Milwaukee-Eight 117 engine and featuring special paint, high-end audio and large-diameter Tomahawk cast wheels. Harley-Davidson trikes had come a long way from the Servi-Car of 1932.

BELOW Batwing fairing and a trio of lights gave the trike a familiar face.

BELOW For 2021 the Tri Glide featured the Milwaukee-Eight 114 unit.

BELOW The trunk offered more than twice the capacity of the Tour-Pak.

FLHXS STREET GLIDE SPECIAL, 2014

The Street Glide Special was new for 2014, incorporating a bunch of features that were optional upgrades to the standard Street Glide. But the year's big news from Milwaukee was the major revamp, code-named Project Rushmore, that incorporated not just those two models but the whole Touring family.

An enlarged, 1,690cc engine, named the High Output Twin Cam 103, used new cams and airbox to increase midrange torque for improved roll-on acceleration, and also introduced a hydraulically operated clutch. Thicker front forks and reworked shocks contributed to a stiffer chassis. New hand controls, gauges, wheels, front fenders and panniers – whose lids could now be opened with one hand – were among the updates.

Both Street Glides featured a redesigned batwing fairing, which incorporated a vent below the screen to smooth the airflow. The Special also incorporated a bigger screen for the new Boom! Box infotainment system, and a linked braking system, both of which were options with the standard model. The result, especially with the new Special, was a Street Glide that was usefully improved in almost every area.

Harley didn't rest on their laurels, either; for 2017 there was a revamped Street Glide Special, now powered by the 1,745cc Milwaukee-Eight 107 engine, featuring four valves per cylinder, oil-cooled cylinder heads and balancer-shaft smoothness. Not to mention new Showa suspension and Brembo brake system. The Street Glide had changed a lot in just a few years, while retaining its distinctive look – and its status as one of Harley's best loved models.

ABOVE The Special's straight-line performance was boosted by the new High Output Twin Cam 103 engine.

SPECIFICATIONS

Engine	aircooled OHV V-twin
Capacity	103cu in (1,690cc)
Transmission	6-speed
Power	80bhp
Weight	775lbs (352kg)
Wheelbase	64in (1,625mm)
Top speed	110mph (177kph)

LEFT Although the familiar Street Glide look was little changed, there were updates in almost every area.

FLHTK ELECTRA GLIDE ULTRA LIMITED, 2014

As Harley's touring flagship, the Electra Glide Ultra Limited highlighted the many upgrades of the Project Rushmore programme, described by CEO Matt Levatich as the "most significant product launch in the company's 110-year history".

The Ultra Limited was of particular note, because it introduced liquid cooling to the 45-degree V-twin line.

Named the Twin Cooled unit, because it used both liquid and air, this version of the new High Output Twin Cam 103 generated five per cent more torque, on top of the five per cent already gained by the aircooled 103's new camshafts and airbox. The cooling system was also adopted by the CVO model and the Tri-Glide trike but could not be used by the other tourers because it incorporated radiators set into fairing lowers.

The Ultra Limited's radiators reduced its fairing's built-in storage space, but along with the extra grunt it benefitted from the pick of Project Rushmore's many upgrades – notably its Daymaker LED lighting, 6.5-inch touchscreen, powerful four-speaker sound system, new dual-seat with extra pillion room, and redesigned Tour-Pak top-box. The additional engine torque, stiffened touring chassis and linked brake system were particularly valuable on such a big, heavy machine, especially when it was loaded with pillion and luggage.

With its subtly reshaped batwing fairing, proudly exposed V-twin powerplant and host of thoughtfully upgraded components, the Ultra Limited was a thoroughly modern giant tourer that was still every inch an Electra Glide. That remained true three years later when it was fitted with the 1,745cc Milwaukee-Eight 107 engine, again in partially liquid-cooled form.

SPECIFICATIONS

Engine	air/liquid-cooled OHV V-twin
Capacity	103cu in (1,690cc)
Transmission	6-speed
Power	80bhp
Weight	896lbs (414kg) wet
Wheelbase	64in (1,625mm)
Top speed	110mph (177kph)

ABOVE The Ultra Limited's stiffened chassis helped give good handling for such a big, heavy bike.

BELOW Although visually similar to its predecessors, the 2014 Ultra Classic was comprehensively updated, notably with its Twin Cooled engine.

FLHRXS ROAD KING SPECIAL, 2017

The Road King Special began an exciting new chapter in the story of the Road King, which had become a mainstay of Harley's range following its launch in 1994 thanks to its 1950s-inspired style and appeal to riders who preferred a naked bike or detachable screen rather than a fairing.

With the Special's launch in 2017 the familiar name adopted a whole new character – a bagger with a low-key look based on monochrome paint, black finish and minimal chrome.

That engine was special in itself: along with the rest of the touring family, the new model was powered by the Milwaukee-Eight 107 unit, named after its doubled number of valves. The V-twin got its larger, 1,745cc (107cu in) capacity from a bigger bore and unchanged stroke, compared to the previous Twin Cam 103, also gaining a new oil-cooling system around its cylinder heads.

In the Road King Special's case the engine was mostly black, with just a few shiny highlights. The big round headlight was also black, as were the fat front forks, raised mini-ape handlebar and hand controls. So too the exhaust system and wheels, which featured a slender multi-spoke "turbine" design. The big front fender and tank-mounted instruments added retro appeal. Longer panniers contributed to the Special's low-slung bagger look.

The Milwaukee-Eight 107 engine made roughly ten per cent more torque than the old Twin Cam unit through much of its rev range. That gave this stripped-down Road King an enjoyably lively feel, with a crisp throttle response from as low as 2,000rpm, and a strong surge of acceleration until even the eight-valve unit began running out of breath at around 5,000rpm.

It was pleasantly

ABOVE Its Milwaukee-Eight 107 unit meant the Special had plenty of punch.

SPECIFICATIONS	
Engine	air/oil-cooled OHV V-twin
Capacity	107cu in (1,745cc)
Transmission	6-speed
Power	80bhp
Weight	781lbs (354kg)
Wheelbase	64in (1,625mm)
Top speed	110mph (177kph)

RIGHT Its single-colour paintwork and blacked-out engine and other components gave the Special a very different appearance to that of the traditional Road King.

RIGHT Unless fitted with its accessory windscreen, the Special was a respectably light naked bagger that was well suited to some gentle cruising.

smooth, too, thanks to the new engine's balancer shaft. The Milwaukee-Eight unit also ran cooler, was more economical, had a lighter clutch action and even sounded better, because its reduced mechanical noise had allowed Harley's engineers to liberate a little more of the characteristic "potato-potato" exhaust note.

The firm's 2017 updates to the touring models also included new suspension, with stiffer 49mm Showa front forks containing more sophisticated, cartridge-style damping; and rear shocks from the same Japanese firm, featuring a hydraulic remote preload adjuster in place of the old air-assisted units. The Special's shocks gave just 54mm (2.1in) of travel, matching the Street Glide and Road Glide.

This allowed a low seat height of just 26.4in (671mm), which helped make it manageable at low speed. At 781lbs (354kg) the Special was light by Harley big twin standards, which aided its agility. It allowed a little more lean angle than the Street Glide, and could be cornered confidently until its footboards touched down.

All of which made the Road King Special both fun to ride and versatile, its long-distance ability easily enhanced by fitting a quickly detachable windscreen. By 2023 the standard Road King, with its shiny chrome, had been dropped from Harley's range. The Special rumbled on in familiar blacked-out style, by now fitted with the even torquier, 1,868cc Milwaukee-Eight 114 engine that had previously powered the CVO models, and gave some useful extra midrange performance.

BELOW The Special's front end specification included a 19in cast wheel, Showa forks and twin brake discs gripped by Brembo four-piston calipers.

BELOW The blacked-out nacelle and fork shrouds contributed to a vintage look but the dual halogen headlight provided plenty of candlepower.

FLH ELECTRA GLIDE REVIVAL, 2021

Harley-Davidson's ability to blend retro style with modern technology shifted up a gear in 2021 with the Icons collection: a series of limited-edition models inspired by the firm's greatest hits, with a new star to be chosen each year.

First up was the Electra Glide Revival, whose tri-tone finish, with white fairing and panniers, turned the clock back to 1969, the year the Electra Glide was first offered with a distinctive accessory fairing that became known as the batwing.

Back in the summer of '69, the Electra Glide's batwing and saddlebags were made from white fibreglass, which the Revival replicated with paint in Birch White. The gas tank's authentic two-tone Hi-Fi Blue and Black Denim was divided by a Birch White stripe, the paint names for once enhancing the period feel. So too did the classical solo saddle with its white cover and chromed rail. Wire-spoked

ABOVE Classical Electra Glide lines, faithfully reproduced colours and details, including a solo seat, gave the Revival a captivating 1960s look.

BELOW LEFT AND BELOW The solo seat was sprung for comfort in period style; white panniers echoed the original Electra Glide's fibreglass items.

SPECIFICATIONS

Engine	air/oil-cooled OHV V-twin
Capacity	114cu in (1,868cc)
Transmission	6-speed
Power	97bhp (claimed)
Weight	862lbs (391kg)
Wheelbase	64in (1,625mm)
Top speed	115mph (185kph)

ABOVE Half a century of brake development had seen the old Electra Glide's front drum replaced by twin discs with cornering ABS.

wheels with whitewall tyres added to the look, as did more chrome on the auxiliary lights and the front fender and pannier rails.

That 1969-model Electra Glide was the last 74cu in (1,207cc) Panhead model before the Shovelhead took over for the following year. More than half a century later, the Revival was powered by the latest 1,868cc Milwaukee-Eight 114 engine, complete with four valves per cylinder, oil-cooled cylinder heads and balancer shaft. It made 118lb.ft (160Nm) at 3,250rpm, well up on the old bike's 70lb.ft at 4,000rpm. Its gearbox had six rather than four speeds but no longer the option of hand shifting.

The chassis and electronics had come a long way too. Back in 1969, the Electra Glide with its push-button starting (plus kick-start just in case) was four years old, and it was barely a decade since the Duo-Glide had introduced rear suspension. By contrast the Revival featured sophisticated Showa suspension and the 21st-century safety aids of cornering ABS brakes and traction control, plus Boom! Box infotainment system with twin speakers in the batwing.

ABOVE The Revival's Milwaukee-Eight 114 V-twin was over 50 per cent bigger than the old Glide's Panhead and made 70 per cent more torque.

The Electra Glide Revival was a stunningly evocative machine that was also expensive and exclusive, with production limited to 1,500 units. It had unique ergonomics, thanks to its solo saddle, which sat four inches (102mm) higher than the Electra Glide Standard's seat, and incorporated an old-style spring underneath. That sat the rider higher but still well protected by a screen that was taller than the Standard's. There was more legroom, and a comfier ride thanks to the seat spring, at the expense of a longer reach to the ground.

For 2022 the Icons series switched models with the Road Glide El Diablo, whose hand-applied red paintwork was inspired by the US West Coast custom scene of the 1980s. The following year the Electra Glide returned, this time as the 1968-inspired Electra Glide Highway King, with windscreen instead of batwing. Like the Revival, it was enjoyably quick, impressively refined, and dripping with period charm.

BELOW For 2024 the Icon was the Hydra-Glide Revival, inspired by the 1956-model FLH with red and white finish.

FLTRXSE CVO ROAD GLIDE, 2023

Harley's range has frequently included a hotted-up CVO version of the Road Glide, the mile-eating V-twin that has been among the firm's most popular models since the turn of the century, and more recently has led US motorcycling's move towards baggers of increasingly high performance.

As well as gaining bigger, more powerful engines in standard form – and a slimmer "shark-nose" fairing in a major redesign in 2015 – the Road Glide has formed the basis of the factory's King Of The Baggers racebike.

It has also been a regular choice for Custom Vehicle Operations treatment, frequently featuring a new engine. This began in 2000, the programme's second year, when the Screamin' Eagle Road Glide debuted the 95cu in (1,556cc) version of the Twin Cam 88 unit that was later widely adopted. Numerous CVO Road Glides followed, several incorporating significant upgrades.

This continued in 2023 with the CVO Road Glide, powered by the Milwaukee-Eight VVT 121 – a biggest yet, 121cu in (1,977cc) V-twin featuring variable valve timing. Along with the extra capacity over the Road Glide Special's 1,868cc Milwaukee-Eight 114 engine, the new variable valve timing gave increased torque through much of the rev range. The result was a 10bhp higher maximum of 115bhp (Harley having recently begun to quote power outputs).

Other changes included a reshaped shark-nose fairing, still with the Road Glide's trademark frame mounting, and slightly higher, flatter bars. The chassis gained stiffer, inverted Showa forks, damping-adjustable shocks with 50 per cent more travel, bigger front brake discs and radial Brembo calipers. Lighter parts including a new triple clamp contributed to a weight saving of 35lbs (16kg). And the Glide featured sophisticated electronics, including a huge touch-screen, cornering ABS brakes and traction control.

The big, free-breathing V-twin engine generated notably stronger performance, with a smoother response at low revs and extra enthusiasm as it revved towards the limit of just over

SPECIFICATIONS

Engine	air/liquid-cooled OHV V-twin
Capacity	121cu in (1,977cc)
Transmission	6-speed
Power	115bhp (claimed)
Weight	862lbs (391kg)
Wheelbase	64in (1,625mm)
Top speed	120mph (193kph)

ABOVE The rider's view includes touch-screen for info and entertainment, plus a powerful pair of audio speakers.

RIGHT This hand-sprayed Whiskey Neat with Raven Metallic paint scheme looked good but added $6,000 to the CVO model's $43,000 price.

6,000rpm. The stiffer, better controlled chassis encouraged enthusiastic cornering. And on longer trips the reshaped screen, which incorporated an adjustable wind deflector, contributed to a comfortable ride.

Even this exotic Road Glide lacked some rivals' high-end features, such as radar-assisted cruise control and semi-active suspension, but it was fast, comfortable and charismatic. Along with the similarly upgraded CVO Street Glide, it was Harley's finest and most comprehensively equipped long-haul companion yet. And like previous CVO Road Glides, it pointed towards the firm's touring future.

RIGHT The famous bar-mounted shark-nose fairing was subtly reshaped but this Harley was still instantly recognizable as a Road Glide.

2023 CVO STREET GLIDE

Since the Street Glide's launch in 2006 it had competed with the Road Glide as Milwaukee's star of the bagger movement, its distinctive batwing fairing generally helping make it the more popular of the two. The Street Glide, too, became a regular choice for Harley's CVO division, including in 2023 when it also adopted the Milwaukee-Eight VVT 121 engine.

As with the standard model, the CVO Street Glide's bar-mounted batwing allowed a slightly lighter bike and a more compact riding position than the Road Glide's frame-mounted shark-nose. The trade-off was heavier steering and a less precise feel at high speed. Harley inevitably chose the Road Glide for bagger racing, but on the highway the CVO Street Glide's blend of stripped-down style and straight-line punch was hugely appealing.

BELOW The batwing-faired Street Glide was more agile than the Road Glide but slightly less stable at speed.

BELOW Its Milwaukee-Eight VVT 121 engine gave the CVO Street Glide effortless roll-on performance.

HARLEY-DAVIDSON

REVOLUTION

In general terms, Harley-Davidson's revolution involved the introduction of liquid-cooled V-twin engines at the start of this century, after almost 100 years of cooling with air and oil alone. More specifically, Revolution was the name given to the 1,130cc, DOHC eight-valve unit, with cylinders set at 60 degrees rather than the traditional 45, that powered the stunning V-Rod on its launch in 2001.

The development had been a long time coming. The V-Rod unit shared its architecture with the engine that had been designed to power the VR1000 racebike in the late 1980s. Links with liquid cooling and Porsche engineering, who had worked on the VR powerplant, stretched back further to the aborted Nova project of the late 1970s.

The V-Rod led to a family of bikes, and in 2015 to a short-lived Street series that combined similar 60-degree layout with smaller 749 and 494cc capacities. In 2021 the Pan America debuted the Revolution Max unit, with capacity of 1,250cc and output of 145bhp, soon followed by a new liquid-cooled Sportster S. Harley's range remained dominated by 45-degree V-twins, but the new generation was gaining strength.

LEFT The Pan America was a step forward for Harley with its 145bhp liquid-cooled Revolution Max engine, and a bold leap into a new world of adventure motorcycling.

VRSCA V-ROD, 2001

Harley-Davidson had built some striking bikes over the years, but never anything remotely like this. With its aluminium finish, angled headlamp, raked-out front end, solid disc wheels and sweeping slash-cut silencers, the V-Rod resembled a show-stopping custom bike or radical dragster.

In reality it was the first of a new and distinctly more powerful breed of roadster from Milwaukee.

The 1,130cc Revolution V-twin engine featured cylinders set at 60 degrees apart, and was based on that of the VR1000, the factory racebike that had been competing, without much success, in the US Superbike championship. Like the racebike, the V-Rod had twin overhead cams, eight valves and fuel injection. Its peak output of 115bhp was getting on for twice that of the aircooled Twin Cam 88 unit.

If Harley's engine team had done a good job, in partnership with Porsche of Germany, the styling crew led by Willie G. Davidson and Louie Netz had also risen to the occasion. The V-Rod could almost have been machined from a giant lump of aluminium. It had neat details everywhere, from the slanted headlamp via the prominent steel frame tubes to the aluminium swing-arm.

From the low seat the V-Rod initially seemed deceptively normal. It set its rider's arms high, with feet well forward. Only the innovative, clamshell shaped instrument panel and alloy tank (actually an airbox cover; fuel lived

SPECIFICATIONS

Engine	liquid-cooled DOHC V-twin
Capacity	1,130cc (69cu in)
Transmission	5-speed
Power	115bhp (claimed)
Weight	594lbs (270kg)
Wheelbase	67.4in (1,713mm)
Top speed	135mph (217kph)

ABOVE With its long, low profile and milled-from-solid finish the V-Rod looked like no bike on earth.

BELOW The 1,130cc Revolution V-twin engine had twin overhead camshafts and cylinders set at 60 degrees.

ABOVE A clamshell-shaped instrument cover curled over the dummy tank.

RIGHT The aluminium disc front wheel held twin front brake rotors.

FAR RIGHT Harley used hydroforming (high-pressure water) to shape the large-diameter steel frame tubes.

under the seat) gave the game away – until the throttle was wound open and the bike hurtled forward like no ordinary cruiser.

The motor was not only powerful at the top end, it was also strong and refined at lower revs. Even from just 2,000rpm and about 30mph (48kph) in top gear, the V-Rod accelerated cleanly and without hesitation. Through the midrange it leapt forward with real enthusiasm, which made for effortless overtaking and meant that the five-speed gearbox was rarely needed.

The rev limit was 9,000rpm, and at higher revs the bike was smooth without being bland, thanks to a balancer shaft plus the Milwaukee development team's efforts to tune-in the right level of vibration. Wind-blast inevitably became tiring well before the top speed of over 130mph (209kph), but the bike was reasonably comfortable at typical freeway speeds.

For such a radical looking bike the V-Rod also handled surprisingly well. Its stretched-out steering geometry allowed it to steer precisely, if inevitably rather ponderously. The suspension was soft, but not excessively so; cornering clearance was generous by cruiser standards. Twin discs with four-piston calipers gave powerful stopping.

The V-Rod was a unique machine that did not appeal to all motorcyclists, or even all Harley riders, and it lacked the aircooled V-twins' lumpy charm. But it took two-wheeled style to new heights, and brought thrilling performance to the cruiser segment. For Harley to launch its new liquid-cooled family in such dramatic fashion was brave. To give it so much power was admirable. And to make it work as well as the V-Rod did was truly impressive.

RIGHT Despite its kicked-out forks and enormously long wheelbase the V-Rod handled well, and even allowed a respectable lean angle in bends.

VRSCDX NIGHT ROD SPECIAL, 2008

If the original V-Rod of 2001 had been the bike that sparked Harley-Davidson's liquid-cooled revolution, then the similarly long and low but distinctly different Night Rod Special that thundered onto the scene seven years later was very much its natural successor.

By cruiser standards, that first silver machine had been powerful, hard-accelerating and refined. The black-finished Night Rod Special turned the dial up to 11 on all counts.

The seven-year gap between the two models was substantial but, after stirring up the cruiser market so dramatically with the V-Rod, Harley had been slow to deliver a follow-up. In 2003 the 100th anniversary V-Rod offered special badges and a wide choice of colours, and the following year's VRSCB V-Rod had a black frame and a handful of detail differences. But that was it for another two years.

The first significant arrival came in 2006 with the Street Rod, which took the V-Rod in a sportier direction, emphasising Harley's ambition to

SPECIFICATIONS

Engine	liquid-cooled DOHC V-twin
Capacity	1,247cc (76cu in)
Transmission	5-speed
Power	123bhp (claimed)
Weight	642lbs (292kg)
Wheelbase	67.5in (1,715mm)
Top speed	140mph (225kph)

LEFT The Night Rod Special had steeper steering geometry than the original V-Rod, and a slightly sharper handling feel.

BELOW Its bikini fairing, stretched-out profile and all-black finish made the Night Rod Special reminiscent of the XLCR Café Racer of the 1970s.

RIGHT Steeper geometry, revised suspension and a more aggressive riding position made the 2006-model Street Rod feel sportier than the V-Rod.

attract younger riders. The DOHC, 60-degree V-twin engine was unchanged, but a new twin-pipe "shotgun" exhaust increased peak output by 5bhp to 120bhp. Shorter, flatter handlebars and relocated, mid-mounted (instead of forward-set) footrests gave a more aggressive riding position.

Chassis changes included a steeper steering angle, new suspension that allowed additional ground clearance, and four-piston Brembo front brake calipers. The result was a slightly quicker, notably more agile machine that felt more like a naked musclebike than a cruiser. In 2007 it was joined by the Night Rod, essentially the same bike with blacked-out engine and frame.

A year later the Night Rod Special delivered the liquid-cooled line's first engine upgrade: a bored-out, 1,247cc version of the eight-valve V-twin. This increased midrange torque and raised peak output to 123bhp. The all-black Special combined its long, low profile with a headlamp fairing and slotted disc wheels, giving a hint of the XLCR Café Racer from the 1970s.

Harley's experiment with a sportier variant was over: the Night Rod Special's forks were less steep than the Street Rod's (though less kicked-out than the original V-Rod's), and it reverted to forward-set footrests. That made the Special more like the original bike to ride, though its bigger, more flexible engine meant it was quicker and required less effort. A wider rear wheel and fatter tyre gave plenty of grip off the line. New Brembo front brake calipers with ABS meant it was among the hardest-stopping bikes Harley had ever built.

A year later the Special was joined by what turned out to be the family's final model. The V-Rod Muscle shared the same 1,247cc engine and reflected its name both by generating more midrange grunt, thanks to a new twin-sided exhaust system, and by requiring more force through the handlebars on a twisty road, thanks to revised geometry that enhanced stability.

Frustratingly for Harley, neither the Muscle nor the Night Rod Special approached the sales of the firm's familiar aircooled V-twins. The liquid-cooled models remained in the range until 2017, before production ended and the revolution that had begun so dramatically 16 years earlier quietly ground to a halt.

ABOVE The Night Rod Special was among the first Harleys fitted with an ABS brake system, developed with Italian specialist Brembo.

RIGHT The V-Rod Muscle handled well but lived up to its name by requiring firm pressure on the bars to make it change direction.

XG750 STREET, 2014

At a glance, the Street 750 and its near-identical sibling the Street 500 resembled Harley's powerful Night Rod Special and that bike's inspiration, the lean black XLCR Café Racer that had been one of Milwaukee's best known models of the 1970s.

The Streets were very different: entry-level machines designed to appeal not so much with performance as with a competitive price.

The Streets were aimed at a fresh generation of riders; replacements for the ageing "baby boomers" who had long been Harley's customer base. Bikes destined for north America, where the 500cc model was more than $1000 less expensive than the cheapest Sportster, were assembled in Kansas City. For other markets the Streets were produced at Harley's plant at Bawal in India, where labour cost less and the bikes were intended to satisfy many Asian countries' growing enthusiasm for premium brands.

Harley coined the name Revolution X for the new engine, which shared its liquid-cooling and 60-degree cylinder angle with the bigger Revolution unit but used single instead of twin overhead camshafts. The 749cc model produced about 50bhp; the smaller-bore 494cc unit slightly less.

The two models were otherwise identical and had areas where they failed to live up to Harley's normal high standard of finish. Some castings were crude, the switchgear was basic, and there was no rev-counter or gear indicator.

Performance was respectable, though. The Street 750 had a lively feel, and accelerated with slightly more enthusiasm than the Iron 883 that was its closest rival in the range. It had enough power for fairly relaxed cruising at 70mph (113kph), and for a top speed of about 100mph (161kph). The 60-degree V-twin was fairly

SPECIFICATIONS

Engine	liquid-cooled SOHC V-twin
Capacity	749cc (76cu in)
Transmission	6-speed
Power	50bhp (estimated)
Weight	504lbs (229kg)
Wheelbase	60.4in (1,535mm)
Top speed	100mph (161kph)

LEFT The Street 750's output of about 50bhp was sufficient for a respectable cruising pace, and it was smooth if slightly lacking in character.

BELOW From a distance the Street models were cleanly styled but closer inspection revealed a basic specification and some untidy details.

ABOVE Both Street engines followed the V-Rod unit with a 60-degree angle but had an SOHC valve layout.

ABOVE The 500cc Street was visually identical to the 750 and was popular with training schools in the US.

smooth, and its six-speed gearbox shifted cleanly.

At over 500lbs (227kg) the Street was heavy by entry-level standards but it steered easily and the low seat helped make it manageable. Handling and ride quality were fairly good. The single front and rear disc brakes were initially weak but Harley quickly upgraded them, and also added the option of ABS.

That helped make the Streets competitive as entry-level models, and they had some success both in export markets and in the US, where the smaller bike was used by training schools. But although the liquid-cooled machines had café-racer style plus that famous double-barrelled name on the tank, they lacked the soulful appeal of the traditional aircooled V-twins.

Harley didn't give up, and in 2017 released the XG750A Street Rod, featuring a tuned, 70bhp engine in an revamped chassis comprising stiffer frame, sportier geometry, new suspension, 17in wheels and twin front brake discs. It was quicker and more exciting to ride than the Street 750, handled better and was still keenly priced.

Even the Street Rod couldn't tempt enough young riders or generate the global sales that Milwaukee had been hoping for, though. In 2020, with emissions regulations closing in on the Revolution X engine, and Harley's "Hardwire" programme focussing on the most profitable areas of business, the firm closed its Indian factory and ended production of the Streets.

RIGHT Its tuned engine and an uprated chassis incorporating 17-inch wheels made the XG750A Street Rod fun to ride but it proved short-lived.

PAN AMERICA, 2021

Two decades after the V-Rod had led Harley-Davidson's cruisers into a new era of liquid-cooled performance, the Pan America revitalized the 60-degree, DOHC V-twin line and took it in a very different direction – into a fiercely competitive but potentially lucrative new world.

Milwaukee's first big adventure model was a belated attack on a thriving market sector – and its striking, arguably brutal styling, with a hint of two-wheeled Jeep, confirmed an imaginative and aggressive approach.

The Pan America's 1,252cc so-called Revolution Max engine shared its basic layout with the V-Rod family unit, but was an all-new design featuring variable valve timing, twin balancer shafts and crankpins offset by 30 degrees to give a 90-degree firing order. Ride-by-wire throttle control allowed multiple engine modes. Peak output was 148bhp at 8,750rpm, substantially up on any of the old V-Rod models.

Alongside the standard Pan America was a higher specification model, the Special. Both used the same engine, which doubled as a stressed member of the chassis, along with bolted-on steel frame sections and a cast aluminium swing-arm. Both used long-travel Showa suspension, the Special differing by having semi-active actuation, plus the option of an innovative adaptive ride height system that lowered the bike slightly as it approached a stop, then raised it again as it pulled away.

The Pan America's list of features confirmed that this was a seriously modern motorbike. Even the standard

LEFT Despite its size and weight the Pan America could perform impressively in difficult off-road conditions if its rider was sufficiently skilled.

SPECIFICATIONS

Engine	liquid-cooled DOHC V-twin
Capacity	1,252cc (76cu in)
Transmission	6-speed
Power	148bhp (claimed)
Weight	534lbs (243kg)
Wheelbase	62.2in (1,580mm)
Top speed	135mph (217kph)

BELOW Nobody could accuse the big, brutally styled and unmistakable Pan America of being just another adventure bike clone.

RIGHT For 2024 the Pan America was given its first CVO upgrade, featuring special paint and accessories including aluminium luggage.

model had a colourful touch-screen instrument panel, adjustable windscreen, Brembo brakes with cornering ABS, and a sophisticated traction control system. The Special's extras included a headlight that illuminated through turns, heated grips, a steering damper for added stability, and a protective aluminium bash-plate.

Entering such a fiercely contested market sector with an all-new model had been a huge ask for Harley, and the Pan America surprised many with its ability to give even long-established rivals a run for their money. Its engine delivered crisp throttle response and a generous surge of torque throughout the range, and stayed smooth without feeling bland. Acceleration to the 135mph (217kph) top speed was thrillingly strong.

The chassis worked well, too, making what was inevitably a big, fairly heavy bike not only a very capable roadster but also a useful off-roader. It steered and handled well, had powerful brakes, provided useful wind protection and a generous fuel range, and was respectably comfortable. Accessories including luggage added to its long-distance potential. The Special's adaptive ride height was genuinely useful, especially for smaller riders (and was soon followed by similar systems from rival firms).

Harley's research, before the firm committed to the project, had suggested that there were plenty of existing customers who would welcome an adventure model, and also many adventure riders who would consider a bike from Milwaukee. Response following the Pan America's launch in early 2021 seemed to bear this out.

By September the bike was top of the US dual-sport sales chart, and Harley had announced that first-year production had sold out. There would doubtless be bumps in the road ahead, but the Pan America looked ready for the challenge.

ABOVE Effortless cruising ability and a roomy riding position helped make the Pan America a capable tourer.

BELOW Brembo radial front calipers came as standard but wire wheels were an option even on the Special.

BELOW The 1,252cc Revolution Max unit was powerful and fairly smooth yet had some V-twin character.

SPORTSTER S, 2021

Although it shared some of the aggressive attitude of recent models with its famous family name, the all-new Sportster S was a very different bike to the familiar aircooled, 45-degree V-twins whose lineage stretched right back to the original 883cc Sportster of 1957.

LEFT Its compact design, fat tyres and unique features, such as its headlight, gave the Sportster S a distinctive, streetwise look to begin the family's new chapter.

BELOW The low-set single seat unit and tailpiece helped make the Sportster manageable and brought to mind the legendary XR750 flat-tracker.

Notably more powerful and refined, the 1,252cc Sportster S was launched in 2021 to lead a new, liquid-cooled family of streetbikes.

The end of the old aircooled line was mourned by many, but Harley's hand had been forced by tightening emissions legislation. By contrast, the S-model's 60-degree V-twin engine was heavily based on that of the recently introduced Pan America, albeit in a lower state of tune. The DOHC, eight-valve layout and variable valve timing remained. Reshaped camshafts, smaller valves and a revised intake system added ten per cent more torque between 3,000 and 6,000rpm, while cutting peak power output by 30bhp to 118bhp.

Style had long been a big part of the Sportster family's appeal, and the S-model had a bold, muscular look that blended some of the streetwise appeal of recent aircooled models like the Forty-Eight with an added hint of menace. Its upside-down forks, fat front tyre and running-track shaped headlight caught the eye up front. The fuel tank, twin "shotgun" exhausts and minimalist seat unit owed a debt to the legendary XR750 flat-track racer.

The riding position combined fairly wide, raised handlebars and forward-set footrests with a low solo seat, which helped make the S-bike manageable despite the bike's 502lbs (228kg) of weight. The cruiser-style ergonomics did not suit every rider but the accessory list included mid-mounted footrests, along with a pillion seat.

SPECIFICATIONS

Engine	liquid-cooled DOHC V-twin
Capacity	1,252cc
Transmission	6-speed
Power	118bhp (claimed)
Weight	502lbs (228kg)
Wheelbase	62.2in (1,580mm)
Top speed	135mph (217kph)

ABOVE Even in detuned form, the 1,252cc liquid-cooled V-twin made this the most powerful Sportster by far.

ABOVE The tubular steel swing-arm and fat rear tyre contributed to a clean rear-end look; final drive was by belt in Harley-Davidson tradition.

Like the Pan America, the Sportster S used its engine – which Harley called the Revolution Max 1250T – as a stressed member of the chassis. Its bolted-on main frame member was made from aluminium, rather than steel like the Pan America's; and the swing-arm was tubular steel rather than aluminium. Also like the adventure model, the S-bike incorporated a host of modern features including TFT instrument panel, multiple riding modes, cornering ABS brakes and traction control.

Straight-line performance was in a different class to that of its aircooled predecessors. The S-bike stormed away from the line in exhilarating fashion, pulled cleanly from low revs and surged through the midrange, before kicking harder as it approached the 8,000rpm redline. It flicked sweetly through its six-speed gearbox, and stayed smooth thanks to twin balancer shafts although Harley's engineers had been careful to allow some vibration to remain.

The chassis also worked respectably well, giving stable handling, although the fat front tyre resulted in slightly heavy steering, and the short-travel Showa rear shock couldn't prevent a harsh ride on a bumpy road. The single front disc and four-piston Brembo brake caliper generated good stopping power in conjunction with the rear disc.

Inevitably the Sportster S couldn't replicate the lumpy charm of its aircooled forebears, and it was also considerably more expensive. But it was fun to ride, solidly engineered, and a stylish and distinctive machine with which to begin a new Sportster era.

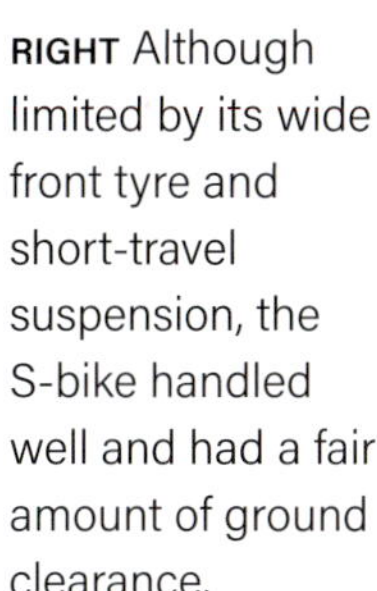

RIGHT Although limited by its wide front tyre and short-travel suspension, the S-bike handled well and had a fair amount of ground clearance.

NIGHTSTER, 2022

A year after Harley-Davidson had begun a new family of liquid-cooled V-twins with the 1,252cc Pan America and Sportster S, the firm added the 975cc Nightster to provide a less powerful but more rider-friendly and accessible entry-level model.

The Nightster name had previously been used in 2008, for a 1,200cc Sportster variant. Despite the new bike's modern, 60-degree V-twin engine, there was a hint of its aircooled ancestry in its look and twin-shock chassis.

The Revolution Max 975T engine shared its basic architecture and DOHC, eight-valve top end design with the bigger unit, but there were more differences than simply a smaller bore and stroke. Each cylinder had a single spark plug, rather than two; and the variable valve timing worked only on the intake side. The smaller unit was revvier, putting out its maximum torque at 5,000rpm and its peak output of 89bhp at 7,500rpm.

There were also significant chassis differences between the Nightster and Sportster S, in addition to the smaller model's use of twin Showa shocks instead of a hidden monoshock. Although the two bikes' tank and seat layouts looked similar, the Nightster held its fuel under its seat, and had a dummy tank that covered the airbox.

Other visible differences included mid-mounted rather than forward-set footrests; a single, low-set silencer instead of twin pipes, and a 19in cast front wheel wearing a narrower, 100-section tyre. The Nightster also had simpler electronics, including three preset engine modes but no customizable options, and basic ABS and traction control systems.

Harley had copied the Nightster's

LEFT The Nightster had some of the look of its aircooled namesake from 2008, but its performance and character were distinctly different.

SPECIFICATIONS

Engine	liquid-cooled DOHC V-twin
Capacity	975cc
Transmission	6-speed
Power	89bhp (claimed)
Weight	486lbs (221kg)
Wheelbase	60.8in (1,545mm)
Top speed	110mph (177kph)

LEFT The small gas tank and minimalist rear end were traditional Sportster features; the 60-degree, liquid-cooled V-twin, not so much.

RIGHT Harleys are typically designed to be viewed from the right side but the Nightster also looked good from the left, especially with just a solo seat fitted.

riding position from its namesake of 2008, which meant a fairly upright posture with hands on the slightly raised bars, and a reasonable amount of legroom despite the low seat. That helped make the bike manoeuvrable and rider-friendly at slow speeds, as did its gentle low-rev power delivery.

This Harley wasn't designed just to be ridden slowly, though. It was a lively machine that pulled adequately strongly through its midrange, before kicking harder as it charged towards the 9,500rpm limit. Rather than being laid-back like its aircooled forebears, it encouraged plenty of action from its rider's right wrist and a busy left foot to flick through the six-speed gearbox.

The chassis was a capable accomplice, helped by reasonably firm and well-damped suspension, notably at the rear where the shocks gave significantly more travel than the Sportster S's unit. Steering was lighter than the larger model's, too, thanks partly to the slimmer front tyre.

The Nightster lacked the old-school charm of its aircooled Sportster predecessors and it was also considerably more expensive, which limited its appeal to new and younger riders. But as a stylish and sporty cruiser it was capable and fun in much the same way as its namesake of 14 years earlier, while outperforming it in almost every area.

LEFT The Nightster Special arrived in 2023 with features including a TFT display and the pillion seat that was an extra with the standard model.

XR
HARLEY-
DAVIDSON
750

RACEBIKES

The first Harley-Davidson racebikes were nothing more than standard production machines in the hands of some adventurous private individuals.

These days, although competition is not what Harley is best known for, it's very much part of the company soul. The Milwaukee firm joined the American motorcycle racing scene in its early years and became the dominant force. Walter Davidson himself recorded the first "factory" win in an endurance trial in 1908. By the First World War, daredevil riders were hurtling along on Harley twins at three-figure speeds – with no brakes and almost no suspension.

Since the innocent enthusiasm of the pioneer years, a huge variety of Harley machines have won races and championships, set records and provided entertainment: from the first eight-valvers, via the booming XR750 that ruled flat track for decades, to the improbably fast and spectacular Road Glide bagger of recent seasons. For Harley-Davidson, as for almost everyone else, racing has improved the breed.

LEFT At the start of its remarkable era of flat-track domination in 1975, the brakeless XR750 was a battle-honed yet still wonderfully elemental racing motorcycle.

EARLY RACERS

Harley-Davidson tasted competition success from 1908 with riders including Walter Davidson, and within another decade the firm was producing rapid purpose-designed competition V-twins, some of them exotic, highly tuned machines featuring four valves per cylinder.

EIGHT-VALVE, TWO-CAM

Although a special "7-E" competition version of Harley-Davidson's first V-twin was built for selected customers as early as 1910, the first model created specifically for racing was the eight-valve twin which appeared in 1916. The multi-valve layout had already been amply proven by the exploits of Indian's similar engine, which had made a big impact in board-track racing. Displacing 61cu in (999cc), the Harley-Davidson eight-valve was the device on which the Harley Wrecking Crew began their domination of the American racing scene.

Private individuals were less fortunate, since the machine's price – $1,500 – was deliberately inflated to ensure that it could only fall into serious hands.

A 65cu in (1,065cc) twin-cam racer followed. Like the eight-valve model, the Two-Cam had inlet-over-exhaust valve layout, no brakes and direct drive by chain to the rear wheel (although some examples may have used three-speed transmissions). Once started – no easy task due to the use of very high compression ratios – these monsters were capable of well over 100mph (161kph). To promote its wares overseas, Harley-Davidson freighted its top racing machines all over the world. In Britain, both Freddie Dixon and D.H. Davidson took the Two-Cam to numerous records at the famed banked Brooklands circuit in Surrey. In September 1923, at Arpajon in France, Dixon rode the same machine to a world-record speed of 106.5mph (171.4kph).

LEFT A handsome 74-inch J-series racer dating from 1924. Note the total lack of any sort of brakes.

LEFT A 1924 74-inch F-head racer. Exhaust silencing was not a prime concern.

OHV TWINS

During the mid-1920s, the F-head Two-Cam was the mainstay of Harley-Davidson's factory twin-cylinder racing efforts, but they were seriously hampered when the AMA introduced the new "Class C" racing formula. This was for production-based 45cu in (750cc) machines, of which at least 25 had to be built. Overnight, the old Class A and Class B factory specials were relegated to the sidelines in much of American racing – especially in the

LEFT Another F-head, a 1920 board racer ridden by Dewey Sims. The plunger on the left side of the tank feeds engine oil.

ABOVE The legendary eight-valve racer, one of the most potent motorcycles in the world in its day.

RIGHT Four overhead valves per cylinder can clearly be seen in this view of the same 1923 eight-valver. Note the single carburettor between the cylinders.

buoyant "slant-shooting" (hill-climbing) scene.

At the time, Milwaukee produced no eligible machine, but by 1926 it did have the remarkably fast 21-inch OHV Peashooter single, and any fool could see that two times 21 wasn't far from 45. Before too long someone investigated the possibility of grafting Peashooter heads on to existing V-twin bottom ends.

The first such OHV Harley-Davidson twin was probably a machine dubbed "Home Brew", ridden with some success by Oscar Lenz in 1927. A similar device, also based on a 61-inch bottom end, was built by Ralph Moore of Indianapolis.

By 1928, Harley-Davidson had given in to popular demand and released "roadster" versions of its Two-Cam racing twins, the 61-inch JH and 74-inch JDH and it wasn't long before Juneau Avenue followed the example of creative privateers with a number of factory specials featuring OHV Peashooter top ends grafted on to JD Two-Cam crankcases.

These first hit the tracks in 1928 at Fond du Lac, just a few miles north of Milwaukee. However, there is some dispute as to whether they were actually created in Harley's competition shop or by a local dealer, Bill Knuth, with the factory's knowledge and support.

In either case, this was an interim measure, because twelve months later a 45-inch factory racer, the DAH, first appeared.

Unlike the Two-Cam-based machines, the DAH was substantially a new engine from the ground up, although it still depended on cylinder heads derived from the Peashooter's.

Displacing 45.44cu in (744cc), the DAH retained the 88.9mm stroke of the JD, but with a bore reduced to 70.6mm.

The DAH was dominant for a while, but Knuth came back with a four-cam hybrid reputed to produce fully 45 horsepower, which continued to give the official factory machines a run for their money. There are even records of a 61-inch OHV racing twin, designated FAR, being built for export.

It is highly likely that, in some measure or other, these exotic racing models were to inspire the later Knucklehead OHV twin. What is for certain is the profound influence that they had on the racing world at large.

RIGHT Compared to the exotic factory eight-valvers, F-head board racers such as this were relatively low-tech, but still capable of frightening speeds.

PEASHOOTER, 1929

As legendary in its way as the exotic Two-Cam, the Peashooter began life as a standard roadster model. The little single would become one of Harley's most successful competition machines, scoring spectacular wins in dirt-track racing, especially, over a number of years.

The Peashooter was based on the overhead-valve Model AA magneto version of the 21.1cu in (346cc) single produced from 1926 to 1935, which proved itself more than amenable to race tuning. Perhaps this was not altogether surprising, as the cylinder head – the most crucial performance element in any four-stroke engine – was designed by the great Harry Ricardo, the British engineering genius. Only a few years earlier, Ricardo had created Triumph's first four-valve motor, the Model R. Sir Harry, as he was later to become, practically invented the art of petrol-flowing and, during the course of developing the concept of octane ratings for fuel, gained an unparalleled understanding of the combustion process.

Central to the Peashooter's success were two things. One was the engine's hemispherical "squish" heads, in which the outer portion of the piston crown almost touches the cylinder head as it rises up the bore. This in turn

ABOVE Joe Petrali kicks up the dirt with his Peashooter's rear tyre in 1935, when he won all 13 national races.

BELOW This single became a legend on the race tracks of the United States.

ABOVE "Speedster" drop handlebars were a feature of the Peashooter.

ABOVE The cylinder head of the Peashooter was designed by Harry Ricardo, a British engineer.

creates a fierce turbulence, promoting fuel/air mixing and combustion. This made the 'Shooter's combustion more efficient than its rivals over a broader range of revs, also permitting the safe use of higher compression ratios. Even in roadster form, the "21" generated only 20 per cent less power than an F-head twin with almost three times the displacement.

The Peashooter's other "ace" was Joe Petrali, who remains one of the most successful riders ever to grace the race tracks of America. In 1935, towards the end of the model's racing career, Petrali won every one of the 13 dirt-track races in the national series. The diminutive Californian was equally adept whether board racing or tackling towering hill-climbs, proving virtually unbeatable until his retirement in 1938.

SPECIFICATIONS

Engine	aircooled OHV single
Capacity	21cu in (346cc)
Transmission	1- or 3-speed
Power	30bhp
Weight	290lbs (132kg)
Wheelbase	55in (1,400mm)
Top Speed	over 80mph (128kph)

ABOVE Chains were commonly fitted for extra grip on hill climbs.

Petrali and the single first hit the headlines when the AMA adopted a new 21-inch racing class in 1925. In the first race under the new formula, fittingly held in Milwaukee before a crowd of over 20,000, Petrali, Jim Davis and Eddie Brock simply blasted the opposition into the Wisconsin weeds. Board-racing versions of the OHV roadster were stripped to the bare essentials, with tiny seats, "Speedster" drop handlebars and neither brakes nor mudguards. Such abbreviated devices were easily capable of speeds in excess of 80mph (128kph). Depending on the type of competition, they were built with single-speed (Model SM) or three-speed (SA) transmission.

Despite the OHV single's instant track success, Juneau Avenue was oddly disposed towards its side-valve sidekick since the flathead roadster was seen as the likeliest seller. However, others quickly saw the potential of high-revving overhead-valve engines, and the Peashooter became the single of choice on the American racing scene (although a speedway version, inspired by the all-conquering British JAP, was far less successful).

The final, flattering piece in the Peashooter jigsaw came with the introduction of the OHV Knucklehead in 1936.

Although the factory was developing overhead-valve DAH competition twins during the late 1920s, the Knuckle bears many detail similarities with the Peashooter top end.

Whether this was by design or accident, no-one can now tell.

WR/WRTT, 1940

Harley-Davidson's racing mainstay of the 1940s, the side-valve WR, was a star of the popular Class C production flat-track racing scene and was also produced as the WRTT for TT (Tourist Trophy) events, road races and others where brakes were required.

The WR had the humblest of beginnings, evolving by degrees from the unpretentious Model D of 1929. Essentially, this was powered by little more than a pair of Ricardo heads grafted from the 21.1cu in (346cc) single onto a common crankcase. The machine developed rapidly year-on-year, becoming the Model R in 1932, at which time its hottest roadster derivative was the RLD Special Sport Solo.

By 1935, the Series R range included five models based on the familiar flathead "45", crowned by the lean and purposeful RLDR Competition Special – a snip at $322. For 1937, a Knucklehead-inspired restyle and a welter of engine improvements metamorphosed the R into the enduring Model W. Other than the change of prefix letter, the 45-inch range continued as before, now with the WLDR Competition Special at its head – a WR in all but name. Harley-Davidson put this right in 1941: the WLDR still existed, but now as a mere Special Sport Solo roadster.

Taking its place as the hottest 45 was the plain WR, a race machine available only to special order. Initially, availability was poor – just 36 WRs were produced in 1941 – but both demand and supply picked up dramatically in the aftermath of war.

These purpose-built racing machines were, of course, very much stripped down compared to their roadster cousins (the WR had not so much as a front mudguard, and later examples also benefited from a lightweight chrome-molybdenum steel chassis). The WRTT, produced as a specific model only late in the WR's career, retained the heavier roadster frame. Being a flat-track machine, the WR also had no brakes, while the road-racing TT machine was equipped with

SPECIFICATIONS

Engine	aircooled side valve 4-stroke V-twin
Capacity	45u in (742cc)
Transmission	3- or 4-speed
Power	40bhp
Weight	300lbs (136kg)
Wheelbase	60in (1,525mm)
Top speed	around 105mph (169kph)

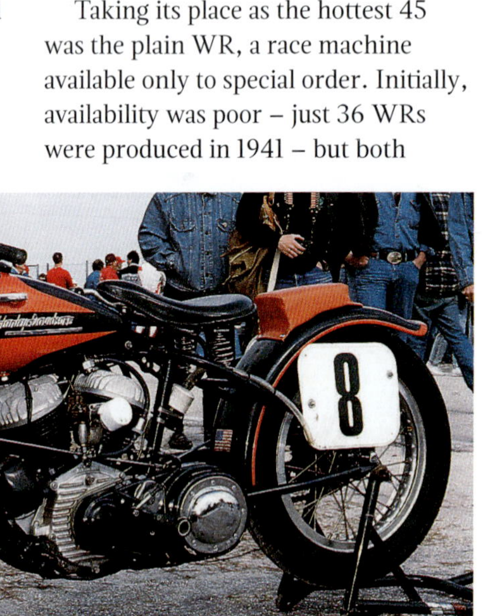

LEFT This "45" wears telescopic forks manufactured long after the side-valve racer was history.

LEFT The "pillion" pad helped the rider stretch out to cheat the wind.

BELOW A competitor fettles his "45" during a modern classic race meeting.

ABOVE AND RIGHT Although substantially similar engines propelled American postmen, the WR carried Harley's racing banner for a decade in both factory and private teams.

standard WL wheels and brakes – scarcely state-of-the-art stopping power. The WR's suspension was no more impressive, with old-fashioned girder front forks and a rigid rear end. For good measure, the gearbox, although available with close-ratio racing cogs, was hand-change. It may have been crude, and 40bhp from 45 inches was unimpressive. Yet this, and sheer weight of numbers, was enough to rival the much more sophisticated but sorely handicapped overhead-valve twins and overhead-camshaft singles from Europe. The brute toughness of the WRTT, in particular, made it a surprisingly capable "Class C" racer.

For more than a decade, these outwardly primitive machines gave a good account of themselves on the race tracks of America – taking 19 out of 23 championship victories in 1948 alone.

This was partly because they were rugged and dependable, and partly because the AMA was as eager then as it has been since to adjust the rules in favour of domestic hardware.

In this case the AMA, which is the governing body of American motorcycle sport, greeted the arrival of fast European overhead-valve machines with a decree that said they would be limited to 500cc, while side-valves of 750cc were permitted. And guess who made the only flathead racers in the frame?

WLDR: CLASS C CONTENDER

Harley's first racing success with the 74cu in flathead V-twin came in the late 1930s with the WLDR, after the AMA had created Class C – an affordable category for standard bikes, with the only permitted modifications being the removal of lights, brakes and licence plates. The WLDR, basically the WL roadster with racing parts, was ideal for Class C, which quickly became very popular.

One of Class C's early stars was Ben Campanale, who won the Daytona 200 on a private WLDR in 1938, then repeated the victory in 1939, this time on a bike provided by the Harley factory. After quitting racing Campanale ran a California Harley dealership, where one of his customers was movie star Clark Gable.

Campanale's successor as Daytona 200 winner in 1940 was Babe Tancrede, a fellow Harley rider and New Hampshire native. The prestigious, attritional Florida race involved repeated blasts up Daytona Beach and back down the A1A highway. Tancrede, on his robust WLDR, was among only 15 of the 77 starters to finish.

BELOW Ben Campanale won the Daytona 200 on a private WLDR in 1938, and on a factory bike a year later.

BELOW Babe Tancrede won another Daytona 200 for Harley in 1940, when only 15 of the 77 riders finished.

KR/KRTT, 1952

What Harley-Davidson needed to replace the elderly WR was a machine reflecting the technology of its era. In the KR, the company most certainly didn't get it. What it got instead was yet another long-stroke flathead racer derived from a road bike.

The model in question was the 45.3cu in (742cc) Model K which was about to be so comprehensively licked by British machines on America's streets. In racing, the KR had an edge: the AMA's 500cc limit on overhead-valve engines still applied.

As with the WR a decade earlier, production began slowly, with just 17 KRs built in the first year. Yet by 1955, the special equipment range encompassed no fewer than five specific models: the KHK Super Sport Solo, KHRM off-roader, KR dirt track racer, and KRTT and KHRTT "Tourist Trophy" machines.

All three KH models boasted the new 55cu in (883cc) long-stroke K-Series engine and were essentially "race replicas" intended as much for the private enthusiast as the racer. Serious racers remained limited to what the regulations allowed: 750cc.

In 1955, the factory built 90 45-inch competition models, declining to 33 by the decade's end. Unlike the WR/WRTT, all variants now enjoyed a lightweight racing frame, although only the road-racing TT model received the new swinging-arm rear end.

The flat track KR had a smaller tank, fatter wheels and tyres and no need of brakes. Bore and stroke were identical to the WR's at 70 x 97mm (the slow-revving 55's stroke was even longer at 116mm).

However, the cylinders were commonly re-bored after bedding-in.

LEFT Few racers have remained competitive for as long as the KR, although it needed help from the rules to survive.

ABOVE The 45-inch (750cc) engine in close-up. The push-rod tubes to the side valves are clearly seen.

LEFT A very original example of a 1962 KR dirt-tracker. Note the lack of rear suspension or brakes.

SPECIFICATIONS

Engine	aircooled side-valve 4-stroke V-twin
Capacity	45cu in (742cc)
Transmission	4-speed
Power	48bhp
Weight	377–385lbs (171–175kg)
Wheelbase	56in (1,420mm)
Top speed	150mph (240kph) (with road-race streamlining)

RIGHT This dirt tracker wears TT-type rear suspension and brakes, although both the shock absorbers and front forks are non-period items.

By using the maximum permitted piston oversize, mechanics could raise the displacement legally to 46.8cu in (767cc).

At 9:1, the compression ratio was high by side-valve standards and a single 33mm Linkert carburettor was standard. Power was around 48bhp at 7,000rpm, with 50lb.ft (68Nm) of torque at 5,000rpm. British Norton, Matchless and Triumph machines, as well as putting out far more specific power than the KR, handled and stopped far better. Yet the old KRs just kept rolling on.

While they were heavy (around 380lbs/172kg) and ill-suited to any circuit with proper corners, they remained surprisingly competitive elsewhere – not least because every race grid in America seemed to be packed with them. Since a dirt-track KR actually cost $95 less than a stock road-going Sportster during the mid-1960s, perhaps this wasn't too surprising.

The road racers, too, were capable of surprising feats. At the super-fast Daytona Speedway, streamlined KRs have been recorded in excess of 150mph (240kph), an astonishing achievement for a side-valve machine.

For all their shortcomings, in the hands of racing aces such as Bart Markel and Carroll Resweber, they managed to win a round dozen American national titles during their 18 years on the grid.

The KR's astonishing span came to an end in 1969 when the AMA ended discriminatory limitations on overseas machines.

Unfortunately for Harley-Davidson, when faced with a level playing field there was no way that the redoubtable old flathead "45" could compete with the overhead-valve machines.

BELOW Rear springing identifies this KR as the TT version.

BELOW A KRTT in Harley's famous orange and black factory racing colours.

XR750, 1970

To many people's eyes – and ears – the XR750 was the most handsome, raunchiest and most purposeful piece of kit ever to rumble out of Milwaukee. And in the XR's case, that subjective gut feeling is backed-up by incomparable statistics.

Certainly no other Harley-Davidson enjoyed so much competition success for so long as the seminal flat-tracker, which won 37 Grand National championships and 502 main event races over more than four decades.

The glory followed a disappointing debut in 1970. Mert Lawwill had won the previous year's title on Harley's KR750, which had dominated for years with the help of AMA regulations that gave side-valve bikes a 250cc capacity advantage, hindering their overhead-valve British rivals. For 1970 the limit changed to 750cc for all, prompting Harley to introduce the overhead-valve XR750.

But Lawwill and team-mate Mark Brelsford could manage only sixth and seventh in the AMA championship. The problem was the engine's iron cylinders, which were heavy and conducted heat less efficiently than aluminium components. This meant compression ratio had to be drastically reduced if breakdowns were to be avoided. In 1970, race boss Dick O'Brien admitted to a lowly 62bhp.

Midway through the following year, Harley replaced iron with aluminium, after which the XR750 didn't look back. The new engine had over-square dimensions, in contrast to the long-stroke iron-head unit. This format, allied to a much stronger crankshaft,

LEFT By 1975 the revised aluminium V-twin with oversquare dimensions had set the XR on the path to success.

BELOW The '75 XR750 was the purest of racebikes, with its aircooled engine, steel-tube frame, tiny tank and seat, and no brakes.

SPECIFICATIONS

Engine	aircooled OHV V-twin
Capacity	45cu in (748cc)
Transmission	4-speed
Power	around 100bhp
Weight	290lbs (132kg)
Top speed	130mph (210kph)

ABOVE The uncompetitive and unreliable iron-engined XR750 of 1970 was revamped in the following season.

ABOVE Mert Lawwill raced the XR for many years after winning the 1969 AMA title on its KR750 predecessor.

permitted more revs and a substantially higher compression ratio. The result was a dramatic rise in power and reliability, initially to about 80bhp.

The XR's lightweight, high-grade steel frame held Ceriani forks and Girling rear shock absorbers. Claimed dry weight was a feather-light 295lbs (134kg), although the XR road racers' fairing, brakes (early dirt-trackers had none) and larger fuel tank added about 30lbs (14kg).

Brelsford took the XR to the 1972 Grand National title, and Cal Rayborn whipped all comers that Easter in the annual USA v Great Britain road-race series. In subsequent seasons the XR was all but unbeatable on dirt, in the hands of riders including multiple champions Jay Springsteen, Chris Carr, Jared Mees and most of all Scott Parker, who won nine titles between 1988 and 1998.

A consistent XR attribute was its ability to find grip on the dirt. "The first time I got to ride one is one of my greatest memories," Parker said. "It had so much more horsepower than anything I had ever ridden, and the way it delivered the horsepower – wow! You could just get it in a corner and give it the gas. It would turn the rear wheel and start putting traction down to the ground, and down the straightaway you'd go."

Harley evolved the XR continuously, maintaining its distinctive look despite the introduction of upside-down forks, cast wheels, a rear brake and huge silencer. From 1980 the factory did not build complete XRs, instead selling engines which were then built into bikes using parts from firms such as frame specialist Champion.

Engine development was less visible but equally vital. Cylinder porting evolved from round to oval. Valve construction went from steel to titanium; valve springs became stiffer. Peak revs increased from less than 8,000rpm to over 9,500rpm. Maximum power output climbed to around 105bhp, good for over 130mph (209kph) on the mile-circuit straights.

Eventually even the XR750 became less competitive, and Harley replaced it with the liquid-cooled XG750R for 2017. But it continued to be ridden by privateers for several more years, its status as one of the greatest racebikes of all time by now secure.

LEFT Scott Parker spent nine seasons with the AMA champion's No. 1 plate on the front of his factory XR750.

RIGHT By the end of its life the XR had become more powerful and refined but retained its traditional simplicity.

RR250, RR350, 1971

The twin cylinder, two-stroke racers built at Varese during the 1970s, after Harley's takeover of Aermacchi, brought the Milwaukee marque a hat-trick of 250cc world championships plus a 350cc title – its sole successes in post-war grand prix road racing.

These were state-of-the-art machines, broadly similar to the stroker twins produced by Yamaha and Kawasaki, with fierce powerbands, strident exhaust notes and performance belying their relatively small engine displacement. To cope with the narrow band of usable revs, the gearbox held six speeds, the maximum allowed by FIM regulations.

The 250's 56.2 x 50mm cylinders were fed via rotary disc valves by twin 34mm Mikuni carburettors. The earliest examples were aircooled but the factory soon switched to liquid-cooling, bringing far greater temperature stability and reliability during long grand prix races. Primary drive was by gear, to a multi-plate dry clutch and thence to the six-speed "box". Power output was prodigious (particularly by Milwaukee's four-stroke standards), with the 250 producing 58bhp at 12,000rpm and the 350 a dozen horsepower more at 11,400rpm. The 250's figure equates to over 232bhp per litre, compared to a mere 65 for the KR750 which had been Harley-Davidson's racing mainstay at the time RR250 development began.

The chassis featured a conventional twin cradle of high-grade tubular steel. Italian Cerianio forks graced the front end with a pair of British-made Girling shocks at the rear. The whole package weighed just 230lbs (104kg).

If the machine had a shortcoming, it was the use of drum brakes (albeit a double-sided twin-leading shoe affair at the front) when hydraulic discs were already in widespread use and far superior. Discs finally arrived in 1976, by which time Italian star Walter Villa had already taken two 250cc world titles.

With better brakes, he repeated the feat in 1976, adding the 350cc title for good measure. RRs also campaigned successfully in American road races, ridden by Gary Scott, Jay Springsteen, Cal Rayborn and others.

ABOVE The great Walter Villa at speed on the RR250 at the notorious Nurburgring circuit in 1978. He failed to finish. Note that the machine still relies on a drum front brake.

SPECIFICATIONS: RR250

Engine	liquid-cooled twin cylinder 2-stroke
Capacity	15.1cu in (248cc)
Transmission	6-speed
Peak power	58bhp @12,000rpm
Weight	230lbs (104kg)
Wheelbase	49in (1,250mm)
Top speed	155mph (249kph)

BELOW A disc-braked factory two-stroke twin shares pride of place with a classic four-stroke single.

BELOW Villa on the RR350 at Hockenheim in 1977, carrying the world champion's Number One. He finished third in the 250cc world championship that year, but the 350 proved less competitive.

MX250, 1977

Harley-Davidson's only venture into mainstream motocross produced a highly competitive machine which could have become better still had Milwaukee not severed its Italian links after just two years of MX production, before the two-stroke had made a major mark.

ABOVE LEFT AND RIGHT Harley's Italian-designed and built MX250 motocrosser benefited from lessons learned in grand prix road racing and might have gone on to great things had Varese not been sold.

By the time the MX250 came on stream in 1977, Varese had developed a formidable pool of two-stroke know-how, not least from its successful grand prix road-racing experience.

Four years after its official demise, the great American dirt track racer Jay Springsteen mischievously used an MX-based machine to win the first AMA event of the 1982 season in Houston. We can only speculate about where this potential might have led.

The single-cylinder stroker used a short-stroke (72 x 59.6mm) engine which drove an integral five-speed transmission via gear primary drive and wet multi plate clutch – a format that endured for years. Initial examples were aircooled, but a liquid-cooled version came later.

A 38mm, Italian-made Dell'Orto carburettor provided the fuel (mixed 20:1 with oil for lubrication), while sparks came from a CDI generator on the left end of the crankshaft. During development, peak power rose to a ferocious 58bhp at a giddy 12,000rpm. Telescopic forks provided a generous 9in (228mm) of travel with a similar degree of movement that came from the twin rear shock absorbers.

Light alloy Akront rims were laced to simple 5½in (140mm) drum brakes (as discs were not yet used on dirt-bikes).

SPECIFICATIONS

Engine	aircooled single-cylinder 2-stroke
Capacity	14.8cu in (242cc)
Transmission	5-speed
Peak power	58bhp @12,000rpm
Weight	233lbs (106kg)
Wheelbase	57.3in (1,455mm)
Top speed	n/a

BELOW Harley later produced this Rotax-engined single.

AERMACCHI OHV RACERS, 1961

Originally an aircraft factory – hence the name – Aermacchi diversified into motorcycle production in 1948, in Varese, Italy. Its first models were 123cc (7.5cu in) singles – two-strokes but already possessing the horizontal cylinder which was to become so typical of the marque.

Overhead valve four-stroke singles followed, both road bikes and the potent Ala d'Oro (Golden Wing) production racer. A generation of elegant racing models were developed from the late 1950s onwards, based on this Alfredo Bianchi-designed machine.

Although the racers were built in both 250cc (15cu in) and 350cc (21cu in) versions, it was the latter which achieved the greater success. Even during the 1960s, a single-cylinder push-rod machine was an anachronism among the exotica then crowding the Grands Prix grids, yet the "Macchi" exploited its fine handling, light weight and slim aerodynamic profile to the fullest. Its best world-championship performance came in 1966 when Renzo Pasolini – who would lose his life when racing the 250cc Aermacchi Harley at Monza in 1973– took third place in the 350cc grand prix championship.

It was as a privateer mount that the little 'Macchi achieved its greatest popularity and success however, although it also had a reputation for being temperamental unless expertly set up. Perhaps its most remarkable performance came in the 1970 Isle of Man TT races when Alan Barnett lapped the daunting Mountain Course at a stunning 99.32mph (159.84kph) on a Syd Lawton 350, recording well over 40mpg (15km/litre) in the process.

Nor were the OHV single's exploits confined to the track. On 21 October 1965, a 250cc Aermacchi established a world mile record of 176.817mph (284.55kph) and kilometre record of 285.21kph (177.225mph) at Utah's Bonneville salt flats. Although nominally a Sprint roadster, the machine in question used a 1966-specification CR racing engine on standard pump fuel. Officially, Milwaukee dubbed its Italian singles CR, CRS and CRTT, although in Europe these designations were largely ignored.

The single was produced with many variations over the years, but the 350's

ABOVE An Aermacchi 250 at speed. Light weight and a slim profile made them astonishingly fast.

BELOW A CRTT 250 in Harley-Davidson factory racing livery.

SPECIFICATIONS: 350	
Engine	aircooled OHV horizontal single
Capacity	344cc (21cu in)
Transmission	5-speed
Power	38bhp
Weight	245lbs (111kg)
Wheelbase	not known
Top Speed	130mph (210kph)

ABOVE Aermacchi's famed horizontal single cylinder, here on a 350 from 1969.

RIGHT A brace of ex-factory racers. Note the racing dry clutch.

typical power output was around 38bhp at 8,400rpm. Bore and stroke were under-square at 74 x 80mm, although this incurred a dangerously high piston speed of 4,400ft/min (1,340m/min) at maximum revs. As a result, other configurations were also built, including short stroke and ultra-short stroke examples. Compression was high – around 11.4:1 – and the engine breathed through a 35mm dell'Orto carburettor tipped almost vertically to feed fuel into the horizontal cylinder. A short megaphone exhaust swept down the right side of the machine.

The racer was available with a choice of "A" or "B" gear clusters, the latter offering the closer ratios, although the engine delivered a reasonable spread of power considering its high state of tune.

The chassis was simple in the extreme, using a large diameter tubular steel spine, which was reputed to flex but in a controlled, user-friendly way which gave the rider ample feedback.

A variety of suspension and brake components were employed, invariably with telescopic forks (usually Ceriani), twin rear shock absorbers and drum brakes. On later versions, the front drum was often twin-sided.

A measure of the Aermacchi single's excellence is its enduring popularity and success in classic racing in recent decades.

ABOVE A 350 'Macchi contesting the 1984 Historic Isle of Man TT. Ironically this was the only TT ever won by an American – on a British Matchless machine.

BELOW In the USA, light and simple Aermacchis derived from the Sport roadster were popular for dirt-track racing.

LUCIFER'S HAMMER, 1983

One of the most revered of all Harley-Davidson road racers is Lucifer's Hammer, the sleek, fully-faired machine which, in the spring of 1983, became the first big twin for a decade to carry Milwaukee's famous black and orange livery on to the Daytona speed bowl.

It certainly did so with distinction, taking the great Jay Springsteen – better known as a dirt-track rider but certainly no slouch on tarmac – to victory in the Battle of the Twins event. In October of the same year, Gene Church began a love affair with the same machine when he rode it triumphantly in the BoT finals, also held at Daytona.

SPECIFICATIONS

Engine	OHV V-twin
Capacity	60.9cu in (998cc)
Transmission	4-speed
Power	104bhp
Weight	286lbs (130kg)
Wheelbase	56in (1,420mm)
Top speed	158mph (254kph)

The Hammer represented one of those bouts of enthusiasm and expertise with the big twin that were often typical of Harley-Davidson. The germ of the project began when Dave McClure rode a prototype XR1000 street bike at Daytona the previous autumn, which suggested that a full-on racer project might succeed. Once race-boss Dick O'Brien got the go-ahead to build what would become the Springsteen machine, he set his hand-picked team into action. Engine work was put in the hands of Don Habermehl, while racing legend Carroll Resweber (four times AMA champion for Harley, 1958 to 1961) put his considerable talents into the chassis, and Peter Zylstra oversaw the design. To some extent, the machine was also a test-bed and publicity statement for the XR1000 roadster unveiled at the same Daytona meeting, another project which very much carried the O'Brien imprint.

The engine consisted of a modified competition XR750 bottom end and light alloy heads mated to iron Sportster barrels. Twin 42mm smoothbore Mikuni carburettors took care of induction, feeding exotic 110 octane aviation fuel – for nothing less would handle the engine's giddy 10.5:1 compression ratio. To improve combustion, each cylinder boasted twin spark plugs, fired by a total-loss racing ignition system.

In dyno tests, this device had put out a brutal 106bhp at 7,500rpm, but fears about reliability caused Habermehl to

BELOW Lucifer's Hammer's engine was based on that of an XR750 competition model.

ABOVE The Hammer with fairing removed, at Daytona in 1983.

impose a rev ceiling of 7,000rpm, which cost a couple of horsepower. Since even this equated to a dizzying mean piston speed of 4,430 ft/min (1,350m/min), the precaution must have been wise. Not only was power prodigious but the spread was enormous, too, coming in strongly by 4,000rpm. A four-speed gearbox was more than adequate. Resweber's chassis employed the very XR750 frame comprehensively crashed by then-AMA champion Mark Brelsford at Daytona fully ten years before the Hammer's 1983 win. The basic single spine and twin tube cradle was heavily reworked with extra gussets and bracing, mated to an all-new box-section swing-arm.

The rest was essentially an Italian affair: front suspension was in the hands of a pair of Forcelli Italia forks, with twin Fox gas shock absorbers at the rear. Brembo supplied the brakes: twin 11.8in (300mm) floating-front disc brakes, with a 9.8in (250mm) disc at the rear. These ran on Campagnolo magnesium wheels, 16in front wheel, 18in rear, shod with Goodyear racing slicks. Dry weight was a remarkably lean 285lbs (130kg) and top speed an even more impressive 158mph (254kph).

After its winning Daytona debut, Gene Church went on to take the HOG-sponsored Hammer to three AMA Battle of the Twins titles.

All of this success was not really too bad for a bike that began its life as a ten-year-old scrap!

JAPANESE RACERS: THE SUNDANCE WEAPONS

Another outstanding Harley-powered racebike was the Daytona Weapon built by Zak Shibasaki of Tokyo-based Sundance Custom Cycles. Alongside custom Harleys, Sundance developed tuning parts, and in 1989 built the Weapon, a Buell-based Battle of the Twins racer. This led in the 1990s to the Daytona Weapon and its successor the Daytona Weapon II – stylish, superbly engineered V-twins that took riders including Jay Springsteen and Yoshiyuki Sugai to victory at the Florida circuit and elsewhere.

BELOW LEFT Willie G. Davidson (second left) pictured at Daytona with the Japanese-built Sundance racer.

BELOW Yoshiyuki Sugai cranks the Sundance Weapon through a turn at the Daytona International Speedway.

SPORTSTER RACERS

Sportsters have been tuned and raced for almost as long as they have been produced. That began in the late 1950s with the lean XLC and XLCH models that were built for competition with tiny peanut tanks, cut-down rear fenders and unsilenced exhausts.

More recently, "one-make" championships for modified Sportsters have provided close, spectacular and relatively inexpensive racing.

The first of these was the 883 Sport Twins series, which was launched in the United States in 1989. The championship was an instant success and was exported to race tracks around the world, where spectators flocked to hear the thunder of a grid-full of Harley twins.

SPECIFICATIONS: XR1200

Engine	aircooled OHV V-twin
Capacity	1,202cc
Transmission	5-speed
Power	95bhp
Weight	517lbs (235kg)
Wheelbase	59.6in (1,515mm)
Top speed	130mph (209kph)

At the series' inception, the general expectation was that it would be an all-American affair. That proved incorrect, when the first American Sports Twins champion was an Englishman, Nigel Gale. But the title soon came much closer to home, with the emergence of Scott Zampach... from, of all places, Milwaukee.

Riding for North Carolina dealer Don Tilley, who had masterminded Gene Church's hat-trick of AMA titles

ABOVE Jay Springsteen is one in a long line of champions that stem from the legacy of the Wrecking Crew of the early part of the 20th century.

LEFT Jeremy McWilliams' UK title-winning XR1200 was prepared for racing by London dealer Warr's, but its engine and frame remained standard.

LEFT Harley's inspired 883 Sportster series even attracted stars such as Jay Springsteen.

RIGHT A race exhaust improved the XR1200's ground clearance and raised output to 95bhp.

on Lucifer's Hammer in the mid-1980s, Zampach proceeded to go one better on the 883. The "Z-Man" won the championship from 1991 to 1993, then finished second to Shawn Higbee in 1994 before taking his fourth title the following season. Higbee later joined Tilley's team, and in 1998 rode a modified Sportster to win the Harley-Davidson Twin Sports World Cup at Daytona.

Harley revived the one-make format a decade later with the XR1200, with similarly successful and widely exported results. As with the 883 series, regulations dictated that bikes remained relatively standard. A racing exhaust system typically boosted the 1,202cc engine's output to 95bhp. The XR's steel frame also had to be retained; chassis upgrades could include new yokes, fork internals, shocks, brakes, wheels and tyres.

In the States, riders entering the Vance & Hines sponsored series could use the firm's website to order a $3,500 box containing almost everything required to convert a standard XR1200 for the track, including 17in diameter front wheel (to replace the standard 18in wheel), front fender kit, steering damper, racepipe (upswept for better ground clearance), racing seat, belly pan, and even a racing number plate and stickers.

The AMA championship ran for five seasons, with Danny Eslick winning in both 2010 and 2014. Former MotoGP star Jeremy McWilliams was an XR1200 race winner in the US and a champion in the UK. On both sides of the Atlantic, the XR1200s' closely matched performance ensured thrilling racing, including flat-track style drafting on the straights. And the chassis' limitations led to some hair-raising handling, which added to the entertainment for spectators.

BELOW Former MotoGP ace Jeremy McWilliams leads Mike Edwards on the way to winning the UK's inaugural XR1200 championship in 2010.

VR1000, 1994

The VR1000 that flew Milwaukee's road-racing flag through the latter half of the 1990s was a Harley-Davidson like no other. It was a V-twin, true, but with twin overhead camshafts, liquid-cooled cylinders set at 60 degrees, and an aluminium frame.

The VR was a pure-bred racebike, conceived as a way for the firm to compete in top-level Superbike racing.

Harley developed the eight-valve powerplant largely in-house, and aimed to use exclusively American-made chassis parts too. Engine development began in 1988, with Harley designer Mark Miller aided by experts including former race team boss Dick O'Brien and tuning ace Jerry Branch. Michigan-based specialists Roush Performance provided input until their engineer Steve Scheibe joined Harley's team.

Erik Buell was also involved, and designed an aluminium frame that held the fuel (an idea he would later revisit with the Buell XB models), but this was dropped in favour of a more conventional twin-spar frame created by Mike Eatough, from the British Armstrong firm that had recently been acquired by Harley. Willie G. Davidson, who supported the firm's return to racing, gave the VR its distinctive look: orange on the right and black on the left, split by a white stripe.

Harley overcame Superbike rules stipulating that 50 roadgoing VR1000s had to be produced and registered,

ABOVE Chris Carr in action on the VR1000 at Daytona. In 1999, the Californian returned to dirt track and claimed the AMA title.

SPECIFICATIONS: 2001

Engine	liquid-cooled DOHC V-twin
Capacity	61cu in (996cc)
Transmission	6-speed
Power	170bhp
Weight	373lbs (169kg)
Wheelbase	55.1in (1,400mm)
Top speed	175mph (282kph)

ABOVE As brutally black as the old XLCR, the factory racer failed to live up to expectations on the track.

although the purpose-built racebike had no chance of meeting US emissions regulations. The 50 bikes were duly announced, offered for sale at almost $50,000 apiece... and one was quietly put through homologation testing in Europe, amid reports that machines had been registered in Poland.

But internal disputes and redesigns of both the engine and chassis had delayed development. Serious testing commenced only in 1993, more than five years after the project's birth. By this time the 996cc engine produced almost 150bhp – less than Ducati's lighter V-twin, the Superbike class yardstick. Development by an independent firm, Gemini, would increase power while adding reliability and reducing weight... but never quite enough to make the Harley competitive.

In the seasons following the VR's debut in 1994 it was raced by a string of star riders, including Canadian ace Miguel Duhamel, flat track champion Chris Carr and former World Superbike champ Scott Russell. But none could manage an AMA Superbike race win, let alone a championship. Carr scored the VR's only pole position, at Pomona in 1996. In the same season Tom Wilson won at Mid-Ohio... until a red flag meant the race was ended a lap earlier, denying him victory. Several riders came close but were denied by crashes, breakdowns or bad luck.

By the end of the 2001 season the VR was producing about 170bhp but required a comprehensive redesign. Harley instead abandoned the project, although the engine in some respects lived on in the V-Rod, which was launched that year with a similar 60-degree, DOHC layout. As a racebike the VR1000 cannot be judged a success, but it had played an important part in the Harley-Davidson story.

ABOVE A private racing VR with bodywork removed, highlighting its engine's 60-degree engine layout and the twin-spar aluminium frame.

LEFT Note the slim lines of the Superbike VR. The ventilated dry clutch would later be replaced by an exotic multi-plate carbon assembly.

RIGHT This prototype roadster VR1000 never made it into production.

XG750R, 2017

Replacing the all-conquering, uniquely long-lasting XR750 was always going to be a huge step, but in 2017 Harley-Davidson finally began a new era of flat-track racing with the XG750R, powered by a production-based liquid-cooled, 60-degree V-twin engine.

The XG's SOHC, eight-valve unit was derived from the Revolution X powerplant that had been introduced three years earlier with the Street 750 and had since been developed to produce about 70bhp in the Street Rod.

The XG750R project was led by Vance & Hines, whose impressive track record included AMA road-race success as well as eight AMA titles with Harley's Pro Stock drag racer. The fuel-injected engine was tuned with parts including CP pistons, Carrillo conrods and a new twin-throat throttle body, and produced a maximum of about 110bhp at 10,000rpm.

The team made new, closer-fitting covers for the engine cases, and bolted the narrower engine into a traditional XR-style tubular steel cradle frame, albeit one whose rectangular-section steel swing-arm worked a single Showa shock unit, rather than twin shocks. Other chassis parts included 19in wheels, no front brake (in flat-track tradition) and a cast iron rear disc gripped by a four-piston caliper.

With its wide, raised handlebar and a big V-twin engine at its heart, the

SPECIFICATIONS

Engine	liquid-cooled SOHC V-twin
Capacity	749cc (45cu in)
Transmission	6-speed
Power	100bhp (estimated)
Weight	300lbs (136kg)
Wheelbase	60.4in (1,535mm)
Top speed	130mph (209kph)

ABOVE Flat-track shape and factory paint scheme were familiar; right-sided exhaust less so.

RIGHT Carbon-fibre heat shields kept the rider's leg away from the high-level exhaust.

RIGHT Orange and black paintwork and the distinctively shaped gas tank maintained links with the past as the XG750R began a bold new era.

BELOW Harley's development team worked hard to make the XG750R find traction as well as its famously hard-charging XR750 predecessor.

XG750R shared much of the XR's look, not least its factory orange-and-black finish. Notably differences included the radiator ahead of its engine, and the high-level, twin-pipe exhaust on the right rather than the left. It was an unmistakably lean and simple racing machine, good for a top speed of about 130mph (209kph) at a fast track like the Sacramento Mile, where it was geared to use only the first four ratios in the box.

The XG immediately showed promise, when debuted by 18-year-old rookie rider Davis Fisher, while factory team-mate Brad Baker continued with the XR. The liquid-cooled, more over-square engine revved harder and, after teething issues were sorted, was more robust than the ageing aircooled unit, which required frequent overhauls to maintain reliability.

If Harley's team had been hoping for a seamless transition, they got a nasty shock, not least from old rival Indian. Recently reborn under Polaris ownership, and keen to establish a racing reputation, Indian entered the 2017 season with a factory Scout FTR750 flat-track bike which, unlike the XG, was a pure-bred racer. They also hired Harley's last three Grand National champions, including Jared Mees, who won ten races en route to another title.

The Street-based XG750R couldn't compete with the purpose-built FTR, which went on to dominate the class. But it was a different story from 2019, when American Flat Track introduced a class for street-based machines. James Rispoli and Jesse Janisch won two of the first four Production Twins championships on the XG750R, beginning a new era of success despite Harley's decision to end the factory flat-track effort in 2021, and instead provide support through dealers.

LEFT AND RIGHT Wisconsin-born Jesse Janisch rode the XG750R to seven race victories and the AMA's Production Twins championship in 2022.

ROAD GLIDE 131R, 2023

Of all the bikes that have lined up on a racetrack with the name Harley-Davidson on their tanks, the heavily modified Road Glides and Street Glides competing in the King of the Baggers series are among the most spectacular.

Producing 150bhp, weighing well over 600lbs (272kg) and rampaging around the circuits like a runaway herd of buffalo, they have enlivened the US racing scene.

Bagger racing began in October 2020 with a one-off event at Laguna Seca in California, sponsored by parts giant Drag Specialities and called the King of the Baggers. Harleys dominated the entry, with 11 of the 13 runners including a turbocharged Street Glide, but the winner was an Indian ridden by Tyler O'Hara. The bikes, featuring tuned engines and lengthened, firmed-up suspension, were improbably fast and the race was a hit, viewed online more than two million times.

Harley struck back the following year, when the King of the Baggers was expanded into a three-round championship. It was won by a factory-built Road Glide Special ridden by Kyle Wyman, who was very much a home-grown Harley hero; along with

ABOVE Kyle Wyman (No.33) and brother Travis pitch their huge and heavy, yet improbably stable-handling, Road Glides into a left-hand turn.

SPECIFICATIONS

Engine	aircooled OHV V-twin
Capacity	2,152cc (131cu in)
Transmission	6-speed
Power	150bhp
Weight	631lbs (287kg) dry
Wheelbase	65in (1,651mm)
Top speed	160mph (257kph)

BELOW The Road Glides' fairings and panniers resemble standard parts but their long suspension and slick-shod 17in wheels confirm racing intent.

ABOVE Hayden Gillim won the 2023 title at a wet New Jersey final round.

ABOVE Winner Gillim with team-mate James Rispoli and Travis Wyman.

younger brother and fellow racer Travis, he was the son of Kim Wyman, owner of Harv's Harley-Davidson in Macedon, New York.

Interest in bagger racing grew rapidly, not least because these belligerent beasts were hotted-up versions of the popular Glides that were being modified by performance-hungry owners across the land. Milwaukee was encouraged, and what had begun as an after-hours project for staffers became a factory race effort in 2022 – with both Wyman brothers signed to ride.

The chosen model was a Road Glide Special, powered by an aircooled, 45-degree Milwaukee-Eight 131R engine – a tweaked version of the 131cu in (2,151cc) "crate engine" that Harley offered as an upgrade for road riders. New camshafts, pistons and fuel injectors helped increase peak output to 150bhp and torque to an equally massive 150lb.ft (203N.m), with a redline at 6,800rpm. Another big number was the estimated $200,000 value of the lavishly produced racebike.

Numerous neat touches transformed the giant tourer, with its deceptively normal looking fairing and panniers, into a dedicated racing machine. Its lattice-like swing-arm was a work of art, machined from a solid lump of aluminium. To increase ground clearance, footboards were replaced by specially machined engine covers with mounts for footpegs.

The Glide's steel backbone frame (which regulations insisted remained standard) supported a much-modified chassis incorporating adjustable yokes, long and strong Öhlins racing forks, Öhlins-built Screamin' Eagle shocks, four-piston monobloc front brake calipers, and forged 17in wheels wearing sticky racing rubber.

The result was a fearsome 160mph (257kph), improbably hard-cornering racebike that proved highly competitive. Series leader Travis Wyman's crash in 2022's final rain-soaked round handed the title to Indian's O'Hara. But the following season's expanded, 14-race series was won by Harley's Hayden Gillim, adding another chapter to one of racing's oldest and hardest fought rivalries.

RIGHT Travis Wyman at speed on the factory Road Glide, showing its two-into-one race pipe and machined-from-solid aluminium swing-arm.

GLOSSARY

Air cleaner: A filter for removing dust from the air entering the engine.
Aircooled: An engine which is cooled directly by the air flowing over it, rather than via a liquid-filled radiator.
Alternator: An electrical generator producing alternating current which must then be converted to direct current by a rectifier.
AMA: American Motorcycle Association (governing body of American bike racing).
Bearing: Placed between two rubbing or turning components to reduce friction. Can be "plain" or with moving balls or rollers.
bhp (brake horsepower): Engine power as measured on a dynamometer, on which the engine is run against a resistance or "brake". Horsepower is essentially torque times revs.
Big end: The connection between con-rod and crankshaft.
Bore: Diameter of the cylinder in which the piston travels.
Bottom end: The engine below the cylinder, containing crankshaft, bearings, oil pump, etc.
CAD: Computer-aided design.
Camshaft: A lobed shaft turning at half engine speed which operates the valves.
Carburettor: Instrument that mixes fuel and air for combustion.
Choke: A device that enriches the fuel and air mixture to facilitate cold starts; also the carburettor venturi.
Clutch: A device which allows the rear wheel to be isolated from the turning of the engine.
Coil: An electrical device which turns low-voltage current into high-voltage for the spark plug.
Compression: The extent to which the piston "squeezes" the fuel and air mixture, expressed as a ratio of maximum to minimum volume.
Con-rod (connecting rod): A (usually steel) member connecting the crankshaft to the piston.
Crankcases: The (usually aluminium) housing containing bottom end components. These are commonly split into pairs.
Crankshaft: An eccentric (cranked) shaft on which the con-rods run, held in the crankcases by the main bearings; it turns the piston's reciprocating action into rotary motion.
Cylinder: A cylindrical "barrel" in which the piston moves up and down.
Disc: A type of brake in which "pads" of friction material are squeezed against rotating disc(s) attached to the wheel.
Displacement: An engine's capacity, i.e. total volume displaced by an engine's pistons.
DOHV: Dual overhead valve.
Drum: A type of brake in which a mechanism forces "shoes" against the inside of a drum in the wheel hub.
Dry-sump: An engine in which lubricating oil is located in a separate tank rather than the sump.
Evo: The 1,340cc V2 Evolution engine produced from 1984.
F-head: An ioe cylinder head.
Flathead: Any side-valve engine.
Flywheel: A heavy disc spinning with the crankshaft which stores engine inertia and "smooths out" power pulses.
Gearbox: A housing in which lie the shafts on which the transmission gears run.
Gudgeon pin (wrist pin in the USA): A steel tube connecting the piston to the small end.
Hardtail: A rigid, i.e. unsprung, motorcycle rear end.
Hog: Nickname given to any Harley-Davidson model.
HOG: Harley Owners' Group.
Horsepower: Torque times revs, the actual power output of an engine. However, in the early years, an engine's rated horsepower was simply a function of engine displacement.
Hydraulic: Operated by pressure in a fluid, as with disc brakes or hydraulic "lifters".
ioe (inlet-over-exhaust): The earliest type of valve arrangement, with a side exhaust valve facing an overhead inlet valve. The latter could be "automatic" or mechanically operated.
Knucklehead: Harley's first OHV engine, 1936–47.
Lifter (USA): A push-rod. Also hydraulic lifters.
Magneto: An early, free-standing device which generates (and times) the ignition spark.
Mudguard: fender (USA).
OHV (overhead valve): Both valves contained in the cylinder head and actuated by rockers.
Panhead: An OHV Harley engine produced 1948–65.
Piston: An inverted cylindrical "tub" in the cylinder which transmits combustion forces to the crankshaft via the con-rod.
Piston ring: A flexible iron or steel ring located in a groove near the top of the piston which seals against the leakage of combustion gases or oil.
Power: *See* bhp.
Push-rod (also, solid lifter in the USA): A metal rod which transmits camshaft motion to the valve via the rocker.
Rake: The effective angle of the front forks, expressed in degrees from vertical.
Revs (rpm): Engine revolutions per minute.
Retro-Tech: Modern technology that mimicks old, such as Springer forks.
Rocker: A rocking arm which transmits motion from lifter to the valve.
Shovelhead: An OHV Harley engine produced 1966–84.
Side-valve: "Flathead" engines with both valves below the level of the cylinder head.
Small end (little end): The connection between the piston's gudgeon pin and the con-rod.
Softail: Rear suspension with swing arm and underslung shock absorbers, that is designed to look like a hardtail.
SOHV: Single overhead valve.
Springer: A modern "Retro-Tech" version of the sprung fork; any Harley-Davidson so fitted.
Sprung fork: Pre-1948 front suspension with solid legs, and (usually) coil spring(s) at the top.
Stroke: The distance travelled by a piston between its top-most and bottom-most points.
Swing-arm: Also known as swinging fork, a pivoting suspension member allowing the rear wheel to move up and down.
Sump: An extension at the bottom of the crankcase containing oil. "Dry sump" engines hold their oil in a separate tank.
Tachometer (rev-counter): An instrument that measures engine revs.
Telescopic fork: Front suspension in which one tube (containing a spring) slides within another, damped by oil.
Timing: Arranging that the spark is delivered (or the valves open and close) at the correct time.
Top end: The engine "above" the base of the cylinder, including the cylinder head.
Torque: The turning force applied to the crankshaft (and ultimately the rear wheel) by the force of combustion on the piston.
Trail (castor): The extent to which the front tyre's contact patch trails the point at which the steering angle intersects the ground. Harley-Davidson favours high trail figures which tend to give slower steering and greater stability.
Venturi: The part of the carburettor through which incoming air passes; also its diameter.
Wheelbase: Distance between the front and rear wheel centres.
Wrist Pin: *see* gudgeon pin.

HARLEY-DAVIDSON MODEL CODES

In recent years Harley-Davidson has mostly used names to identify its models, but for more than a century the firm used letters and numbers as a main – sometimes the only – form of identification. The model code began as a way of denoting the year of production and level of specification, and became more complex as new engines and bikes were added.

The first machine produced in significant numbers was the 1908 Model 4, the number indicating the fourth year of production. The basic model was known by its year number alone; a suffix letter identified the model type, such as "A" for magneto ignition.

Model 5 followed in 1909, then Model 6 in 1910 and so on, until 1916, when all models adopted the last two digits of their year of manufacture. Thus, Model 16B was the basic 1916 single, 16E was the basic twin and 16J was a three-speed twin with full electrics.

The suffix letters became more numerous as the range grew, but the basic year-prefix system continued publicly until 1969. Not all letters of the alphabet were used, but several had different meanings at different times.

Similarly, the same feature was denoted by different code letters. For example, electric start was indicated by both B and E, while the latter also represented the 61cu in Knucklehead and Panhead engines (as opposed to F for the 74-inch models) and even police spec.

More recently, aircooled Sportster models kept the XL designation that began with the first 833cc model of 1957. And FL, originally used in 1941 for the 74cu in Knucklehead, expanded to FLHR for the Road King family, FLHT for the Electra Glides, FLTR for the Road Glides and FLHS for Street Glides.

Inevitably the proliferation of different models within each family resulted in increasingly long and complex model codes. The Tri Glide Ultra, for example, was the FLHTCUTG, its eight-letter code dwarfed by the ten of the FLTRKSEANV CVO Road Glide LTD Anniversary.

Which perhaps explains why, although each current model can still be identified by a series of letters – and sometimes numbers, as with the RA1250S Pan America Special – these days even Harley generally sticks to calling its bikes by name.

The accompanying table outlines some of the more commonly used letters.

Suffix	Recent meaning	Historical meaning
A	–	Army/no tow-bar (Servi-Car)
B	Bad, as in Bad Boy, Belt Drive	Electric start; previously aluminium piston(s)
C	Custom, Classic, Café (as in Café Racer)	"Competition"/Commercial /Canadian spec
D	Dyna, Daytona, Deuce	At least four other uses
DG	Disc Glide	–
E	Electric start	Knucklead, 61cu in OHV engine
F	Fat Boy	As a prefix, 74-inch OHV engine; as suffix, foot change
G	-	Servi-Car
H	Highway frame; Hugger (XLH883); Notionally extra power but largely redundant	Hand shift/High peformance/Heavy duty
I	Fuel injection	–
J	–	Battery electrical system (as opposed to magneto)
K	-	
L	Low (seat); Wide front tyre (and Hydra-Glide style forks)	Sports specification; LD signified Special Sports models
LR	Low Rider	–
N	Nostalgia; Iron model, eg XL883N	Iron piston; Deluxe model
P	Police moel	sprung fork on 1949 OHV models
Q	–	Two passenger sidecar
R	Road King	Racing/pseudo racing (XR1000)
RA	Pan America	–
RH	Liquid-cooled Sportster	–
S	Springer, front end; Sport, eg, FLHS Electra Glide Sport	Sidecar specifications/ sometimes Sport
SE	Screamin' Eagle	–
SP	Sport Edition, eg FXRS-SP Low Rider Sport Edition	–
ST	Softail	–
T	Touring, with frame-mounting fairing	Reverse gear/Twin
U	Ultra	Side-valve big twin, 74/80cu in; Restricted engines
V	Revolution engine; Seventy-Two model (SL1200V)	–
WG	Wide Glide	–
X	Some Sports models; narrow front tyre	Rear wheel clutch
XG	Street	

INDEX

ACKNOWLEDGEMENTS

This edition is published by Lorenz Books
an imprint of Anness Publishing Limited
info@anness.com
www.lorenzbooks.com

A CIP catalogue record for this book is available from the British Library.

Publisher: Joanna Lorenz
Editorial Director: Helen Sudell
Editor: Keith Ryan
Editorial Consultant: Shaun Barrington
Designer: Nigel Partridge
Indexer: Valeria Padalino
Production Controller: Ben Worley

Author and Publishers' note

In recognition of the uniquely American pedigree of the motorcycles featured, engine capacity is generally expressed in imperial units (cubic inches) with the metric equivalent (cc) in brackets. However, even Harley-Davidson employ units somewhat arbitrarily, favouring cu in for heavyweight twins, but ccs for Sportster models, a practice we have also adopted.

The capacity of Harley engines should also be treated with some care. Even from the early days, the inch sizes quoted and used by Harley fans were a sort of numeric shorthand, relating only approximately to measured reality. More recently, even the "80-inch" Evo engine actually measured 81.8cu in – a difference of no less than 29cc. In general, where an engine is referred to as something-inch, this refers to popular usage. Dimensions expressed in cu in and/or cc are as accurate as records permit.

We trust that this historical ambiguity will not reduce the reader's enjoyment.

Captions

Page 1: 1909 Single. Page 2: Hydra-Glide revival, 2024.
Page 3: Softail Rocker C, 2008. Page 4: Model E, 1936. Page 5: Fat Boy, 2000 (tl), Road King Classic, 2000 (tr), Pan American, 2021 (bl), Low Riders S, 2016 (br). Above: CVO Road Glide, 2023. Front jacket: Electra Glide Ultra, 2014. Endpapers: WL45 Knucklehead, 1942 (front), Street Glide Special, 2014 (back).

The publisher would like to thank the following for their kind permission to reproduce their photographs:
John Bolt: 48t, 85t, 97tr, 118bl/br, 130t/m, 131m/b, 177tl.
Roland Brown: 30tl, 32tl, 36b, 51b, 52b, 53tr, 54t, 74b, 75 all, 76, 99tl, 108b, 118t, 130bl, 132 both, 133 all, 134b, 143t, 189 both, 198–99, 207tl, 210b, 211b, 214 both, 215 tl, 227tr, 235b, 236t, 257 tl/tr, 259t, 260b, 261 tl/tc/tr, 281t, 307br, 308b, 309tr.
John Caroll: 111b, 122t, 180br, 186t/m/bl, 187br.
Alan Cathcart: 152br, 306, 307t.
Bob Clarke: 30tr, 47br, 71bl, 96tl/m, 97ml, 98 all, 107m/b, 114bl, 122m/bl/br, 123t, 165b, 183tl, 187m, 221t, 296t/br, 299bl/br, 302bl, 304b, 307bl, 311 all.
Classic Bike: 172t, 222b, 224b.
Neil Dalleywater: 82br, 180bl, 202t.
Don Kates: 116t/bl, 117t/br.
Kobal: 114t/m, 115br, 149bl/br.
Mac McDiarmid: 8–9, 28bl, 29tr, 39m, 45tr, 47b, 68t, 69bl, 70br, 71tl/br, 72t, 79tr/b, 80t, 81br, 82br, 104–5, 112–13, 115t/m/bl, 124 both, 125 all, 126tr, 131tr, 145t, 150t, 164b, 170b, 171b, 176t, 177tr, 178bl, 190–1, 192t, 193t, 194t/b, 203t, 204t, 206bl, 207tr, 224 all, 228m/b, 229tr, 232tl, 233t, 253bl/br, 255t, 303tl, 305tl/tr.
Don Morley: 13br, 44t, 152t, 302t/br, 303b, 304t, 305m.
B. R. Nicholls: 148t.
Garry Stuart: 1, 11t, 12tl/tr, 13bl, 14bl/br, 15t, 16t/bl, 18b, 19t/m, 20t, 21tr/b, 22 both, 24 both, 25 all, 26 all, 27 both, 29b, 31t, 32b, 35tl/tr/bl/br, 36t, 37tl, 38t/b, 39b, 44b, 45tl, 46bl/br, 48m/b, 69b, 70b, 78 both, 80b, 81t/bl, 83 all, 84b, 85b, 86b, 97tl, 106br, 108tl/tr/br, 110t, 116br, 117bl, 126tl, 145bl, 150b, 154t, 160 both, 162 both, 163 all, 164t, 165t/m, 166–67, 168 all, 169bl/br, 170t/m, 171tr, 172b, 173 all, 176bl/br, 177bl/br, 178t/br, 179 both, 180t, 181 all, 182 both, 183tr/m/b, 185 all, 186br, 187br, 188b, 193m/b, 195 both, 196 all, 197b, 200br, 202b, 203b, 204b, 205bl/br, 206t, 207b, 208t, 209tl, 218–19, 220b, 221ml/bl, 225b, 226 all, 227b, 229b, 230m, 231tl, 232b, 235t, 236 both, 237b, 254tl/tr, 259b, 292 all, 293 all, 294b, 295 all, 296br, 297tr, 298m/b, 299t, 303tr, 305b, 310t.

KEY: t=top b=bottom l=left r=right m=middle.

All other photographs courtesy of Harley-Davidson, Inc.

Harley-Davidson